Smarter Investing

Tim Hale

Smarter Investing

Simpler decisions for better results

Second Edition

**Financial Times
Prentice Hall**
is an imprint of

Harlow, England • London • New York • Boston • San Francisco • Toronto • Sydney • Singapore • Hong Kong
Tokyo • Seoul • Taipei • New Delhi • Cape Town • Madrid • Mexico City • Amsterdam • Munich • Paris • Milan

PEARSON EDUCATION LIMITED

Edinburgh Gate
Harlow CM20 2JE
Tel: +44 (0) 1279 623623
Fax: +44 (0) 1279 431059
Website: www.pearsoned.co.uk

First published in Great Britain in 2006
Second edition published 2009
©Tim Hale 2006, 2009

The right of Tim Hale to be identified as author of this work has been asserted by him in
accordance with the Copyright, Designs and Patents Act 1988.

ISBN: 978–0–273–72207–6

British Library Cataloguing-in-Publication Data
A catalogue record for this book is available from the British Library

Library of Congress Cataloging-in-Publication Data
A catalogue record for this book is available from the Library of Congress

10 9 8 7 6 5 4 3 2
13 12 11 10

Designed by Sue Lamble
Typeset in Stone Serif 9 point by 3
Printed in Great Britain by Henry Ling Limited., at the Dorset Press, Dorchester, DT1 1HD

The Publisher's policy is to use paper manufactured from sustainable forests.

For Emma, Tilly and Betsy – my gorgeous girls
It's getting closer to a pamphlet!

Contents

Preface / x

Author's acknowledgements / xii

Publisher's acknowledgements / xiv

Foreword / xvi

Introduction / 1

I.1 *What should I do with my money? / 1*

I.2 *Some eye-openers to get you thinking / 1*

I.3 *How this book will help you / 5*

I.4 *How this book works / 6*

I.5 *A few points to note / 8*

Part 1: Smarter investing basics

1 **Simplifying the confusion / 13**

1.1 *Choices, choices, choices / 13*

1.2 *How did we get here? / 14*

1.3 *Battling for investors' money / 17*

1.4 *Reducing confusion and complexity / 18*

2 **Covering the basics / 21**

2.1 *What is smarter investing? / 21*

2.2 *Ten points of focus for smarter investors / 24*

2.3 *The two distinct phases of investing / 32*

2.4 *There are no perfect answers / 36*

2.5 *Summary: smarter investing basics / 37*

3 **It only takes a minute / 38**

3.1 *Twenty tips for smarter investing / 38*

Part 2: **Smarter thinking**

4   Get smart – find your philosophy / 47

4.1 Don't be a loser / 47

4.2 The foundations of your philosophy / 50

4.3 The path to establishing your philosophy / 56

4.4 Can active managers win? / 57

4.5 Do a few managers outperform over time? / 66

4.6 Can you identify them in advance? / 70

4.7 Don't just take my word for it / 71

4.8 Summarising what you now know / 75

4.9 A personal philosophy / 76

4.10 Your investment philosophy rules / 79

5   Get smart – manage your emotions / 83

5.1 You are your own worst enemy / 83

5.2 Challenges to decision-making / 87

5.3 Thirteen questions for you to answer / 89

5.4 Ms Rational versus Mr Irrational / 98

5.5 Wise words to leave you with / 102

5.6 Behavioural rules and tips / 102

Part 3: **Building smarter portfolios**

6   Understanding your emotional risk tolerance / 109

6.1 What is your risk profile? / 109

6.2 Why is it so important? / 111

6.3 Exploring your risk profile / 112

6.4 The process from here / 116

7   Sorting out your goals / 118

7.1 Well thought-out goals underpin success / 118

7.2 Five steps in defining your goals / 121

7.3 Basic financial survival goals / 128

7.4 A working example / 138

7.5 Useful calculations / 141

7.6 Summary: investment goals / 142

8   Smarter risk taking / 143

8.1 2008 – a violent introduction to risks / 144

8.2 The cost of capital / 146

8.3 Focusing on market risk / 148

8.4 The risks and rewards of being a lender / 149

8.5 The risks and rewards of being an owner / 151

8.6 Therefore, risk choices are fortunately limited / 153

9   Smarter portfolio construction / 154

9.1 The portfolio building process / 155

9.2 Construction goals and approach / 155

9.3 Deciding on the asset class menu / 159

9.4 Ground rules for the growth portfolio / 164

9.5 Building your growth-oriented portfolio return engine / 171

9.6 Building a robust defensive asset mix / 175

9.7 Portfolios along the risk spectrum / 180

10   Smarter portfolio choice / 183

10.1 Understanding and using the matrix / 183

10.2 Smarter Portfolio insights / 186

11   An insight into key asset classes / 193

11.1 The thrills and spills of equities / 193

11.2 Voting machine v. weighing machine / 195

11.3 An insight into equity market returns / 198

11.4 Developed equity market returns / 204

11.5 Emerging market equities / 206

11.6 Value (less financially healthy) companies / 208

11.7 Smaller companies / 210

11.8 In summary – equity asset classes / 213

11.9 Commercial property – a diversifier / 214

11.10 Commodity futures – a bit esoteric / 216

11.11 Defensive assets / 219

11.12 Key asset classes excluded / 222

11.13 Summary of asset class assumptions / 223

Part 4: Smarter implementation

12   Hire an adviser or do it yourself? / 229

12.1 Hiring an adviser / 229
12.2 What attributes will a leading adviser have? / 231
12.3 Checklist for finding a leading wealth advisory firm / 234
12.4 The do-it-yourself option / 234
12.5 Don't forget about tax / 244

13   Smarter product choices / 247

13.1 The serendipity of index-fund investing / 248
13.2 Choosing your market index / 249
13.3 Product structures / 252
13.4 Selecting the best passively managed index funds and ETFs / 254
13.5 Passive providers / 257
13.6 A possible shortlist – caveat emptor! / 262
13.7 Using active funds (if you must) / 263

14   Costs – what a drag / 267

14.1 Why do we throw our money away? / 267
14.2 More than just management fees / 268
14.3 Summary: costs – what a drag / 275

15   Standing firm on index funds / 276

15.1 Common put-downs / 276
15.2 Bond investing: active or index? / 281
15.3 Summary: favour index strategies / 282

Conclusion / 284

Bibliography / 286

Websites / 286
Insightful books / 286
Data-orientated books / 287
Asset allocation software / 288
Additional sources / 288

Appendix 1 / 289
Index / 291

Preface

This book was first written with a certain degree of frustration with the investment management industry as a whole; it plays an important part in our lives as we seek to secure our financial futures through sound investment programmes, yet much of the information and advice on investing in our daily lives, on the television, in the press and from cyberspace, is often confused by fuzzy thinking, frequently tainted by vested interests, and occasionally reeks of exploitation. This makes life difficult for anyone faced with making decisions about how they are going to invest. That, nowadays, means nearly all of us.

As 2008 passes into recent history, that frustration is perhaps even higher. Investors again find themselves at the wrong end of an industry that created overly complex, opaque and expensive products that neither they nor their advisers understood or investigated properly. The result has been great disappointment and the unnecessary destruction of hard-won wealth. Surely this time the better end of the investment and investment advice industry needs to stand up and say enough is enough. Let's get back to understanding what we are doing, structure sound and transparent portfolios that we can believe in and have a good chance of helping us to achieve our financial goals.

Fortunately some aspects of the industry are moving in a positive direction. These include the increasing prominence of small, dynamic and professional fee-based wealth advisers using passive investment solutions, along with the rapidly increasing availability of passive products available to them, as well as to those investing on their own. The essence of *Smarter Investing* is to do a few simple things exceptionally well and as cheaply as possible.

Investment decisions are extremely important parts of our lives and affect us profoundly. As such, you owe it to yourself to begin to put your investing in order. It can appear complicated out there, but if you have a few solid and simple rules to hand, then you can use or discard information and advice as you see fit and make investing decisions with confidence. I hope this book contributes to your understanding in some small way.

Tim Hale
Exeter
United Kingdom
2009

Author's acknowledgements

Writing is an adventure. To begin with, it is a toy and an amusement. Then it becomes a mistress, then it becomes a master, then it becomes a tyrant. The last phase is that just as you are about to be reconciled to your servitude, you kill the monster and fling him to the public.

Winston Churchill

To those who asked me to write a pamphlet, this second edition is a step closer!

Special thanks to Emma, my wife, and my girls who put up with the late nights at the office and my weary mind at the end of each day's writing. Thanks too to my sister Sian Lamb who proofed and prepared the manuscript for this edition and deciphered my illegible notes.

I would also like to thank the team at Pearson for their enthusiasm and encouragement in getting this second edition finished. I would particularly like to thank my former editor Liz Gooster who suggested it and Chris Cudmore, Senior Commissioning Editor, who suffered my one false start with good grace and helped to push the project through. Thanks also to Karen Mclaren who put the edition together, along with Laura Blake who struggled through the permissions process.

Over the years I have received inspiration from many sources that have shaped and influenced this book. They include my colleagues from the Chase Manhattan days, who sowed the seeds of my understanding. Also to the institutional sales group who made going to work fun, particularly when it dawned on many of us that active management was the emperor with no clothes! Special thanks must go to some of the other fund managers I have worked with without whose egos, bull and lack of sustainable outperformance the angst to write this book would never have existed.

I would also like to thank my clients, the professional wealth advisers who strive to deliver robust and meaningful guidance to their clients in an unconflicted and evidence-based approach, for their vision and passion for what they do that makes my consulting business fun. They know who they are.

Finally, I am indebted from an intellectual standpoint to two people: first, Richard Dawkins, who I first encountered when I was a (somewhat distracted) zoology undergraduate at Oxford and was privileged to hear him lecture on quite a few occasions; and the second is John Bogle, the founder of Vanguard, who kindly reviewed the first edition of this book. The common theme between the two is their unswerving pursuit of 'the truth' in their respective fields based on the evidence before them and their passion for sharing their arguments with others in a rational and understandable way. Their writing is immense. If this book achieves those values in any small way, I will be both relieved and delighted.

Publisher's acknowledgements

We are grateful to the following for permission to reproduce copyright material:

Figures 11.5 and 11.7 use data from Elroy Dimson, Paul Marsh and Mike Staunton, *Triumph of the Optimists: 101 Years of Global Investment Returns*, Princeton University Press, 2002 and the *Credit Suisse Global Investment Returns Yearbook 2009*; Figure 7.1 from MASLOW , ABRAHAM, MOTIV-ATION & PERSONALITY, 1st Edition, © 1970, Adapted by permission of Pearson Education, Inc., Upper Saddle River, NJ; Table 4.4 and Figure 15.1 from WM Company (1999) *Comparison of Active and Passive Management of Unit Trusts* with permission from WM Performance Services; Table 4.3 from Bogle, John C., *The Investment Dilemma of the Philanthropic Investor*, 31 October 2002; Figure 6.1 from Davey, G., (2009), 'Risk Tolerance Revisited', FinaMetrica Pty Limited (www.riskprofiling.com), p.1; Table 14.2 and Figures 14. 1 and 14.2 from Lipper Fitzrovia; Table 14.2 from an FSA Occasional Paper entitled 'The Price of Retail Investing in the UK' by Kevin R. James, dated February 2000; Table 15.1 Standard & Poor's Indices versus Active Funds Scorecard (SPIVA™) Fourth Quarter 2008; Figure 15.2 from Bernstein, William The Intelligent Asset Allocator © 2001, McGraw-Hill, reproduced with permission of the McGraw-Hill Companies; Dilbert cartoons reproduced with permission from Knight Features.

We would also like to thank those who have kindly given their permission to use their data sets either directly or as underlying constituent components of data series compiled by others. These include:

Dimensional Fund Advisers for the use of the Dimensional UK Value Index and the Dimensional UK Small Cap indices; We would like to thank Elroy Dimson, Stefan Nagel and Garrett Quigley for their permission to use the underlying data for the Dimensional UK Value Index computed by Dimensional Fund Advisors from "Capturing the value premium in the UK", *Financial Analysts Journal* 2003, 59(6): 35-45 and the updated series in Elroy Dimson, Paul Marsh and Mike Staunton, *Credit Suisse Global*

Investment Returns Yearbook 2009, Zurich: Credit Suisse, February 2009. We would like to thank Elroy Dimson and Paul Marsh for permission to use the underlying data from January 1970-June 1981 representing the Hoare Govett Smaller Companies Index 2009, ABN-AMRO / Royal Bank of Scotland, January 2009 which forms one of the underlying data sets for the computation of the Dimensional UK Small Company Index. Permission to use a reconstructed back-history of the UK equity market from Elroy Dimson, Paul Marsh and Mike Staunton, *Triumph of the Optimists*, Princeton University Press, 2002 prior to the start of the FTSE data series in 1962 is appreciated.

We thank Dimensional Fund Advisors for permission to use the Dimensional US Small Cap Index; Eugene Fama and Kenneth French for the use of the Fama/French Emerging Markets Value Index and Standard & Poor's for their permission to use the underlying data used to compile the latter. Standard & Poor's, MSCIBarra, and FTSE have all kindly granted permission to use a number of their data series.

Data is sourced on each figure or table and detailed citations and data compilation processes can be found in Appendix 1 to this book, where applicable.

Every effort has been made by the publisher to obtain permission from the appropriate source to reproduce material which appears in this book. In some instances we may have been unable to trace the owners of copyright material and would appreciate any information that would enable us to do so.

Foreword

If you are concerned about how money is invested you should read this book. If you are responsible for, or are the beneficiary of, moneys invested to meet your or your family's future needs, you must read this book. It matters not whether you are a 'do-it-yourself' investor or you are employing others to make investment decisions for you. In both cases you will be richer and more capable of critically judging the options available to you if you do so. Whether you like it or not, the quality and enjoyment of your future is likely to be heavily determined by investment decisions. You fail yourself and your family if you leave them naively to others or rely on chance.

Tim Hale has distilled, into less than 300 easy-to-read pages, the building blocks for you to construct a portfolio that's best for *you*. He puts together a solid case for low cost, low turnover investments that are easily understood. It is the most coherent and well constructed argument that I have come across in more than 30 plus years working in the financial services industry.

We know that investing is an uncertain activity. What Tim does is tell you why and how to build portfolios which have the greatest likelihood of achieving your goals. This does not mean that they come with a guarantee of portfolio performance. The financial world is too fickle for that. You might be the one in 50 or the one in 100 that will not be happy with your results. However, what you will learn from this book will leave you unsurprised by the portfolio returns and outcomes over time. You may be disappointed in the results but you should know that they are possible.

There are two distinct parts of Tim's argument. One is concerned with helping you solve a very personal issue: how much investment risk you should take on in your investment portfolio. The second gives you a practical 'how to' strategy for both constructing and managing your portfolio over time.

So how much investment risk should you take? Tim shows that you need to quantify and prioritise three competing expressions of risk in your life: risk required, risk capacity and risk tolerance (sometimes called risk appetite).

Risk required is the amount of risk associated with the return required to achieve your goals. You might want to live well in retirement, travel internationally on a regular basis, support your children and give generously to charity. You would not be unusual if you needed to take a reasonable amount of risk in your investments to do so. Most of us do not have sufficient existing or potential assets to meet our preferred future spending from cash-like returns. One of the basic laws of capitalism is that shares in businesses will, in the longer term, give you a higher return than lending money to a bank or government. So for those needing a higher return than cash or bonds, investment in shares is necessary. The downside is that there is a possibility that some of the companies you invest in might fail outright whilst others will vary in value over time. In simple terms shares should give a higher return than cash but with greater likelihood of variation above and below.

Risk capacity is the amount of money you could lose without putting your important short and long term goals at risk. Risk tolerance is best understood as the amount of financial risk you would naturally be comfortable with taking, all else being equal. Risk required and risk capacity vary with individual circumstances over time whereas risk tolerance is an enduring and generally persistent personal trait.

So here's the rub. Rarely do all three line up. More often than not the risk we need to take (risk required) is more than we could afford to take (risk capacity) and more than we normally prefer to take (risk tolerance). Which is the dominant one for you? What is the right mix? Many individuals would prefer to say this is just too hard. But you and your family will live the outcomes of these decisions and they must be made based on your values not someone else's. It's just not fair to your family to leave it to someone else to decide. Worst of all do not leave it to a common risk profiler or portfolio picker. These are usually idiot quizzes offered by lazy life companies, indolent fund managers and apathetic financial advisers. More akin to the more lurid women's magazines astrology predictions than science, they seek to box unsuspecting investors into such groupings as 'You are a balanced investor seeking inflation protection, tax efficiency and regular income' from the answers to half a dozen unrelated questions. They might just as easily say 'You are an Aquarian. You like new floats, holidays by the sea and highly liquid investments'.

While it might seem a little difficult to define and establish the portfolio that best suits you, this turns out to be relatively straightforward compared to the challenges of managing that portfolio over time as markets move, the media bays and as a consequence your confidence sags. More often than not individual investors make the mistake of buying at the top of the market and selling at the bottom. Tim firstly gives you the underlying disciplines to build a solid portfolio that meets your needs and secondly tells you how to minimise the behaviour that results in poor investment performance in the longer term.

The best thing about Tim's arguments is that they are almost invariably supported by both hard evidence and intuitive common sense. In summary they are: invest in things you understand, use transparent, cheap and robust products and control yourself when markets get tough. Whether you manage your own investments or use a financial adviser your responsibility to yourself and your family demands that you at least read and make sense of the arguments presented.

Paul Resnik, Melbourne, July 2009

Paul Resnik has had many roles in the financial services industry over the last 40 years including setting up in Australia a national financial advisory practice, an asset management business, a life insurance company and many retirement income products. He has spent the last 15 years developing practical solutions to better match portfolios to investors' needs. He is a co-founder of FinaMetrica which robustly assesses financial risk tolerance for investors in more than 12 countries.

Introduction

I.1 What should I do with my money?

Have you ever asked yourself this question? I bet you have, and quite right too. I would also wager that you probably feel a little uncomfortable that you haven't come up with an answer that you feel truly comfortable with either, or where to turn to for the help and advice that you need. Have you ever wondered how much you should be investing in for your future, or how big your pot needs to be to be able to take a good income from it, no matter how long you live? Even if you have these things in control, do you ever ask yourself what you should be doing with your investments today, to make the most of your money?

If you haven't asked yourself such questions, then you have the wealth of Bill Gates, or are already a smart investor, or have taken the ostrich approach to investing.

If you have asked such questions, and know that you really do need some help in answering what appear to be such simple questions, then this book is for you. You are not alone because nearly everyone is in the same boat. If you have taken the ostrich approach, this is a great chance to get your head out of the sand, and to take some easy positive steps towards unravelling the conundrum. Read on.

I.2 Some eye-openers to get you thinking

A good place to start is by looking at some facts that should make you sit up and take notice. If they don't, then either you are a very well informed investor, or you need to go away, drink a strong cup of coffee and start again. Don't despair though if you are shocked, because the solution to smarter investing is straightforward and this book shows you how. Smarter investing is simple investing – a mantra we will return to time and again. Perhaps now is the time to begin to commit to doing things differently and so avoiding some of the pitfalls that many investors fall into, including: failing to invest in the first place; investing too little to have any real chance of achieving your goals; asking too much from your portfolio; and chasing last year's best performing markets and managers – a fool's errand.

Eye-opener 1: It is not too hard to be a great investor

It is actually quite easy to be a great investor. Have faith in capitalism; there may be stormy weather at times, but capitalism still works. Own global capitalism (i.e. companies) by owning a global equity index tracker fund that puts as much of the market return that it generates in your pocket, not someone else's. As a balance, lend your money to the UK government with their promise that they will preserve its purchasing power for as long as they borrow it (inflation-linked investments), plus a little more. Get this balance right, execute it with the lowest costs and hold the balance firm over time. That's about it. This book shows you how.

Eye-opener 2: The market beats the 'average' investor

Over the long term the market will beat a majority of investors, professional or otherwise. This is a mathematical fact, not supposition. The market is made up of all investors; as such, the return of the average investor is by definition the return of the market before costs. After paying professionals to manage money, administration costs and costs associated with the buying and selling of shares, the average investor's return will inevitably be below that of the market. In the UK, investment professionals trying to beat the market represent the majority of investors, so for all of them to beat themselves is not possible. You might be surprised to hear that well over 80 per cent of all UK investors' money (90 per cent in the case of individual investors) is invested in strategies that try to beat the market. A lot of people will lose out – fact. Not everyone can be a winner.

Eye-opener 3: The average investor is terrible at investing

In the USA, the average individual investing in equity funds reduced $100 of spending power to around $90 over the nineteen-year period from 1984 to 2002 (Dalbar, 2003), most of which was during one of the greatest bull markets. This occurred because investors chased returns, moving from the funds they were in to those that seemed to be performing better, destroying their wealth with this buy-high and sell-low strategy. Such behaviour in all likelihood applies to investors around the world, not just those in the USA. During this time, the equity market itself turned $100 of spending power into a little under $500. Investors are simply throwing away wealth.

Recent research on UK investors (Schneider, 2007) reveals that they also chase fund managers who have performed well, with the same unfortunate consequences. From 1992 to 2003, investors' returns were around 2 per cent per year below the return delivered by the funds they were invested in as a consequence of the timing of their entry and exits into the funds. On average, UK equity funds underperformed the market (FTSE All Share) by around 2 per cent per year. In total that means that the average fund investor received a return around 4 per cent a year below the market. That is approximately equivalent to the entire reward that you can expect for owning equities rather than placing a deposit.

Eye-opener 4: The market beats most professionals

Over this same period the market beat the average professionally managed US equity fund by around 3 per cent a year (Bogle, 2003). An investor who started with $100 and remained invested in such a fund ended up with around $300 of purchasing power compared with around $500 generated by the market. That's a huge amount of your future wealth to give up by paying professionals to make decisions for you.

Eye-opener 5: Industry costs are excessive

The average 'on the road' cost of a UK equity fund exceeds 3 per cent a year. In the long run equities have produced a real return, i.e. after inflation, of around 5 per cent a year over the past 109 years or so (Barclays, 2009). In the long run, the industry croupier takes almost 60 per cent of your returns. Is that really fair or sensible? As the title to Fred Schwed's classic book about New York's Wall Street asks: *Where are the Customers' Yachts?* (Schwed, 1995).

Eye-opener 6: Past performance tells you almost nothing

A track record of good past performance for a specific fund provides few clues as to whether performance in the future will be good or bad. Performance in most cases appears to be random over time. As an investor, it's extremely hard continuously to outsmart all the other smart people trying to outsmart you. Some investors will get it right, either through luck or judgement, some of the time, but very rarely all of the time. You probably need fifteen to twenty years of performance data to be able to differentiate between the two. Yet for most investors, short-term past performance is the sole criterion for selecting a manager. How are you going to choose a good manager to manage your money without using performance data? If you find a way, let me know.

To be fair, a small handful of managers, such as Warren Buffett in the USA and Anthony Bolton in the UK, have excellent track records as a result of outstanding skills and investment processes. The challenge, as you will see, is picking them in advance.

Eye-opener 7: Picking winners is hard

Looking for a manager, then, who will beat the market for you over the next twenty or more years is like looking for a needle in the proverbial investment universe haystack. With 3,000 funds managed by more than 100 firms, let alone managers, in the UK, and with the average investment manager hopping from one firm to the next every three to four years, you'll be kept busy trying! A recent piece of research (Bogle, 2007), covering a thirty-five year period in the US, revealed that of 355 US equity mutual funds in 1970 only 3 (less than 1 per cent) delivered statistically significant and consistent performance through to 2005. Now that should get the alarm bells ringing. For all the claims of the market-beating active management world, the emperor still has no clothes!

Eye-opener 8: Many will be poor in their retirements

People in their twenties spend around £150 a month on booze and cigarettes yet only half save anything and of these, half save less than £50 a month according to a Birmingham Midshires Bank survey (2004). *Carpe diem.* Forty per cent of UK workers told an AON survey in 2003 they didn't think the state and company plans will provide them with a decent retirement yet only one in five is doing anything about it. The average annual contribution rate into defined contribution pension plans, where the employee makes the investment decisions, is only 6 per cent, when it should be at least 15 per cent for a comfortable retirement (NAPF, 2003). A recent report for the British government estimated that three-quarters of these type of pension plan members have contribution rates 'below the level likely to be required to provide adequate pensions' (Pensions Commission, 2004). Half of all employees in the UK have no occupational pension plan at all (TUC, 2002). That doesn't sound very encouraging. My advice – don't be one of them.

Eye-opener 9: You can easily avoid these pitfalls

Hopefully, I now have your attention and we can focus on the task of making sure that you avoid the many investment pit falls that lie in wait for the unsuspecting investor, not by any complicated investing strategy, but by doing a few plain, easy-to-understand things well. Please read on.

1.3 How this book will help you

Who are you?

It doesn't really matter because the fundamentals of investing are the same whoever you might be, whatever you are hoping to achieve and however much money you have to invest. Perhaps more contentiously, it shouldn't matter how much you think you know about investing, because it's always good to challenge your beliefs. If you are just starting out, excellent, this book is for you too. Investors generally fall into three categories: those who have no interest in doing anything themselves; those who want to be involved but don't want to spend too much time or effort on it; and those who are keen to run the entire show themselves. Whichever you are, the one thing you need to do is at least understand the basics of what investing is about.

Why did you pick this book up?

I imagine it's because you know that maybe all is not as good as it should be in terms of getting your investment life in order. Maybe you feel that you ought to start investing for your future, but feel at a loss where to start. Perhaps you feel that your money should be working harder for you, but are unsure what to do, or are not sure how you should invest your pension contributions, surplus income, an inheritance or your bonuses. Read on if you have a suspicion that what you are doing at present is not optimal. It's an important business that deserves some of your time.

Most of us don't build our own houses or service our own cars, but increasingly we have to take on the responsibility for investing money without any formal training. You may well have some questions on your mind:

- Who should I turn to for advice?
- How do I know what is good advice and what is not?
- What type of investments should I make?
- How should I choose managers/advisers for my money?
- What type of products makes sense?
- How should I monitor my investments and manage them?

This book is a chance to arm yourself with what you need to know to answer these questions yourself.

What this book will do for you

■ Develop a simple set of rules to make your investment decisions by (or to understand those suggested by your adviser).

■ Help you to control some of your demons that will tempt you into being a bad investor.

■ Help you broadly to define what you want to achieve from your investing.

■ Help you to construct a portfolio that meets your financial needs.

■ Help you to construct a sensible portfolio of investments that you can live with.

■ Suggest some practical ways of being an efficient, good investor.

■ Provide some practical pointers about using advisers and products.

■ Help you to relax and enjoy your investing responsibilities.

Why am I qualified to write it?

While I am not a fund manager by trade (thank goodness), my career has revolved around the process of advising wealthy individuals and institutions on their investment strategies. I have probably heard most of the crazy notions that investors have about investing, discussed many of the old chestnuts they argue about, which we will throw around too, and had the privilege to meet and listen to some very smart and experienced investors.

Today, my company, Albion Strategic Consulting, focuses on helping wealth managers to provide valuable, clear and well-articulated advice to help clients meet their lifetime spending goals. I have spent many years thinking that there must be a better way to try to educate investors than the tools and books that the industry provides; in the end I decided to tackle the issue myself, both through my business and this book.

I.4 How this book works

The basic principle of this book is to provide a clear and balanced view of investing and some simple rules and practical tools to help you to make your own decisions. It will provide access to research, data, concepts and hotly contested debates that are central to the industry and from which good investing rules arise. It provides an understanding of investment ideas at a level that you decide and is broken down into four parts:

Part 1: Smarter investing basics

This is a foundation course on investing. It introduces some of the basic things that you need to understand before you go any further. Failing to take these basic concepts on board may prove to be very costly. If you are familiar with them, there is no harm in spending a few minutes in bringing them into the forefront of your thoughts. Even if you intend to employ an adviser to help you with your investment programme you should make sure that you understand the concepts that are raised. It is rounded off with twenty investing tips, although I urge you to read beyond this point!

Part 2: Smarter thinking

Here, you will build a simple and practical investment philosophy to develop rules that give you the highest chance of success in your investing, avoiding the many pitfalls set by the industry. It also provides an insight into the bad-investing demons that tempt you towards poor investment practices. Your emotions have the potential to destroy your wealth.

Part 3: Building smarter portfolios

Defining your goals is the first step to creating a suitable investment programme and you will find guidance and some useful tools to help you to work out what they are. The concept of building a smart but simple portfolio is covered and an insight into why equities and bonds form the structural core of this portfolio is provided. We'll take a refreshingly straightforward, novel and leading edge approach to finding the portfolio that is right for you including how and when to introduce other building blocks into the investment mix.

Part 4: Smarter implementation

It's no good getting to this stage of the book and failing to do anything because you are swamped by choice when you put the book down. This part of the book arms you with some down-to-earth advice and ideas about how to put into action what you have decided upon in Part 3, right down to website and product provider details.

I.5 A few points to note

UK and US bias to data

This book focuses on the UK marketplace using data from it and practical solutions that relate to it. Many of the better books on investing have a US orientation and I thought it was about time that UK investors got a chance to hear the story from their own perspective. You will see that much of the data and research is based on the UK and US markets. This is largely a consequence of availability of data and academic research. Experience in other markets such as Japan helps to bring added perspective and I have introduced facts from these places where I believe they add to the argument. Remember that the fundamentals of good investing are universal and as such it does not matter where you live.

Denomination

Throughout this book try to think about your own domestic perspective. I have used '£' and 'pounds' throughout this book frequently as the means of denominating units of currency rather than as a representation of a purely UK perspective.

An apology to active managers

I want to make clear that this book is not meant to be a direct assault on active managers or their efforts. There are some very smart and hard-working people in the industry, but that just raises the bar for all in a game of winners and losers. Rarely is an industry so brutally cruel on its skilled and dedicated participants, and rarely too are the chances of success (from an investment perspective) so stacked against them throughout their careers. As you will see from the evidence, hard-working and smart does not necessarily translate into outperformance of the market after costs, the measurement of success in this industry.

There are undoubtedly a few managers who outperform over long periods of time as a consequence of their superb skills. I congratulate them.

References

Barclays Equity Gilt Study (2009).

Birmingham Midshires Bank survey (2004).

Bogle, J. C. (2003) The Emperor's New Mutual Funds, *The Wall Street Journal*, July 8, p. A16.

Bogle, John C. (2007) *The Little Book of Common Sense Investing*. John Wiley & Sons.

Dalbar, Inc. (2003) *Market chasing mutual fund investors earn less than inflation – Dalbar study shows* [online]. Available from: http://dalbarinc.com/content/printerfriendly.asp?page=2003071601.

NAPF (2003) *Annual survey commentary*, London: NAPF (National Association of Pension Funds), December.

Pensions Commission (2004) *The first report of the pensions: challenges and choices*. Norwich: TSO (The Stationery Office), October.

Schneider, L. (2007) Diploma thesis: 'Are UK fund investors achieving fund rates of return?' Submitted in July 2007, Fachhochschule Kufstein, Tirol, Austria

Schwed Jr., F. (1995) *Where are the customers' yachts?* 3rd ed. New York: Wiley.

TUC (2002) *Uncovered: workers without pensions*. London: TUC, July. Available from: http://www.tuc.org.uk/pensions/tuc–5429–f0.cfm.

1

Smarter investing basics

A foundation course for the rest of the book. Understanding a few basic investment ideas and spending a few minutes thinking about them will give you the basis on which to move forward and design and implement your own portfolio. The chapters in this part of the book include:

Chapter 1: Simplifying the confusion

To many investors, the world of investment can seem both confusing and complicated; yet it can be reduced down to a simple process. Product proliferation, conflicts of interest and market noise are the culprits. Identifying and filtering out the industry's noise is a good place to start.

Chapter 2: Covering the basics

What is smarter investing actually about? Your understanding of a few simple concepts will allow you to focus on the really important issues. For some, this may seem trivial, but take a look anyway because it really is important stuff that you cannot afford to misunderstand or ignore.

Chapter 3: It only takes a minute

In recognition of the fact that some readers may not be able to find the time to read the whole book in one sitting, this chapter provides a summary of the rules, tips, hints and guidelines that you should be following. In fact, applying these ideas will put you at the forefront of investors, although you may well be doing the right things but without necessarily understanding why. I strongly urge you to read beyond this chapter.

1

Simplifying the confusion

It would not surprise me if the world of investing seems a confusing and complicated place; the number of investment choices is vast and making sense of it all may be daunting. Fortunately, it need not be so.

1.1 Choices, choices, choices

The menu of potential investments has the capacity to leave many new to the game mesmerised by choice; a little like when you go into a restaurant and have to choose what to eat from a menu ten pages long. Dishes on offer include bank deposits, corporate bonds, investing in China, UK companies, gold, property, commodities, the USA, Japan, stamps, wine and vintage cars to name a few. Your choice is as wide as it is confusing. Don't worry though; this book narrows down the menu to a sensible one-pager and gives you help on what to choose.

In the UK there are around 3,200 funds (unit trusts or OEICs) registered for sale that you can choose from, managed by 260 investment management firms, of which 100 are based in the UK. It would take a year or so, reviewing ten funds a day, to cover them all, by which time about a third of the fund managers would have moved! That's a lot of choice. Add to this the fact that there are at least 150 private client investment managers, who would like to manage your money, three hundred investment trusts listed on the stock market that you can purchase, and forty authorised property unit trusts to consider. To make things worse, you face a constant barrage of noise and information from the industry, in its widest sense, trying to influence what you should be doing with your money.

This 'advice' comes from a wide range of sources. Journalists write articles in the Sunday papers along the lines of 'Is now the right time to be investing in [substitute the flavour of the month]?' creating a convincing spin on what to do with your money. Unfortunately it is usually just a return-chasing story encouraging you to jump out of one investment that is doing badly to one that is currently doing well – not a good strategy, as we saw in the Introduction. Fund managers advertise their spectacular market-beating returns over the past three years for a chosen fund, or laud their market-beating 'star' manager in the press. Financial advisers all seem to have their list of 'best performing managers'. Even the TV news gets in on the act with its valueless daily comments that the 'Footsie Index of the leading 100 shares was up 47 points today' or 'The pound fell by a cent against the dollar'. The magazine racks in the newsagents are full of investment magazines that provide stock and fund tips, the bookshelves groan with books on investing that try and teach you about how to pick stocks, day trade, make a million and time when to be in or out of markets, and your poor postman delivers sacks full of junk mail on what ISA to pick before April comes around again. Throw in the thousands of search results from a Google search on any investing topic, and if you weren't already confused, you are now!

The natural response to this confusion is to think about employing someone to unravel the mess and help make the decisions for you. This may well be a sound thing to do, provided you find the right person. Yet here too, uncertainty reigns: investors' confidence in the advice industry has taken a beating from a series of scandals and broken promises, from pension and endowment mortgage misselling to Equitable Life reneging on the payment of its annuity promises to some pensioners. It's not really surprising that many investors don't know which way to turn for advice they can trust.

Finally, let's not forget the stock market crash of 2000–2002 and 2008 when the market fell by more than 40 per cent and 30 per cent respectively, which bruised a good few investors and brought real meaning to the term 'risk'. You can quickly understand the temptation to put investing in the 'I'll deal with that later' category; but face the problem you must and this book is a good starting point.

1.2 How did we get here?

A potted and generalised history provides an insight into how this complexity has arisen, and why the noise from the industry has been turned up so dramatically in the past few years. We can then work out how we can try and make your investing a calmer, simpler and more enjoyable process.

The best way to invest has shifted dramatically

This is really a story about the way in which the best means of investing has evolved. Many investors seem to believe that beating the market is the goal of their investment programme, somewhat ignorant or blind to the fact that the world of investing is one of winners and losers and that costs (in the form of fees, commissions and taxes) result in more losers than winners in aggregate. The active management industry has done a good job in encouraging them to do so, and will try to do the same to you. Today, the battle for investors' money rages around whether you should try and beat the markets through active decision-making, or simply try and capture the market return as closely as possible, adopting a buy-and-hold strategy, as you will see. It is a question of where the probabilities of success lie in your favour. This is how the story unfolds.

The stockbroking model is on its last legs

Before the early 1970s, investors had little option but to buy securities through stockbrokers, or employ a stockbroker to manage a portfolio for them, an optimal way of managing money at the time. Information about companies was disseminated largely in print, and portfolio reporting was commonly just a list of stocks showing their purchase and current prices. Online trading, powerful computers and financial software were still science fiction. Brokers usually made money based on transaction fees, thereby encouraging the churning of investors' portfolios. This was fine at the time, but is not the best option today. Most stockbrokers are moving towards annual fee-based models, as investors wise-up. Those who don't may be living on borrowed time.

Professionally managed 'active' funds

Fortunately, the world has moved on. In the 1970s the mutual fund marketplace in the USA and other markets around the world, began to take off. Professional active managers looked after collective pools of money for a large number of investors, providing diversification by holding a wide number of securities, and a professional eye dedicated to watching over your money. Some managers provided individually managed investment services aimed at more wealthy clients.

Fund managers are remunerated via a management fee, calculated as a percentage of assets managed, so their interests are more closely aligned with their clients than the old stockbroking model. For many, this rightly became a better option than using a broker or investing on their own. These managers strove (and still do) to beat the markets and their peers by making active investment decisions – hence the term 'active managers'. With annual management fees of 1 per cent to 2 per cent and sales fees paid upfront of 5 per cent, this can be an expensive business, unless the manager is able to cover their costs and more. The problem with being paid good fees based on assets is that it has placed the gathering of assets as a higher objective than investment quality, in some firms.

The index fund challenges active management

A few visionaries in the USA began to question the blind belief that professionals could consistently outperform the markets and cover their increasing fees. They began to explore whether there was a better way of investing by simply replicating a market index rather than trying to beat it. Empirical research seemed to indicate that it made sense. The first index (tracker) funds were born in 1973 and run by Wells Fargo and the American National Bank of Chicago. This happened a few years later in the UK, as seems the case with most investment developments.

In the 1970s and 1980s computers were a scarce resource and analysis of data from the money management industry was largely confined to academics. The advent of cheap processing power in the early 1990s provided the means to analyse large amounts of data, the means to run market-replicating portfolios efficiently, and via the Internet, disseminate information and monitor and administer a portfolio.

Index investing has slowly become mainstream, overcoming hurdles as extreme as the charge of being unpatriotic, levelled against it in the USA (no American should accept that they can't beat the markets!) and the vociferous attacks on them by the active management industry. Recognition in the institutional world, and increasingly by individuals in the USA and more slowly elsewhere, has created significant challenges for the active management industry. Today, a battle exists between the two camps.

The rise and fall of product engineering and hot air

Over the 2000s the investor has been faced by an ever-increasing barrage of product engineering by investment banks and investment managers. Opacity, high costs and unidentified and unquantified risks were taken on by investors sold on a convincing story by a conflicted industry. Products such as structured notes were revealed not to be without risk. Ask anyone whose capital was guaranteed by Lehman Brothers (around $8 billion of investors' money was allegedly in these structures). Hedge funds failed to deliver their 'skill-based' returns and were revealed in the main to be selling market exposures at usurious prices, enriching themselves at the expense of gullible investors. No more gullible than those professionals who 'approved' and invested in Madoff's $50 billion Ponzi scheme, uncovered at the back end of 2008.

The time has come for transparency, value for money and the fulfilment of the fiduciary responsibility of all in the industry including fund managers, product development and marketing teams, and advisers. The outlook for impartial fee-based advice and evidence-based, transparent passive investing has never been so promising, or important to us.

1.3 Battling for investors' money

The great equity bull market from the early 1980s to 2000 created vast wealth and power for the active management industry, which captured the bulk of the inflows in the UK. In 2003, the UK fund management industry generated revenues from its clients of £7.5 billion from an asset base of £2.8 trillion (IFSL, 2004), a tenth of which is money invested for individuals either in funds or by private client portfolio managers. Not surprisingly, fund managers are reluctant to give this position up without a fight to the index usurper.

The active management industry works on the premise that the markets can be beaten, after costs, and over the long term. We will test the efficacy of this premise in some depth a little later on in the book, where you can make up your own mind. Each manager has to believe that they will be the winner and can persuade investors to believe the same. Unfortunately, the maths doesn't work. Market-replicating managers, on the other hand, defend their position on logic and abundant empirical evidence, as you will see.

Even so, the active management industry has been remarkably successful, remaining as the default choice for the majority of individual investors, often by default. It has five weapons that it uses remarkably effectively to maintain its dominant position, evidenced by the fact that today more than 90 per cent of individuals' money and still 80 per cent of institutional money remains in active beat-the-market strategies in the UK.

■ The first and most legitimate claim is that picking and investing with an active manager who beats the market can have a very substantial positive effect on your investment outcome, compared with just gathering the market return by owning an index fund. I whole-heartedly agree. Yet, this powerful claim that plays on the hopes and emotions of investors fails to point out the fact that your chances of identifying such a manager upfront are simply too long for most individual investors to consider as a core strategy.

■ Second, human beings tend to be impressed by short-term success and treat it as a proxy for long-term success, which makes them believe that they can pick the long-term winning managers by looking at two or three years of outperformance. Short-term performance tells you next to nothing, I'm afraid, as you will find out. Canny product selection by managers means that most firms have one or two good stories to sell.

■ Third, for investors who may be confused but are trying their best to be sensible, choosing a reputable firm to manage their money, which is staffed by bright people as most investment firms are, with a seemingly strong recent track record, appears like the safest thing to do and is a convenient way of passing on their investment responsibilities to someone else.

■ Fourth, the advice industry that many individuals turn to, which accounts for around three-quarters of all fund sales to individuals in the UK, runs on a business model that is driven by the need to sell actively managed products rather than index fund products, as only the former have upfront fees and high enough annual fees to share. Most advisers are acting in the best interests of their clients, as far as the constraints of self-survival allow. Fortunately a few professional wealth advisers, who operate on a fee basis (a percentage of assets under management or advice), are carving out a niche for themselves at the forefront of the industry. More on this in Chapter 12.

■ Fifth, the industry has incredible firepower to influence investors. Marketing and branding strategies are backed with big bucks. In the USA, in 2000, media advertising alone came to around $1 billion (Bogle, 2001).

1.4 Reducing confusion and complexity

Imagine that the top edge of the triangle in Figure 1.1 represents your current interface with the market. It is crowded, noisy, confusing and all based on the premise that if you are smart, and have access to enough infor-

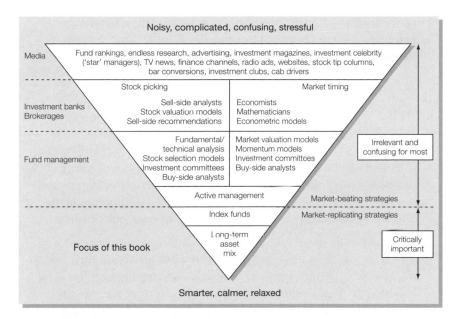

Figure 1.1 **Turning down the volume***

*Unless otherwise stated, all data analysis that appears in this book is by Albion Strategic Consulting.

mation, you can beat the market, or at least choose a manager who can. The lower layers give you an idea of the resources that are positioned in the industry that is trying to beat the market – smart, hard-working, diligent, well-paid but like alchemists of old trying to do the impossible. Remember that all the layers are being paid for by you, the investor, in one way or another.

The position this book takes

The premise of this book is that you can avoid most of the noise by focusing on the tip of the triangle. This is concerned with building and holding a sensible portfolio that gives you the greatest chance of success, not because you want an easier life, but because that is what the empirical evidence and logic tells you is the right thing to do.

In support of this position, a pertinent observation was made in the 2001 Myners Report commissioned by the government to look at pension plan management in the UK:

'A particular consequence of the present structure is that asset allocation – the selection of which markets [long term], as opposed to which individual stocks, to

invest in – is an under-resourced activity. This is especially unfortunate given the weight of academic evidence suggesting that these decisions can be critical determinants of investment performance.'

That's why this book focuses on constructing the right mix of investments above all else, followed closely by making sure that you capture the bulk of the returns that are on offer from this mix. It's as simple as that.

Three unassailable benefits accrue if you take this route:

■ You dramatically reduce the noise and confusion associated with investing, which is predominantly focused on which stocks to invest in and whether to move your mix of investments around over time, with the hope of doing better than your long-term chosen mix.

■ By avoiding the noise as your default position, you provide yourself with the greatest chance of success in meeting your investment goals. You are stacking the odds in your favour and you can't ask for more than that. The alternative, active management, is a high pay-off proposition with a low chance of a successful outcome for most individuals.

■ You narrow the choices that you need to make dramatically, making it easier to identify products that have a very good chance of delivering what you want them to, and have little portfolio maintenance to do.

That sounds a lot easier, doesn't it?

References

Bogle, J. C. (2001) *After the fall: what's next for the stock market and the mutual fund industry?* Bogle Financial Markets Research Center. Available from: http://www.vanguard.com.

IFSL (2004) *Fund management – City Business Series.* London: FSL, August.

Myners, P. (2001) *The Myners review of institutional investing in the UK.* HM Treasury.

2

Covering the basics

Let's start by getting some basic concepts straight. These form the foundations on which you will build an investment programme. While you may be familiar with some or all of them, it makes sense to cover the ground, because they are so important. Even if you feel that you are reasonably well versed in the basics, it's never a bad idea to refresh your thinking.

2.1 What is smarter investing?

As you saw from the Eye-openers in the Introduction, there is a lot of bad investing about, so it is important to make sure that you and I are on the same page when it comes to what we think smarter investing is about. For some, investing is about buying and selling investments through an online brokerage account, feeling that they are in control and enjoying the buzz from the excitement of the markets; for others it is about deciding where to put their money based on which markets will do better in the next year or two, often using funds to reflect their ideas. For a few, it means putting money into an interest-bearing account, because they are cautious and want to preserve the money that they have. Smarter investing is not any of these things.

Smarter investing is not about gambling with your money

When markets are going up, a combination of self-confidence and excitement encourages people to get involved in investing, particularly on their own – just witness the growth in online broking accounts in the late 1990s and the obsession with property in the 2000s. The buzz and excitement of seeing your money growing every day you log into your account is a powerful drug, and reinforces people's self-confidence to play the markets. The bull market of the 1980s and 1990s influenced many people's perception of what good investing is about. Yet they conveniently forgot that a rising tide raises all boats. Many got caught up in the notion that it was about making significant money over the long term, defined as two to three years, and if you had any nous, you could beat the market. Always remember short term is two to three years and long term is twenty-plus years.

Online trading, day trading and a plethora of expensive, complicated and ultimately wealth-destroying products rode on the back of the euphoria of the raging bull. That is gambling and end in tears for most, except for a few who get lucky. Gambling, unlike investing, is looking for long shots with high payouts and this includes: cards, horses and roulette; dipping in and out of the markets; trying to pick stocks that will outperform the market based on some sort of analysis, or guesswork; or picking professionals who you think will be able to beat the markets, and switching between them, as one falters and another shines. This may be a surprise, but as you will see in this book, you are entering a casino if you adopt such an approach, and one in which the croupier has a big fat hand in your pocket. The bank always wins in the long run.

One of my favourite quotes on the problems that investors face when trying to decide what is investing as opposed to what is speculation (gambling) comes from Fred Schwed's book (1995) on the brokerage industry:

'Investment and speculation are said to be two different things, and the prudent man is advised to engage in one and avoid the other. This is something like explaining to the troubled adolescent that love and passion are two different things. He perceives that they are different but they don't seem quite different enough to clear up his problems.'

Throughout this book you will get plenty of guidance to clear up any problems you may have.

Smarter investing is not about saving

There is nothing wrong with saving, i.e. putting your money into a interest-bearing account if you either want to maintain a small contingency reserve for bad times or have a specific short-term goal that you need to accumulate cash for. However, if you have quite a few years until you need this money, one of the cardinal sins is to be recklessly prudent and 'save': placing your money on long-term deposit with a bank or building society makes little sense. The future wealth that you give up as a result is likely to be significant, as is the risk that unexpected inflation will eat up the spending power of your money.

In the UK, the government has promised to give each child born £250, which they can't get their hands on until they are eighteen. Yet nearly half of all parents in a recent survey said that they would put the money in an interest-bearing account rather than invest it. Why?

Some individuals, having spent considerable time and effort in accumulating wealth in their business lives, for example, may decide that simple wealth preservation is what they want to achieve. That's fine: however, they still face the erosion of their money by inflation if they don't act sensibly – long-term saving is simply not an intelligent option.

Smarter investing is a dull process

It is the boring process of deciding what you want your money to do for you in the future, putting your money into a mix of investment building blocks that has good chance of getting you there, using products that allow you to keep as much of the market returns you make in your pocket rather than giving it to the industry croupier, and sticking to your planned mix through thick and thin – no chasing last year's winning markets or managers please! In a nutshell that is it. How dull! Where's the excitement in that? My advice to you is that if it is excitement that you want, book a turn on the Cresta Run with some of the money you make from being a smarter investor.

As you can see in Figure 2.1, good investing is about aiming for pay-offs you can survive with, along with chances of achieving them you can live with, not shooting the lights out with a wild bet or being certain of an unacceptably poor outcome.

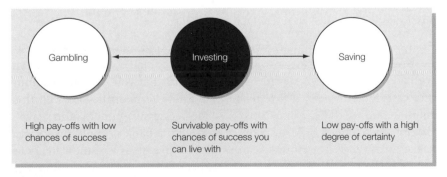

Figure 2.1 **Focus on the middle ground**

Good investing is about playing the probabilities in your favour for every investment decision that you take. To know where the favourable probabilities lie requires a basic knowledge of the markets, an insight into the research that has been done, and a good dose of common sense.

2.2 Ten points of focus for smarter investors

One of the things that I have noticed about the smart investors that I have met is that they all have a very firm grasp of the game they are playing, and I don't mean about understanding economics, or how to read a company's balance sheet. What I am talking about is that they understand the basic concepts that drive success: they understand first and foremost that this is about playing the probabilities in your favour: that time is your friend; the power of compounding is immense; that using history and research are valuable tools in raising their chances of success. They realise too that inflation, emotions and giving away too much to the industry croupier savage wealth creation. Let's take a closer look at the things that you should focus on.

Focus 1: Make better evidence-based decisions

Smart investors make investment choices that give them the greatest chance of achieving survivable outcomes, basing these decisions on evidence, not hope or heresay.

Smart investing involves three key decisions

Perhaps somewhat surprisingly, you only have three big decisions to make on how you should be investing:

- What mix of blocks should you own?
- Should you alter this mix over time to try to improve returns?
- Should you implement it using a strategy that seeks to beat each market or deliver the returns of each market, as near as possible?

Figure 2.2 illustrates the three main decisions you face and what your choices are. As you will see, one of the paths provides a greater chance of success than the other. This book provides you with the knowledge and evidence to see why. At this stage just take my word for it.

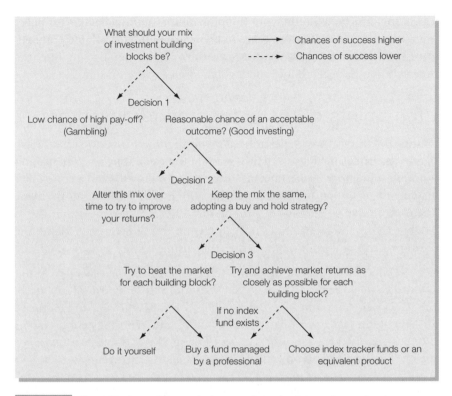

What should your mix
of investment building
blocks be?

→ Chances of success higher
----→ Chances of success lower

Decision 1

Low chance of high pay-off?
(Gambling)

Reasonable chance of an acceptable
outcome? (Good investing)

Decision 2

Alter this mix over
time to try to improve
your returns?

Keep the mix the same,
adopting a buy and hold strategy?

Decision 3

Try to beat the market
for each building block?

Try and achieve market returns as
closely as possible for each
building block?

If no index
fund exists

Do it yourself

Buy a fund managed
by a professional

Choose index tracker funds or an
equivalent product

Figure 2.2 **Smarter investors only have a few decisions to make**

Focus 2: Accept that higher returns come with more risk

This is one of the inescapable facts of investing. In a capitalist society, capital and labour should be allocated to achieve the best returns for the risk being taken. Investments that incur higher risks will be required by investors to deliver higher expected returns. If they did not, no one would invest in them. Smart investors question any product or opportunity where high returns apparently come with low risks. They also avoid risks for which they are not rewarded adequately.

Focus 3: Spread your investments around

Diversification, diversification, diversification – a central tenet of the smarter investor. Realising that markets could go pear-shaped is at the fore-front of their minds. They build portfolios that will hopefully help to protect their wealth if some markets do not go in their favour. As such, spreading risks between different building blocks to provide a portfolio for all seasons, and making sure that within each building block your money is well diversified between securities, is critical.

Focus 4: Use history and research wisely

Knowing how different investment building blocks, such as equities and bonds, have performed in the past provides both guidance and warnings. Studying their behaviour over the past one hundred years or so helps you to understand why such generalisations as 'equities for the long run' are made and, as importantly, to understand the magnitude and longevity of the exceptions.

Some advisers and investors claim that using history is 'investing by looking in the rear-view mirror'. I've always thought that is nonsense. Of course, blind use of data from shorter-term periods without placing it in the context of the long term, or using generalisations as being true all the time, are likely to land you in investing trouble. Look at Figure 2.3 and compare the long-term (109 years) data against that for the ten-year period ending 1999. If you used the ten-year data to 1999 blindly as a means of extrapolating into the future, with no reference to the long-run averages, then you would be likely grossly to overstate the returns that you are expecting and as a result would be sorely disappointed with the outcome of your investment.

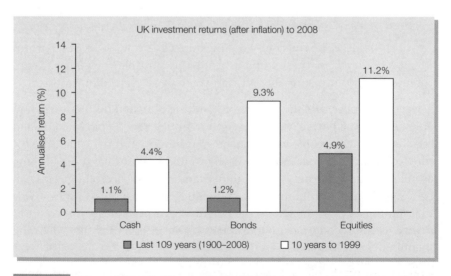

Figure 2.3 **Use returns in the context of history** *Source: Barclays Equity Gilt Study, 2009.*

However, use history wisely and you will find that there is much to be gained. This book allows you to take a good look at the history of different investments and to draw your own conclusions. Reviewing data from several markets helps you to explore a wider range of circumstances than just those in your domestic market. Always bear in mind that the unobserved may occur, hence the need to own a diversified portfolio.

Using research helps to get through to the truth of what investing is about and provides the foundation on which to make decisions. Research also illustrates that some issues remain unresolved.

Focus 5: Understand your portfolio

Knowing how your investment portfolio could behave is extremely valuable, particularly the consequences of being wrong about your expectations. It's no good resorting to a 'no one ever told me that could happen' defence – by then it is too late. Good investors understand what their hoped-for outcome is, but as importantly what the risks are they will not be successful, and just how bumpy their investment journey will be along the way. Being sprung surprises is the surest way of invoking an emotional (and probably wealth-destroying) response. Understanding history and anticipating the magnitude of market crises you could face is essential, before you start. This book provides plenty of opportunity to discover what you are letting yourself in for.

Focus 6: Obsessively seek to minimise costs

As will become apparent later, keeping your costs low, or in other words keeping as much of the returns generated as possible for yourself, contributes more to investing success than you may, at this point, realise.

Always remember that the success of investing is shared out between you, your adviser, the people who manage your money, the people who buy and sell shares for the people who manage your money, and the Chancellor of the Exchequer. It is your money and you should be obsessive about keeping as much of it as you can. As such, understanding and controlling costs will be a significant contributor to your investing success. Investing in a way that minimises costs, including the potential cost of manager underperformance, is the second most important decision in investing after defining the mix of your investments.

Good investing should not cost more than 0.5 per cent to 0.75 per cent a year at most, as you will see – and hopefully even less in the future.

Focus 7: Try to keep your emotions in check

If you are able to keep your emotions in control, you have a good chance of becoming a good investor. Understanding the emotional demons that divert you from the path of good investing is a good starting point. If you understand and are convinced that the way you invest and the mix of investments that you hold is right, then you have a base on which to stand firm when the markets get tough, as they inevitably will. Without this footing you will be sucked into the world of 'maybe I should have done that instead' and begin the fateful return chase. Understanding the characteristics of your portfolio allows you to prepare yourself for short-term and long-term outcomes and avoid being surprised by them. In doing so, you will create defences against being swayed by your emotions when markets get either very depressing or very exciting.

Focus 8: Plan for inflation

Inflation eats away relentlessly at your investments and on occasion in the past, such as the 1970s and early 1980s, voraciously. As a long-term investor, you need to protect your purchasing power by investing in ways that provide a strong hedge against inflation. To get some jargon out of the way, returns that are calculated after the effects of inflation are called *real returns* and relate to how your purchasing power (spending power) grows. Returns calculated before inflation is taken into account are *nominal returns*.

Look at the serious effect inflation can have over time: Table 2.1 shows you how much inflation leaves you with if you hide £100 under the bed instead of investing it.

Table 2.1   **Sticking £100 under the bed is not a good strategy**

Inflation	5 years	10 years	15 years	20 years	25 years	30 years	35 years	40 years
1%	£95	£90	£86	£82	£78	£74	£70	£67
2%	£90	£82	£74	£67	£60	£55	£49	£45
3%	£86	£74	£63	£54	£47	£40	£34	£30
4%	£82	£66	£54	£44	£36	£29	£24	£20
5%	£77	£60	£46	£36	£28	£21	£17	£13
10%	£59	£35	£21	£12	£7	£4	£3	£1

| Table 2.2 | Your £ is worth less every year | | | |

Shopping Item	1980	2004	Annual price increase	Buying power End 2004 (£100 = 1980)
Pint of beer	£0.55	£2.35	6%	£21
Pint of milk	£0.17	£0.35	3%	£47
Sliced white bread	£0.34	£0.55	2%	£61
Average house price in SE England	£31,670	£276,698	9%	£9

Source: Housing OPDM, 1980. FT 1 July 2003. End 2004: Land Registry.

In a low-inflation environment, like today, the temptation is to ignore inflation. Do so at your peril. Five per cent inflation over thirty years leaves you with only £21 spending money out of £100 at the start. Table 2.2 illustrates some common purchases in the UK comparing 1980 prices with those in 2004, which gives you a feel for the effect of inflation on your daily life.

Many investors suffer from 'money illusion', a mental state that fails to take inflation into account. A return of 17 per cent sounds far better than a return of –1 per cent. However, if inflation is 20 per cent in the former case and 2 per cent in the latter, these returns are the same from the perspective of purchasing power. Figure 2.4 illustrates the dangers of looking at investment returns in nominal terms rather than real terms.

In this book, the focus is on real returns because this avoids the money illusion trap. By thinking in this way, you can understand clearly the increase in purchasing power your money may generate. Put simply, there is not much value in knowing that your nominal money has doubled but then discovering that the prices of the goods you want to buy have tripled. By using real returns, you don't have to worry about scaling up income and capital amounts to reflect tomorrow's debased money.

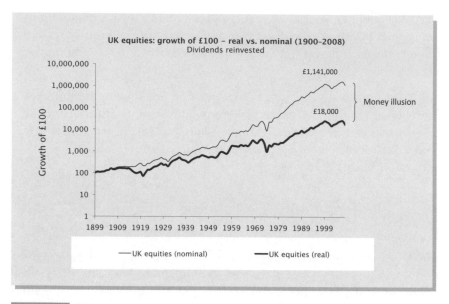

UK equities: growth of £100 – real vs. nominal (1900–2008)
Dividends reinvested

Figure 2.4 **The money illusion trap catches many investors**

Source: Barclays Equity Gilt Study, 2009.

Focus 9: Understand the power of time

A common attitude among the young is that the future is too far off to worry about and it is boring to be thinking about pensions and investments, so the thought is buried in the 'to-be-dealt-with-later' pile. Yet that is the time to begin to plan your investing, as time is a powerful ally. Some older investors adopt a similar head-in-the-sand strategy because the consequences of their lack of investing action to date are too dreadful to think about, and they believe it is too late to rectify the problem. It's never too late or too early to begin investing. Start now. The point to remember is that longer is better for three reasons.

First, time goes hand-in-hand with compounding, which is explored below. The longer you can give yourself to reach your goals, the greater the effect of the mathematical phenomenon of compounding.

Second, each investment building block exhibits certain characteristics that are often turned into generalised statements such as 'equities have higher returns than bonds'. From studying and understanding the history of the markets, it is evident that there are exceptions, and at times rather harsh exceptions that go against this generality: bonds have, for some prolonged periods, outperformed equities. The longer you have to invest, the higher the probability that your investments will behave like their generalisations, rather than like their exceptions. Time gives you the opportunity to work through the difficult, yet not unexpected periods when these exceptions to the rule arise.

Third, time moderates the range of returns that investments exhibit. Over short periods, some investments have very wide ranges of returns. However, over many years, these more extreme returns, generally but not always, tend to cancel each other out, generating much narrower ranges of returns and thus investing outcomes.

Focus 10: Harness the power of compounding

Compounding, as I am sure you are aware, is the effect of interest-on-interest. For example, a portfolio of £100 that compounds by 10 per cent a year rises to £110 in year one to £121 in year two, £133 in year three and so on. The effect of compounding returns is central to investing success and goes hand-in-hand with time. Its effects are exponential. Albert Einstein is commonly credited with the often-quoted statement that:

'[Compounding] is the greatest mathematical discovery of all time.'

You may be familiar with the ancient story where, in return for a favour, a wise man asked a young sultan for one grain of wheat on the first square of a chessboard to be doubled each square, to two on the second, four on the third and so on. The sultan acceded, bankrupting the kingdom well before the sixty-fourth square on which the wise man was owed 9,223,372,036,854,780,000 grains or about 165 times the world's annual harvest today! However, many investors will not have sat down and worked out the parallels when it comes to investing. Table 2.3 illustrates some simple rates of return compounded over different periods of time.

As you can see, compounding and time make a significant difference. While the difference between £100 compounded at 8 per cent versus 10 per cent over five years is only small (£147 versus £161), over forty years you would lose out on over half of your potential future wealth, i.e. £2,172 instead of £4,526. You may think forty years is a long time but if you start your investing at twenty-five and retire at sixty-five you have clocked up forty years. A favourite quote of mine about time and compounding comes from Sidney Homer in *A History of Interest Rates* (Homer and Syllar, 2005), a book far more interesting than it sounds.

| Table 2.3 | Value of £100 with compound interest rate over time |

Interest rate	5 years	10 years	20 years	30 years	40 years
2%	£110	£122	£149	£181	£221
4%	£122	£148	£219	£324	£480
6%	£134	£179	£321	£574	£1,029
8%	£147	£216	£466	£1,006	£2,172
10%	£161	£259	£673	£1,745	£4,526

'One thousand dollars left to earn interest at 8 per cent a year will grow to $43 quadrillion in 400 years, but the first hundred years are the hardest.'

Good investors always try to keep money in their portfolios for as long as possible. You should always be aware that any money that you withdraw, any income you receive from your investments and spend instead of reinvesting, pay out in tax, or in management fees, brokerage commissions, initial fees, etc., is going to cost you dearly in the long run because it will not benefit from compounding over time. Seemingly small differences make big differences in the long run.

In summary: Do these things exceptionally well

Smart investors realise that investing is not about trying to be an economist, or knowing how to read a company balance sheet, or having the ability to pick and choose when to be in or out of markets, or what stocks to buy or sell. What they do know is that their mix of assets has a good chance of delivering them a successful outcome and will not lose them too much if things do not go as planned. They ruthlessly pursue options that increase the chances of success: they stick with their mix, avoid chasing returns, try and be rather than beat the market, and eliminate costs in whatever form they take to keep their money in their pockets. They focus ruthlessly in pursuing these few things exceptionally well. That's all there is to it!

2.3 The two distinct phases of investing

Having quickly highlighted where smart investors focus their time and effort, it is important that you take a quick look at the two phases that all investing falls into. The ultimate goal of investing is to build the purchasing power of your wealth to a level that allows you to fulfil your

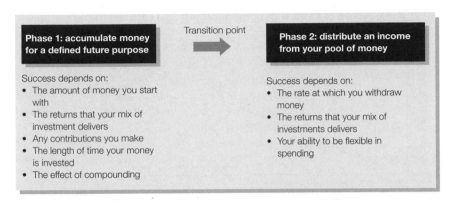

Phase 1: accumulate money for a defined future purpose

Transition point

Phase 2: distribute an income from your pool of money

Success depends on:
- The amount of money you start with
- The returns that your mix of investment delivers
- Any contributions you make
- The length of time your money is invested
- The effect of compounding

Success depends on:
- The rate at which you withdraw money
- The returns that your mix of investments delivers
- Your ability to be flexible in spending

Figure 2.5 **Are you accumulating wealth or distributing wealth?**

lifestyle plans, which usually involves either the distribution of income or the disbursement of capital at some time in the future. As such, most investors can break down their investing into two main phases: the accumulation of wealth and the distribution of financial benefits from this pool of accumulated wealth. Which phase your investments fall into at the moment will be unique to your own personal circumstances.

A thirty-year-old investing for retirement still has thirty years or more of the accumulation phase left and will be concerned with maximising the chances of accumulating enough in his or her investment pot to generate a decent income in the future. On the other hand, retirees no longer pay into a pension plan but draw an income from their investment pool: they are primarily concerned with maintaining the purchasing power of their income, and avoiding running out of money before they die, although some may be seeking to grow their money if the risks are acceptable. Figure 2.5 provides a generic representation of the two phases of investment.

For each pool of money that you have, representing a specific future goal, you will have to decide which phase of investing you are in and how long you have to go before you reach the transition point between the two. An example of this transition point comes at the time of retirement where occupational income stops and investment income takes over.

A quick look at the accumulation phase

Let's look at the accumulation phase of investing in a little more detail. The generic process of accumulating wealth is a simple one: you start by choosing a mix of investments that has a good chance of delivering a rate

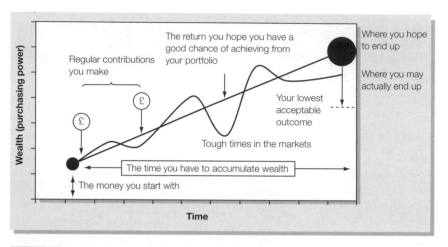

Figure 2.6   The generic accumulator of wealth

of return that, in conjunction with any contributions you may make, and the time you have available, will deliver a pool of assets that is sufficient to meet either your requirement for capital, or deliver an acceptable level of income to you. Figure 2.6 helps to highlight some of the issues that you need to think about.

In reality, your investment life is not going to generate straight-line returns, but fluctuating returns that at times will leave you wondering whether you are doing the right thing when markets take a beating (as they will at some stage) and the outlook looks bleak. Your final pool of money will depend on what the actual returns have been like in your investing lifetime. The real risk is that they are disappointing, despite the fact that the chances of success were in your favour. You need to decide what the lowest acceptable outcome is for you, and make sure that the combination between the mix of assets you choose and the contributions you make, offers you a high enough chance of achieving a successful outcome. The accumulation stage of investing begs answers to the following questions:

■ How much capital or income do you need at the end of your accumulation period to achieve the things you want to do?

■ How long have you got to achieve this growth in your wealth?

■ What is the lowest acceptable outcome you can stomach?

■ What combination of portfolio returns and contributions will provide you with a high chance of successfully meeting your target, or at least your minimum?

■ What mix of assets will generate these sorts of returns with a high degree of comfort?

■ What are the worst-case times in the market that you could suffer with such a mix of investments and can you stomach it?

Part 3, Building Smarter Portfolios, leads you step-by-step through the process of unravelling these issues. With the right tools, it is easier to do than you may think.

A quick look at the distribution phase

The distribution phase of investing is generally concerned with wealth and income preservation rather than wealth accumulation. The commonest example is that of retirees who have accumulated a pool of assets to live off in retirement. The risk they face, if this income is critical to them, is running out of money before they die. The goal of the distribution phase is to find the combination of portfolio investment mix (and thus returns) and rate of income withdrawal that preserves the spending power of the pool of money and thus the spending power of the income derived from it. This is generically represented in Figure 2.7.

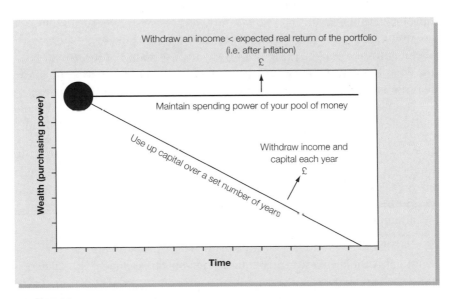

Figure 2.7 The distribution phase is commonly about preserving spending power

When you reach the distribution phase of your investment life, there are really only two important questions that you need to answer:

- How much can I sensibly take out of my portfolio every year?
- What mix of assets will allow me to do this (a) without eroding my capital or (b) using up my capital over a defined period of time?

These questions can be answered in terms that you can understand by asking and answering questions such as 'If I am invested with mix A and withdraw 5 per cent of the value of my portfolio each year, what chance do I have that I will run out of money before I die?' Finding the balance between maintaining your capital, or decreasing it at a prescribed rate, and generating a suitable income is critical.

2.4 There are no perfect answers

Finally, let me tell you that there are no perfect answers to investing and this book does not seek to provide any. Instead, it aims to provide enough insight to allow you to understand the trade-offs and risks that investing entails, and to build yourself an investment portfolio that gives you what you believe is the highest chance of success to achieve your goals and should protect your wealth in poor markets.

We can't see into the future, yet we have to make assumptions about a range of events; many of the measurements that we make and use in coming to decisions vary depending on the time periods we are looking at; and the process of forecasting is littered with the bodies of those who have tried. Add to this the fact that we are all emotionally different as investors and the science of investing quickly becomes the art of common sense.

What we do have on our side is the ability to learn from history, to read and evaluate the empirical research that exists, to maximise the use of all the things that we know to be proven and minimise uncertainties that we know have the power to divert us from achieving our goals. This book pulls all these together to allow you to make your own decisions with confidence. Just remember that common sense and rational thinking are your friends and that emotions and spurious accuracy are your enemies.

The marketplace abounds with software that will spew out pie-charts saying what you should invest in; risk questionnaires to evaluate your tolerance for losses; and investment calculators for retirement or school fees. These will all claim to tell you how much you should save and provide what seem like definitive solutions to how you should invest down to three decimal places. Just remember that these are all just estimates made by someone else, embedded with their own assumptions and imperfections – useful guides, no more. In addition, most of them don't tell you what chance you have of succeeding, which is what you really want to know. At the end of the day it is your money and you need to understand how you arrived at the investment strategy that you do.

In this book you will find few complicated algorithms, calculations, forecasts or models for allocating assets between building blocks – just the application of standard investment rules, common sense and a determination to keep things simple not for simplicity sake, but because that is fortunately what the empirical evidence tells us we should be doing.

2.5 Summary: smarter investing basics

■ Investing is about playing a game that has long-term high probability of success, not about long shots and get-rich-quick strategies.

■ Focus on the few things that good investors do: make sure you take decisions that improve your chances of success; get your mix of assets right for you; use history and research wisely to help you do so; understand what you are letting yourself in for; keep the croupier's hand out of your wallet; control your emotions; be aware of and plan for inflation; and use the powerful effects of time and compounding to your benefit.

■ As an investor you are in one of two phases: the accumulation phase or the distribution phase. As you plan your investment strategy, you will be trying to find answers to questions relevant to each stage – bear these in mind as we move forwards.

■ Remember there are no perfect answers, only some that have a greater chance of success than others.

References

Homer, S. and Syllar, R. (2005) *A history of interest rates.* 4th ed. New York: Wiley.

Schwed, Jr. F. (1995) *Where are the customers' yachts?* 3rd ed. New York: Wiley.

3

It only takes a minute

When I talked to friends and colleagues about my plan to write a book the unanimous response was: 'Great, but please make it a pamphlet'. They are to a large extent right. The 80/20 rule applies in investing – you gain 80 per cent of what you need to know from only 20 per cent of the effort. To that end, the summary below provides a brief list of some of the guidelines commonly used in the investment industry when giving advice.

These tips can help you to become a better investor by way of a kind of investing by numbers, without a real understanding of why or the consequences of the actions you take. They may help you to avoid some of the pitfalls that lie in wait. Some use gross oversimplifications and assumptions about your personal circumstances, but, by and large, they will put you in the right ballpark.

I hope that the list at least makes you ask yourself whether this is how you are currently investing. But only by truly understanding what you are doing and why will you be able to bear the emotional pressures that force many investors to destroy their wealth. I encourage you to use this section as an aide-memoire for later.

3.1 Twenty tips for smarter investing

First of all . . .

1   *Start investing now* If you haven't begun investing yet, then better late than never. The effect of time will be hugely beneficial to you through the power of compounding, i.e. the effect of interest-on-interest. The longer you give it the more powerful it becomes. Time also gives you a greater chance that the investments you choose will act as you hope they will rather than as the exceptions to the rule that inevitably occur over the shorter term, from time to time. Invest whenever you have the cash to do so, regularly if possible.

Choosing your mix of investments

2 *Investment period* Decide how long you can invest for each pool of money, whether it be pension, nest egg or school fees. Getting this right is very important. A mismatch between your mix of investments and your investment period could result in either having to sell investments when markets are down to meet your obligations, or giving up potentially higher levels of future money by being too conservative if your investment period is actually longer than you say it is.

3 *The mix of investments is the most critical decision you will make* At the end of the day, it is the mix of investments that you own that drives your portfolio returns (along with keeping as much of this as you can by keeping other people's hands out of your pockets). Messing around with this mix and trying to pick market-beating investments or managers will add little, for most. Choosing this mix carefully is the first step towards smarter investing.

4 *Rules of thumb for defining your mix* A couple of simple rules provide a sensible starting point for deciding the appropriate mix between equities and bonds, the building blocks of your portfolio. Both provide similar outcomes. Think about them carefully.

Rule 1 Own 4 per cent in equities for each year until you need the money as defined by your investment period above and own bonds for the rest.

Rule 2 If this money represents general funds to support your future lifestyle, own your age in bonds and the rest in equities. Own more in equities if you are more aggressive and able to weather market falls, or more in bonds if you want more certainty of your outcome.

These mixes are based on the probabilities that equities and bonds will perform something like they have over the long run. You could, however, be one of the unlucky investing generations for whom markets stink; it is a possibility. Only you can decide whether you can tolerate such an outcome. If not, you may need to be less aggressive (by owning more bonds), save more, invest longer or scale down your expectations.

5 *Be conservative in your estimates of future returns* It is far better to be conservative about the returns your portfolio will generate than to be overly optimistic. If you pay in more and expect less, most surprises will be on the upside – a far more pleasant place to be than the flip side.

Practical investing

6 ***Diversify using funds or equivalent baskets of investments***
Own your bonds and equities through some sort of pooled fund
vehicle, such as a unit trust in the UK. This allows you to own a large
number of securities to spread the risk of any one security being a
duffer and damaging the value of your investments.

7 ***Don't try to beat the market, be the market*** Buy index funds,
known as tracker funds in the UK, that seek to track the market as
closely as possible, or similar products such as exchange traded funds,
usually referred to as ETFs. Don't try to move in and out of different
building blocks just because the story for one sounds bad and for
another good. Accept that trying to beat the market is a mug's game
for most investors.

8 ***Own the broad (total) equity market*** Your equity fund should
reflect the broad base of companies that make up the market as a
whole and not one or a few sectors of it. In the UK this would be the
FTSE All-Share index, which covers the whole market. In the USA this
may be an index such as the Wilshire 5000. Look for words like *total
market* or *broad market* when selecting products.

9 ***Own high-quality domestic bonds*** Your bond investments should
be high quality. Look for the words 'investment grade'. If you see the
words 'high yield', 'high income', 'extra income', 'sub-investment
grade' or 'junk' avoid them. The safest bonds are issued by the
government and are called gilts in the UK and treasuries in the USA.
Corporate bonds should be investment-grade only and generally rated
AA or above on average. If the threat of inflation worries you, allocate
some of your bond holding to index-linked (inflation proof) gilts
issued by the government.

10 ***Reduce costs at all times*** As costs, which include initial fees,
management fees and brokerage charges, destroy your wealth, always
buy cheaper product equivalents. Never buy any product until you
are sure of the stated and hidden costs. Never pay an initial fee for
investments. Understand what a *total expense ratio* is and always check
what it is for each investment.

11 ***Don't buy products you don't understand*** If products are
confusing or opaque, which includes most insurance-wrapped
products such as with-profits endowments, and guaranteed or
principal-protected products, avoid them. If you can't understand it,
don't invest in it.

12 ***Beat the taxman – legally of course*** Make use of all legal tax breaks. In the UK, like many other countries, there are breaks on contributions you make to your pension, tax-free investment wrappers, such as ISAs and capital gains tax allowances. Make sure you are using these to the best effect and get independent advice if you need to. However, make your investment decisions first and then seek to maximise the tax advantages.

On investing for retirement

13 ***How much to contribute*** You need to save regularly to build a suitable pot and it may surprise you just how much this is for a half-decent retirement. Start early.

Rule 1: Save £1 in £6 for retirement If you are saving for your retirement invest 15 per cent to 20 per cent of your gross salary every year of your working life. If you don't, be prepared to have a quiet retirement. You need to balance the pleasurable and gratifying feeling of spending today with what feels like the nebulous and remote comforts of investing for tomorrow. In effect, you are buying all of your future fun today, with a little help from the markets and compounding to get you there.

Rule 2 Your *age less twenty-five*: If you are starting later in life then your contributions, as a percentage of your gross salary, should be equivalent to your age less twenty-five years, for an income in retirement that is half to two-thirds your final salary – a scary thought for many! Alternatively, invest half your age as a percentage of your gross salary in your retirement savings pot.

These all come out to a similar level of contributions. The resounding message is the same: saving fifty quid here or there is not going to do it for you; retirement investing needs to be a systematic and financially significant process.

14 ***Lifecycle investing*** As you approach retirement make sure that you take the investment mix (point 3) into consideration. If you really want to protect your wealth from equity market falls and inflation as you approach retirement, own *index-linked bonds*, such as National Savings Certificates, and hold them to maturity, this being the date you need the money as cash, which may be when you retire or when you buy an *annuity*.

15 ***Taking an income from your portfolio*** If you need to take an
income from your portfolio and you don't want to run out of money
before you die, withdraw a maximum of 4 per cent per year from
your portfolio. A portfolio that is half bonds and half equities over
the long term has a good chance of returning inflation plus 3 per cent
to 4 per cent. So, withdrawing 4 per cent should, if you are lucky,
allow you to maintain the purchasing power of your capital and thus
your income. Be sensible; if you have a sustained run of bad markets
you may need to rein in your spending. To up your chances, only
withdraw 3 per cent.

Ongoing maintenance

16 ***Maintain the mix*** Rebalance the proportion of equities and bonds
back to your plan (points 3 and 4, above) if they are out of line by
more than a tenth of the value of your total portfolio. If you are a
regular investor you could redirect new cash flow to the underweight
investment to rebalance the portfolio. Check that the bond and
equity investments have performed in line with the broad markets
they reflect. If they have not, find out why. If the answer is
unsatisfactory, then replace them with a better option.

Controlling your emotions

17 ***Stick with your mix through thick and thin and avoid
chasing returns*** One of the greatest risks to good investing is you.
Hold tight when markets get bumpy, as they inevitably will.
Remember buying high and selling low is the worst, but most
popular, investment strategy. Never chase what seems like better
performance with another type of investment or manager. Investors
tend to be prone to emotional excesses that cloud their judgement
both as markets go up and as they inevitably come down. Staying
calm and staying the course is easier said than done, but is critical.

18 ***Don't look at your portfolio too often*** Try to avoid looking at the
value of your investments more than once a year. Any more than that
and you will begin to get short-termist and jumpy about irrelevant
short-term market movements.

19 ***Avoid the noise*** Do not be taken in by articles that begin 'Is now the
right time to be investing in ...?' Ignore most of what you hear and
read about the state of the markets, as most of it is nonsense and fluff

– interesting but unimportant. Much of it is telling you to be happy or distraught at the wrong time. Generally it makes you covet investment products that have already gone up in price: a bizarre yet real emotion. Also, remember that if a product or idea looks too good to be true, it is too good to be true. If you get offered any sort of product that provides high returns for no or low risk to your capital, then look very carefully and reject it. Free lunches like this just don't exist in investing.

And finally

20 *Pay for truly independent advice if you need it* If any of this confuses you, get independent advice. Employ a fee-based adviser who will manage your wealth on an ongoing basis over time. Anything above 1 per cent on your invested assets is getting costly. It may seem expensive but in the long run good advice will pay for itself many times over. Don't give up your future lifestyle for the cost of good advice upfront. Question it if it is markedly different from the points above. Check that the advice is truly independent before you commit. Ensure you know that this is their only remuneration – no kickbacks, no commissions, and no other hidden fees or charges. Never pay upfront fees on funds (sales fees, commissions, etc.) – it is not necessary. As a starting point, go to the Institute of Financial Planning's website, www.financialplanning.org.uk, and choose a fee-based Chartered Financial Planner to meet and discuss your issues.

Ask questions of your adviser that relate to your chances of meeting your goals such as: 'What are the chances of me not running out of money before I die if I withdraw £50,000 a year from my portfolio?' If they can't give you a satisfactory answer, go elsewhere.

If you need more meat on these bones, then read on – after all, that is why you bought the book.

2

Smarter thinking

Perhaps one of the biggest mistakes that investors make is focusing on 'doing' rather than 'thinking' about investing or their own behaviour in relation to it. Before we talk about *what* you should invest in, it is critical that you formulate some simple rules about *how* you should invest. To that end, the following two chapters provide an insight so you can come up with some guiding principles to help you make decisions and curb your emotions on your investing journey.

Chapter 4: Get smart – find your philosophy

Defining and believing in a set of investing rules lies at the heart of successful investing. Although you can't control how the markets will perform during your investment lifetime, you can stop throwing money away needlessly. Much of the industry noise, either directly or indirectly, encourages you to do just that. Having some clear guidelines through which to filter the nonsense from the valuable is the key. By the end of this chapter you will have formed a clear set of rules to live your investment life by.

Chapter 5: Get smart – manage your emotions

Without doubt, one of the hardest aspects of investing is having the courage to stick with an investment plan when times get tough, as they undoubtedly will from time to time. Failing to curb your emotions will be costly – one of the few things you can truly guarantee as an investor. This chapter helps to identify some of the pitfalls that you face. Understanding them is the first step to avoiding them. Take a long, hard, look at yourself.

4

Get smart – find your philosophy

Too often, investors fail to spend enough time trying to sort out what will work and what will not work, but instead dive into the markets and end up being thrown around, chasing returns and damaging their wealth. To avoid being one of them, you need to determine a set of guiding rules and beliefs that will provide the basis for making astute investment decisions. These rules form your investment philosophy. This will become the central perspective from which you evaluate all investment options and ideas, providing a filter to eliminate the industry noise and help focus on what is truly important. By the end of this chapter you should have a pretty good idea of what it should be. This book can guide you, but at the end of the day you need to convince yourself, based on the evidence.

4.1 Don't be a loser

The following scenario reflects the way in which many people go about their philosophy-free investing. It uses the late 1990s and early 2000s as the backdrop.

It is 1998 and James, a corporate banker in the City, is keen to put some of his hard-earned cash to better use than just sitting in a bank account. He is fully aware of the clamour surrounding the rising stock market and decides that he should think about investing a lump sum in equities. In the weekend money pages of a respected broadsheet, three things catch his eye: an article about the outstanding returns being made from the market; an advertisement expounding the

▶

excellent market-beating performance of an equity fund managed by Top Wealth Investors; and a small column on the fact that index tracker funds have tended to outperform professionally managed funds over time. He rips out and sends off the coupon for some literature on the stellar-performing fund.

Over a beer after work the following week, James is given the name of a financial adviser that one of his colleagues uses. At home, in the glossy pile of literature that arrives, he is impressed with Top Wealth Investor's sophisticated process, global resources of over a hundred analysts and fund managers and a UK equity fund that has done really well over the past three years, pasting the market and its peers.

He sets up a meeting with the adviser his colleague recommended to ask for some advice on how to go about things – he really doesn't want all the fuss and bother of doing it himself. The adviser agrees that investing in equities makes sense, as James doesn't need the money in the foreseeable future and concurs that equities have a strong positive outlook, both long and short term. James shows him the literature about the stellar-performing fund and his adviser agrees that it is a reputable firm, but suggests that he should also look at a couple of other funds on his recommended fund list, which have good track records of beating the market over the past couple of years. James doesn't ask how much the adviser will get paid for selling them to him.

James raises the story about index tracker funds, but the adviser suggests that he should give himself the chance of beating the market by picking a good actively managed fund rather than accepting the inevitable defeat of an index tracker fund. He also adds that active managers, who seek to beat the market, have the chance of protecting his money in down markets by holding cash or defensive stocks, and picking better-performing stocks when markets are rising, which sounds good. James should get the upside of beating the markets when times are good and some protection in down markets. He feels that this seems reasonable.

He decides to split his investment between Top Wealth Adviser's fund and a fund his adviser suggests. He writes the cheque then and there, thankful that he doesn't need to waste any more time dealing with his investments. Within a few days, his account is set up and he has access to his portfolio online. The first thing he does each morning is to check how much he is worth, and feels elated watching his money grow.

All goes well for the first year and James adds his annual bonus into the funds, which have both outperformed the market. However, shortly into 2000, the market begins to fall and before long he has lost an amount equivalent to a few months' salary. James hangs in there, assured by a friend that the market bounced back quickly after the crash in 1987. But in 2001 the market falls by more than 10 per cent, and further at the start of 2002. At this point he is beginning to panic as he has lost more than 30 per cent of his wealth and both his funds have done significantly worse than the market.

Two articles catch his eye in Sunday's money section: 'Is this the death of the equity cult?' and 'Is now the time to be investing in corporate bonds?' James feels unnerved at the losses on his portfolio and he doesn't want to lose any more money. He decides that it may make sense to get out of the equity market and perhaps buy corporate bonds instead: these have performed well and are being touted as a safe, income-producing haven from the turbulence of the equity markets, with good future return prospects.

He doesn't feel he can hold out any longer: why stay in equities that may well go down further when he could be in something that is doing well? He rings his advisor, who concurs that the outlook for equities looks poor but that for bonds looks good. He sells most of his equities and switches his portfolio into bonds. His adviser is happy with the additional commission.

James initially feels happier as the market falls further. But in 2003 the equity market rallies by 30 per cent and bond returns have been flat; there is talk that the bond market rally has run out of steam. A nagging doubt exists as to what you should do next. He calls his adviser . . .

Without a sound investment philosophy the dangers of James destroying his future wealth are exceedingly high. He has made a number of fundamental mistakes, because he has no guiding principles to help him to manage his investment. Our hypothetical investor James has:

■ Not thought about what he really wants to achieve with his money.

- Not set up a long-term plan for the mix of investments that he will use. Investing is a journey, which needs to be planned.

- Chased returns and entered a cycle of buying high and selling low, which is a certain recipe for wealth destruction, based on short-term market and emotional pressures.

- Paid fees upfront for advice based on the value of his assets, has bought high-cost products and has incurred switching costs by moving funds.

- A remarkable belief in his ability to pick an outstanding manager. For some reason he believes that he has the skills to select one of the very few managers who will outperform the markets consistently over the years by looking at an advertisement.

- Chosen a manager who has a low probability of beating the market in the long term and a high probability of losing out to an index fund tracking the market.

- A pretty good chance of destroying a significant part of his wealth in the long run like the Dalbar study referred to in Eye-opener 2 at the start of the book so clearly shows.

All in all his investment programme is a mess. Fortunately, he is only a hypothetical investor and not you!

4.2 The foundations of your philosophy

The time has come to build yourself a smart philosophy that gives you the highest chance of achieving your investment goals. This is not a difficult process. It is a matter of looking at the evidence and weighing up where you have the greatest probability of success and acting accordingly. Your resulting investment philosophy is the set of rules that you can use to guide you through the decisions you face.

Establishing your philosophical mindset

The best place to start as you begin to establish your philosophy is with the central message in Charles D. Ellis's superb book *Winning the Losers Game* (Ellis, 2002) as it provides the mindset that you will need to adopt in all the decisions that you face through your investing lifetime: it is that the ultimate outcome of investing is determined by who can lose the fewest points, not win them. It is as simple as that!

I cannot stress how important and central this subtle statement is to your future wealth and financial security. When you look at investment success in this light, it becomes a lot easier to devise a set of rules that will give you a high chance of success – actions that revolve around minimising the chances of eroding the returns that your portfolio mix as a whole can generate for you. If you persist with the view that success comes with winning points by beating the market you are on a very complex, angst ridden road to likely failure, as you will see. In the pages ahead, you will be able to review for yourself the evidence that will hopefully make you believe in this simple statement as well.

Throughout this book we will ruthlessly apply this philosophy. First, though, we need to see why it is this philosophy, alone, that forms the basis of smarter investing.

Your starting point is your long-term mix of assets

As an investor, the choices include cash, bonds, equities, property, hedge funds, gold, art, commodities and stamps, each of which has its own return characteristics and risks. Depending upon what you are trying to achieve with your money, and the time frame you can invest for, you can put together a sensible mix of investment building blocks that will provide you with a reasonable probability of achieving your goals.

The mix that you choose will determine the level of potential returns of your investment programme, the chances that an acceptable outcome will be achieved, such as having enough income in your retirement, and how bumpy the investment road that you take is likely to be. Getting this mix right is critical.

The chosen mix is often referred to as your long-term *investment policy* or *strategic asset allocation*. All sophisticated investors have investment policy statements that set out exactly what this long-term strategy is – you need to do the same. We will not try and answer what this mix is for you until we reach Part 3 of the book, where we will explore the process you need to go through to decide what it is in some depth. Let's explore instead the fundamental philosophical questions that all investors face.

Should you try to beat the returns from your mix?

The central tenet that will underlie the investment philosophy is whether or not you believe that you have a *reasonably high chance* of beating the returns that your long-term investment policy portfolio will generate (simply through buying and then holding it), by making investment decisions during your investment lifetime that move your portfolio away from this long-term mix of investments, asset classes and securities.

Ultimately you face a choice: either try to identify an active manager who, through either personal skill or a robust investment process, adds returns relative to the market, which in the long term could be highly beneficial, or simply make sure that you capture the bulk of the market returns on offer. It comes down to your chances of success. Smart investors always make decisions that maximise their chances of being successful. Make up your own mind where you stand by the end of this chapter. Three potential ways exist to beat your investment policy mix.

1 Improving returns by moving between asset classes

The biggest decision you face and the one that is most likely to govern the success of your investment programme is whether you always keep your investment policy mix constant or whether you move money around to take advantage of investments that are performing, or appear likely to perform, well and sell those that are or are anticipated to perform poorly.

Moving your mix around to try to beat the returns from a static mix is called *tactical asset allocation*, *investment strategy*, or *market timing*. Proponents of this approach are *market-timers*. Seeking to add returns over and above those expected from your long-term investment policy from market timing is often referred to as being a *top-down approach*. Such a strategy 'looks down' on the portfolio and moves chunks of it around either at the asset class level, for example between bonds and equities, between countries or at the sector level by preferring, say, the oil sector of the economy over the financial sector. The jargon is worth remembering, as it is the common language of managers and advisers. Much of what you read in the papers is about market timing decisions such as: 'Should you be investing in Japan (or read: oil, timber, art, wine, etc.) at this time?'

2 Improving returns by picking better securities

Irrespective of your answer to market timing, you also need to decide whether or not you believe if it is possible consistently to pick (or ignore) individual stocks or bonds, generically referred to as securities, that will beat those that make up the market as a whole. This process is known as *stock selection* for equities, or *security selection* in generic terms. Proponents of this approach are referred to as *stock-pickers*. Because it focuses on the smallest element of decision-making, stock-picking is referred to as a

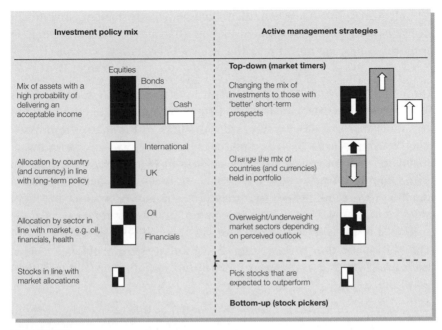

Figure 4.1 **Ways to try to beat a long-term buy-and-hold strategy**

bottom-up approach. TV pundits, stock-tip columns and investment magazines and stockbrokers are the conduits of stock-picking noise.

3 Improving returns by picking market-beating managers

You may feel that you cannot achieve the first two options above yourself, as you have neither the expertise nor the time to do so, but you may feel that you have a good chance of selecting a manager who does, or finding an adviser who can find one that can. It is tempting to be drawn into the comfort of passing the responsibility over to the professionals, who after all should be best placed to beat the market, as they spend their lives working with valuation models, work with bright colleagues, meet and analyse companies, and have good access to information. Surely if anyone can beat the markets, they can?

Figure 4.1 illustrates how active managers attempt to beat the returns from a long-term investment policy mix of investments.

The route you choose is a question of probabilities

Managers who believe that they can beat your investment policy mix returns by market timing and security selection are known as *active managers*. The funds they manage are known as *actively managed* funds.

Investors who do not believe that they can improve upon investment policy returns through market timing or security selection are referred to as *passive* or *index investors*. Using the word passive is a misnomer, at least when it comes to managing funds that try to replicate, rather than beat, markets i.e. index tracker funds, as you will see later.

The difference between an active and a passive approach is actually about the probability of success, not skill, intelligence or hard work of those involved. Passive managers believe that the odds of success, through capturing as much of each market's available gain as possible, for your given mix, and thus losing the fewest points, lie in their favour. Active managers, on the other hand, believe that they can win points because they have superior insight and the ability to use information better than others in the market, and their process and people will allow this superiority to be sustained into the future. As you will see shortly, the probability of being successful is higher through avoiding losing points than trying to win them.

The attraction of active management is similar to that of smoking. It lies in a hope of beating the odds and enjoying a lifetime of rewards, despite that fact that the probabilities of financial and physical ill-health are high in both cases, in aggregate. As human beings, we seem to have an innate sense that we will escape the probabilities and be the lucky winners. After all, many people gamble on the lottery, despite the odds that a thirty-five-year-old man buying a lottery ticket on a Monday has a greater chance of dying than winning the jackpot!

For some reason, we hate to be considered average. We seem to aspire to want to be winners, which is fine if it is winning an egg and spoon race, but dangerous in the less-than-zero-sum game that we play as investors. In investing, there is nothing wrong with being average if by average you mean achieving the market return for your buy-and-hold portfolio, as you will see.

The problem with many investors is that they are attracted to active management because they have not thought through the issues clearly, and have not seen or read the evidence that exists that helps them to decide which course of action is likely to be best for their investing health. Others see the evidence, which is now widely available, but still can't stop themselves from being attracted to trying to beat the markets. This is compounded by our propensity erroneously to value short-term success as a good proxy for long-term success, abrogate investing responsibility to others, and to be influenced by the apparent absolute (as opposed to relative) levels of expertise that reside in investment firms. Fortunately, you have the opportunity to see the evidence and weigh up the probabilities yourself.

Before we begin the process of establishing which approach has the greatest chance of success, you need to be aware of the zero-sum game that investing represents in aggregate.

Understanding the zero-sum game

As we unravel the chances of success from adopting either a passive or an active approach to your investing, you need to make sure that you understand the game that is being played by active investors in aggregate. It is a zero-sum game, assuming that we ignore for the moment the significant issue of costs, where one investor's gain is another investor's loss. For every winning position, there has to be a corresponding losing position, relative to the market. Factoring in the costs of investing, it becomes a significantly less-than-zero-sum game.

If you buy a share at a certain price believing it will rise faster than the market, and it does, you win and the person who sold it to you loses – you cannot both be right. Take a look at the simple market in Table 4.1, which consists of just two investors, me and you, and two shares, ABC plc and XYZ plc. As you can see, the combined returns over one year of our two-stock market must be the market return. You win and I lose relative to the market.

Table 4.1   **We can't both be winners**

	My portfolio	Your portfolio
Start of year	ABC plc (1 share)	XYZ plc (1 share)
Price	£100 per share	£100 per share
Trade	I buy XYZ plc from you for £100	You buy ABC plc from me for £100
Performance during year	XYZ plc up 10%	ABC plc up 20%
Portfolio value at end of year	£110 = **10%** (absolute)	£120 = **20%** (absolute)
Market performance	Total market value now £230 instead of £200 = **15%**	
Relative to market	Loser with −**5%**	Winner with +**5%**

The same applies for all investments. So, if you sell equities and buy bonds, again it has to be a zero-sum game before costs. Only one of the seller or buyer of the bonds can win in the short term. In order to believe that you can be one of the few who can consistently win over time at someone else's expense, you have to believe the following:

- You are superior to the average investor, and are able to access and interpret information in a way that others can't, in order to make market-beating decisions.
- There are enough consistently dumb investors to be the losers funding your wins.

It should therefore come as no surprise that the investment management industry has more than its fair share of overly confident and prima-donna fund managers throwing tantrums, computers and phones around the trading desk (all of which I have seen). To believe that they have the key to above-average wealth generation is a powerful drug, particularly given the talent of their peers in competitor firms. Not to believe it means that your professional worth is meaningless.

Who are the losers that make winning possible?

That's a good question, given that in the UK professional active investment managers make up around 80 per cent – 90 per cent of investors, the losers by definition, are likely to include a fair number of this group. Perhaps it's the small minority of individual investors, who are providing the huge market beating opportunities for all the professionals. Don't bank on it.

A study of 60,000 individual investors in the US trading their own brokerage accounts, a group that is at most risk of being persistent zero-sum-game losers, found that the average gross return, i.e. returns before costs, was more or less in line with the market return (Barber and Odean 1998). So, as a group, these individuals are not being fleeced by the institutional managers, who you would expect to be the consistent winners.

4.3 The path to establishing your philosophy

Whether active management can beat the markets with a reasonably high chance of success over the long term, and is thus a philosophy worth adopting, depends on resolving three questions:

- Can active managers beat the markets after costs?
- If so, do some managers beat the markets consistently over time?

■ Third, do you have a reasonable chance of identifying them in
  advance?

Remember that we are not trying to answer these questions with specific
examples where a forecast has been right, or a particular manager who has
performed well over the past few years. What you need to decide for yourself is whether you can be *reasonably confident* that there is a *high chance*
that you can identify and exploit anomalies consistently over time, or find
a manager who can. If you believe that this is a tough thing to achieve,
then you need to adopt a 'lose the least number of points' strategy. As
simple as that! The rest of this chapter deals with answering these three
questions, the outcome of which will drive your core beliefs and the rules
by which you will manage your money.

4.4 Can active managers win?

To answer this question, we need to review some of the evidence on the
active management industry's success or otherwise. First, though, consider
the following logical argument that immediately puts the active managers
case on the back foot, with the probabilities favouring a passive (index)
approach.

Passive investors will beat the majority of active investors

As we have discovered in the zero-sum game above, all investors are the
market. So, the average investor will generate the market return before
fees, transaction costs and taxes. In the real world these costs cannot be
avoided so the average active investor must inevitably be below the
market by the amount of these costs. If index funds have lower costs than
the average active investor, which is the case, then they will beat the
average active manager by the difference between these costs. Index
funds will thus beat the majority of active funds over the long run. As
Professor William Sharpe, a Nobel Prize winning stock market economist,
puts it:

*'The laws of arithmetic have been suspended for the convenience of those who
pursue their careers as active managers.'*

Opportunities abound for the active manager

Active managers have a wide range of opportunities to deliver above-
market returns: many asset classes to switch between; the choice of

domestic and non-domestic markets and currencies; and a very wide number of securities to pick from. On the face of it, the scope is there for them to outperform. The question is whether they can do so after costs, with a high chance of success from an individual investor's perspective.

The allure of market timing as a route to active returns is easily apparent. Let's look at a simple scenario. In Figure 4.2, the annual return for UK cash, bonds and equities over the past twenty years or so are ranked from highest to lowest. The first thing you see is that, over this short period, the rankings of each jump all over the place. Surely it can't be that difficult to work out which investments are likely to do well and which are likely to do badly? Surely a paid professional manager with their access to market information, economists, analysts, MBAs, etc., should be able to work it out?

To a believer in market timing, this is great news. Their superior skills and insight should provide them with the opportunity to move into and out of these investments to the benefit of their clients. To be able to do so successfully implies success in forecasting future asset prices.

As a simple exercise, let's look at what the consequences are of being right and being wrong. Take two market timers, Ms Lucky and Mr Unlucky, who both have £100,000 to invest at the start of 1990. The former calls the market right, investing all of her funds in cash in 1990. On New's Year's Eve 1990 she decides to move all of her money into equities and so on, receiving the full returns of the top line. Mr Unlucky on the other hand chooses the loser's line each time. Ms Lucky would have ended up with over £1 million and Mr Unlucky would have lost money and ended up with less than £40,000 of his original £100,000 when the effects of inflation are factored in. So, the rewards are there if you can get it right and the trade-off looks good. Can you get it right though? It seems so tempting to give it a go but research points strongly towards a conclusion that even most professionals struggle to do so.

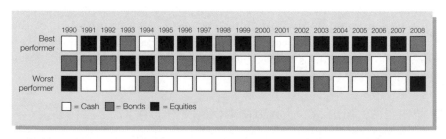

Figure 4.2 **Annual winners and losers – UK cash, bonds and equity returns**   *Source: Barclays Equity Gilt Study, 2009.*

Winning points from market timing is very tricky

In the next few pages you should be acting like a jury and asking yourself whether beyond reasonable doubt, active management can beat the markets consistently. If you believe it can, then active management is for you, and good luck to you. If there is a level of reasonable doubt in your mind then you need to drop any notion of a points-winning philosophy and adopt a lose-the-fewest points philosophy. Here are some of the hurdles that you face:

Forecasting is notoriously difficult to get right, consistently

As economic forecasts are the basis for making forecasts about markets and securities, an active investor needs to be able to make consistently above-average forecasts to win. Wide scepticism by many acknowledged investors, backed up by empirical evidence, tells us this is so. Here are a couple of sceptical quotes about economists and forecasting to set the tone. The first I have always loved, its source unknown to me:

'An economist is an expert who will know tomorrow why the things he predicted yesterday didn't happen today.'

The second is attributed to Ray Marshall, a former US labour secretary, and is an example of the healthy scepticism that we all would do well to adopt.

'When it comes to forecasting, there are only two kinds of economist, those who don't know, and those who don't know they don't know.'

Your forecasting average needs to be Bradmanesque

A study in the USA (Sharpe, 1975) using data from 1929 to 1972 (and others since) estimated that if you employed a market-timing approach, moving your money between equities and short-term bonds, you needed to call the up markets and down markets over 70 per cent right throughout this period just to make the same return as buying and holding equities. That's a steep hurdle to set. In addition, the study calculated that even if an investor managed to avoid all declining markets and to get back into half of the rising markets, they still would not have beaten the return of the market. In reality the hurdle is higher because no tax or transaction costs were included in these numbers.

Each decision you make actually requires two decisions

As the research above indicates, you need to be smart enough to make the call when to get out of the markets and to make the call when to get back in. If you have even a 50 per cent chance of getting one decision right, you only have a 25 per cent chance of getting two consecutive decisions right and so on. You need to be pretty consistently good at forecasting to be successful.

You need to act very quickly to win

To make matters tougher, many investors underestimate the rapidity and magnitude of the movements that markets make. Look at Table 4.2, which uses the Dow Jones index in the USA as a source of data. It demonstrates that if you miss the best ten days, in over twenty-two years of trading, you miss out on 40 per cent of returns. Miss the best fifty days, which is still less than 1 per cent of days, and you lose out on over 85 per cent of all the returns of the market. In this simple analysis, costs and taxes are ignored, which would only make the picture worse. As you can see, not only do you have to make two decisions as to when to move out of the market and back again, but also the exact timing of each move is critical.

Being right is quite a challenge. Being wrong can be very costly. The odds of success are beginning to stack up against you.

Alternatively, you need to be lucky

Napoleon's response of 'send me lucky generals' when asked what type of generals he needed to turn things round against the British could apply to the type of market-beating strategy to adopt when choosing active fund managers.

In the past decade or so, particularly with the rapid expansion of the financial media, the cult of the star investment manager has grown. In fact it probably takes less than three years of market, or peer-beating perform-

Table 4.2 **Missing just a fraction of good days can be very costly**

Nominal returns for Dow Jones Industrial Average (start Q1 1981, end Q2 2003)

	Value of $100	Annualised return %	Contribution of missed days	Days missed %
Invested at all times	$932	10.4%	n/a	n/a
Top 10 days missed	$536	7.7%	42%	0.2%
Top 20 days missed	$353	5.8%	62%	0.4%
Top 50 days missed	$134	1.3%	86%	0.9%

Total number of trading days = 5679
Source: Dow Jones Industrial Average.

ance and some good public relations to make a star manager and be pushed into the limelight as the new 'guru'. Yet how can we tell whether this performance is down to skill or judgement?

A lucky run is probably what you get more often than not when you employ an active manager on just a good short-term track record. Imagine that there are 300 funds investing in the UK equity market and each manager at the start of each of the past three years had made a decision to allocate a portion of the fund into cash or not – a market-timing decision. Just by flipping a coin you would expect around forty of them to get the correct answer ($300 \times 50\% \times 50\% \times 50\%$). That's more than 10 per cent right. Marketing departments can now use these 'exceptional' results to push product and support the case for active management. Sure, some may be geniuses but most will just be lucky over a short period. The problem is, can you tell which is which?

The hurdles faced by active managers are significant

To be a successful active manager, you need to be able to forecast well, get a high percentage of your forecasts right, get your timing spot on as markets move so rapidly and with such great magnitude, or just be one of the lucky few. The hurdles to success are high, but that does not matter if you or managers out there have the ability to overcome these hurdles consistently and you can identify who they are in advance. So, do they exist and can that be done? Just how difficult this is, is revealed by a recent piece of research (Cuthbertson et al., 2006) that shows that only around 1.5 per cent of UK equity funds demonstrate positive market timing ability. Despite the claims made by the active management industry, the evidence simply does not support their wishful thinking.

This is nicely summed up in the comments made by John Bogle (2003), one of the patriarchs of losing-the-fewest points investing. He founded Vanguard, one of the USA's largest managers, which focuses on index investing to replicate the market.

'A lifetime of experience in this business makes me profoundly sceptical of market timing. I don't know anyone who can do it successfully, nor any one who has done so in the past. Heck, I don't even know anyone who knows anyone who has timed the market with consistent, successful, replicable results.'

Winning points through security selection is no easier

Quite a few active managers would happily go along with the proposition that trying to time markets is difficult, and put little effort into trying. They do, though, believe that they can beat markets by picking stocks. They are, however, up against a concept known as market efficiency. The concept is a simple one. It suggests that all known relevant information is incorporated in the current price of a security. Collectively, all the individual shares aggregate to form the market, which as a consequence is efficiently priced. Intuitively, the more analysts, journalists, brokers and lenders digging around companies, the more likely that all information is known about them. Some research estimates that new information is fully priced in within sixty minutes (Chordia et al., 2003). As such, in an efficient market it is hard to find securities that are anomalously priced. The price of the security will only move again on any news that is unanticipated. Price movements are therefore random in their nature.

You would, in this case, not expect to achieve continuing superior profits from investment decisions that you make because any short-term market-beating investment ideas, reflecting the mispricing of assets, would be quickly spotted by all the other smart professionals and the misalignment between price and value would disappear. If a market is efficient, you would conclude that it should be difficult to beat it, particularly after all costs are taken into account. Rex Sinquefield, an economist and proponent of index investing, provides his own humorous slant on the debate:

'So who still believes that markets don't work? Apparently it is only the North Koreans, the Cubans and the active managers.'

This theory is known as the Efficient Market Hypothesis or EMH and is eloquently described in the seminal text *A Random Walk Down Wall Street* by Burton G. Malkiel, which I would recommend you to read if you want to pursue this topic further.

Academics and professional investors argue endlessly about the degree to which markets are efficient. Some mine data for anomalies, which others seek to disprove. They are fortunate to have the luxury of time to do so. Burton Malkiel's overall conclusion, as you will see from active manager returns illustrated later, is hard to disagree with (Malkiel, 2000).

'I remain sceptical that markets are systematically irrational and that knowledge of such irrationalities can lead to profitable trading strategies. Indeed, the more potentially profitable a discoverable pattern is, the less likely it

is to survive. This is the logical reason one should be cautious not to overemphasize the apparent departures from efficiency.'

For the rest of us, we don't have to prove whether markets are efficient or not. What we should be interested in is whether, after all the costs incurred in investing are accounted for, any inefficiencies that exist can be exploited by active managers to generate market-beating returns consistently over time. To draw a conclusion we need to look at the track record of active managers as a collective group, to see if they do. We study the evidence a little later. Signs of efficiency include a narrow dispersion of longer-term returns between the top and bottom managers, as no one has a truly sustainable advantage or disadvantage. On this basis, the fixed income markets are reasonably efficient, as are equity markets such as the USA and the UK.

Active managers invariably claim that their market-beating approach will work better in less-efficient markets, such as small company stocks or small overseas equity markets, as they theoretically have the ability to exploit these inefficiencies. However, always remember that even in markets where information is deemed to be less than perfect, if the anomalies cannot be exploited to exceed the transaction costs involved with investing in them, then active management for you or me is worthless. Transaction costs are significantly higher in smaller, less efficient, markets, negating much of the benefit. Remember that they are still playing in a zero-sum game, but with higher costs.

What does the research tell us?

The reality is that research suggests that few investors outperform the market portfolio consistently over time, especially after transaction costs and taxes are taken into account. The magnitude and consistency of this research, from a wide number of angles, supports this emphatically. Let's look at the case more closely.

Even major investors have failed the active test

Some of the world's most renowned market timers have failed the test of time. The story of George Soros, perhaps the best known and a very successful international market timer for a long time, provides a sobering indication of what a tough game it is. Commonly known as the man who broke the Bank of England, betting against the UK's ability to stay in the failed Exchange Rate Mechanism in the early 1990s, he was a major market timer. His investment firm, which managed $14 billion at the start of 2000 lost $5 billion of this before the year was out. The activities of the firm were dramatically reorganised thereafter. Ironically, Victor Niederhoffer, a protégé of George Soros, set up and ran his own fund, until that closed in 1997 after large losses.

Other notable examples of just how difficult it is to exist: Julian Robertson's Tiger Funds were highly revered until they closed down; John Meriwether's Long Term Capital Managements, complete with two Nobel Prize winning economists, threatened to drag down the global financial system with it – the company had a $100 billion balance sheet when it got its view on Russia wrong and markets behaved out of line with expected, at least in their eyes, norms.

Then there was Jeff Vinik, formerly of Fidelity, who made one of the largest market timing mistakes recorded on the largest mutual fund in the world, The Magellan Fund. The latter's demise was recorded in BusinessWeek.

'When Jeffrey N. Vinik ran Fidelity Investment's huge Magellan Mutual Fund, he was known for his large – and often short-term – bets on stocks and sectors. Vinik's record was stellar – until the end of 1995, when he shifted a big chunk of the $50-plus billion portfolio into bonds. Not smart. Rates rose, returns collapsed, and he departed in June, 1996.'

In aggregate, active management deducts value

Research by John Bogle compared the performance of the average, actively managed balanced fund, where investors could market time between the mix of bonds and equities and select securities, with an index fund that invests in bonds and equities at a fixed mix, replicating as closely as possible the underlying markets and rebalancing its mix back to the original proportions regularly (Bogle, 2002). Table 4.3 illustrates the results of this study looking at US-based balanced funds over the period from 1970 to 2002.

Table 4.3 **Average active balanced fund vs. average balanced index fund (1970–2002)**

	Average annualised return %	Growth of $1	Level of risk
Index funds (no market timing)	10.2%	$22.1	12.2%
Active funds (scope for market timing)	9.4%	$17.2	14.1%

Source: Bogle (2002).

The difference in return between the two can largely be accounted for by the likely difference in fees between them. However, the active funds must be making active market timing and/or stock selection decisions as the volatility of their returns, otherwise known as risk, is higher than the index fund that merely tries to replicate the balance and the markets as closely as possible. The explicit conclusion is that the average balanced-fund manager has not only failed to add value through the active management techniques of market timing and stock selection, but also did so with greater fluctuations in returns. The implicit conclusion is that these smart and dedicated professional managers were, as a group, no smarter than other participants in the markets.

Most active UK equity funds were beaten by the market

We can come at this from another angle, by looking at how many actively managed UK equity funds beat the market. WM Company, a research company, compared actively managed unit trusts in the UK all-companies sector against the FTSE All-Share index, a broad market equity index, for the twenty-year period to the end of 2000.

The main findings were that the market return was in the top quarter of unit trust returns and forty-four out of fifty-five unit trusts with a twenty-year record, failed to beat the market over this period. The first index tracker funds were established by the start of 1989. Over the subsequent twelve-year period, eighty out of 115 active funds failed to beat the index tracker funds and index funds themselves underperformed the market by 1 per cent a year due to costs. This study was updated in 2003 and looked at twenty-year data to the end of 2002. Of forty-eight trusts with a twenty-year history over this period only ten outperformed the index. Similarly, in the USA, over the twenty years to the end of 2003, more than 80 per cent of active managers failed to beat the market (fewer still over thirty years) and the average index fund beat the average active fund by 2 per cent or so (Malkiel, 2004).

Investment policy outweighs investment strategy

A classic study (Brinson et al., 1986) relating to actively managed US pension plans and the role of long-term policy versus short-term active management decisions concludes that:

'Investment policy dominates investment strategy, explaining on average 93.6 per cent of the variation in total plan returns.'

This has also become one of the most misquoted pieces of research in investment academia. When I started work in the industry, I too was led to believe that an investor's total return was therefore about 90 per cent due to asset allocation and 10 per cent due to active decisions. What it refers to is the variation, i.e. changes in returns over time, not what proportion of total return is attributable to investment policy. You'd be amazed how many people still misquote this study.

The relevance of this study is that it implies that even sophisticated players implicitly accept that it is difficult to beat markets and constrain their active decision-making. A similar study was undertaken in the UK looking at 300 pension funds (Blake et al., 1999). It concluded that:

'Strategic asset allocation accounts for most of the time-series variation in portfolio returns, while market timing and asset selection appear to have been less important.'

Where do you stand now?

The evidence against using active management as a high probability points-winning philosophy is mounting up: markets are competitive and probably reasonably efficient; forecasting has some serious hurdles to success, few active managers appear able to do it consistently; and research studies show that the majority of managers fail to outperform the index (and index funds) over the longer term. In its favour there appear to be a few managers who do. As a rational investor the probability of success lies in favour of an index approach over active management at this point.

4.5 Do a few managers outperform over time?

If, however, some managers do have exceptional skills that allow them to beat markets, rather than luck, and they can consistently use these skills to generate outperformance (after all costs) of the markets over long periods of time, then employing them to manage your money would make sense as each incremental point is extremely valuable, when compounded over time. A few do, and the UK's most celebrated manager is Anthony Bolton, with a remarkable track record (see the box at the end of this chapter). Perhaps you could do this by picking funds with persistent past performance, as a guide to future performance. Let's see whether this is the case.

Testing whether performance persists

Significant amounts of research have been undertaken to test whether investment managers' performance does persist over time. In other words:

are the few who outperform over one time frame the same managers who outperform over subsequent time frames? If performance persistence exists, then you could act on that information. Two recent and comprehensive reviews of the literature on performance persistence have been published. The conclusions of which are laid out below. The first was a paper commissioned by the Financial Services Authority, the UK's industry regulatory body (Rhodes, 2000). The conclusion that was reached was as follows:

'The literature on the performance of UK funds has failed to find evidence that information on past investment performance can be used to good effect by retail investors in choosing funds. The general pattern is one in which investment performance does not persist. Small groups of funds may show some repeat performance over a short period of time. However, the size of this effect and the fact that it is only short-lived means there is no investment strategy for retail investors that could be usefully employed. The results of the US literature are similar.'

This is further indication that the UK market is pretty efficient, or that any inefficiency cannot be profitably exploited. If it were not, some managers would have been able to generate long-term persistent records of performance due to their superior skills. Bear this in mind the next time you see an advertisement in the paper for a stellar fund.

The UK study undertaken by WM Company, which is in the full text of the FSA paper, illustrates the general conclusion nicely. The methodology was to take the period 1979–1998 and track the performance of the top quartile of funds in one five-year period and record which quartile they ended up in the subsequent period. If performance persistence were in evidence, then a high proportion of top-quartile funds would remain there. Even distributions across quartiles would indicate that performance was random. Table 4.4 shows that the evidence fails to indicate performance persistence. It seems that those at the top of the pile rotate and, as a result, a consistent

Table 4.4   Performance persistence – what persistence?

		Quartile position in period 2			
		1	2	3	4
Quartile	1	22.2%	22.2%	33.3%	22.2%
position	2	19.1%	34.0%	17.0%	29.8%
in period	3	13.0%	17.4%	32.6%	37.0%
1	4	43.8%	25.0%	16.7%	14.6%

Source: WM Company (2001).

performer, relative to the market, such as good index fund, will, over time slowly float towards the top of the pile. As you will see in a moment, the evidence seems to support this.

The report concluded:

'Over the entire period of the study the probability of selecting a top quartile performer based on historic top quartile performance was no better than would be expected by chance.'

Another paper was commissioned by the Australian Securities and Investment Commission (Allan et al., 2002). The study again took the form of a review of the literature in the USA, the UK and Australia. Three of its general conclusions were:

'Good performance seems to be, at best, a weak and unreliable predictor of good performance over the medium to long term. About half the studies found no correlation at all between good past and good future performance. Where persistence was found, this was more frequently in the shorter term (one to two years) than in the longer term.'

'More studies seem to find that bad past performance increased the probability of future bad performance.'

And:

'Where persistence was found, the "outperformance" margin tended to be small. Where studies found persistence, some specifically reported that frequent swapping to best performing funds would not be an effective strategy, due to the cost of swapping.'

Again, as a rational investor, you have to admit that the weight of evidence backs the claim that 'past performance is no guide to future returns' always quoted as a disclaimer on investment literature.

Are longer-term outperformers lucky or skilful?

Earlier you saw that luck might well play a part in short-term market beating track records of some managers.

In the event that investment performance of active managers was down to luck rather than skill, one would expect these returns to be 'normally' (bell-curve) distributed. In a seminal piece of work Mark Carhart demonstrated that manager returns were similar to randomness less costs, i.e. a bell curve shifted to the left. He also revealed that active management adds additional uncertainty as it exhibited a greater chance of large losses. Persistence was evident in very few outperformers, but higher in terms of underperformance. In other words, bad funds tended to remain bad. A skilled active manager should be able to generate returns in excess of the level of returns expected from a portfolio of equivalent market risk. The risk that the manager takes over and above that inherent in the general market, for example by choosing a few specific equities to hold in the portfolio, can be measured. If you work out the ratio of the excess return (known in the industry as *alpha*) to the excess risk taken on (known as *residual risk*), you can get a measure of how well an active manager manages money. In plain English, it describes the active bang of return they get for their active buck of risk they take. This is known as the *information ratio*.

A number of studies have calculated the information ratio of top-quartile managers, tends to be around 0.5 on a gross basis. After fees and costs this is likely to be considerably lower. The point I am getting to is that for an information ratio of 0.5 you need sixteen years of data for you to be 95 per cent sure that the returns are due to skill rather than luck. At 0.33, which may be nearer reality for these 'top' managers after costs, you would need thirty-six years of data. At 0.2 you need one hundred years. The reality is that you rarely get more than five years of data, let alone twenty.

A recent piece of research (Cuthbertson et al., 2008) shows that of 675 UK funds only nine (less than 2 per cent) showed positive market-beating skills, after taking into account their long-term exposure to less healthy (value) and smaller-company returns (which is just tilting to market risks, not skill) and adjusting for false positives, i.e. luck being identified as skill. That's hardly a number to base your investment strategy on.

Who can tell as managers move around so frequently?

As food for thought, you may want to ponder on recent data in the UK relating to fund manager turnover on unit trusts, which is quite staggering: In the UK, a quarter of fund managers have been in their current role less than one year, half have been with their present funds for under two years, only a third have been with the same fund for three years or more and alarmingly fewer than one in five for more than five years! Few have served twenty years. Just whose track record are you looking at?

In fact a few truly talented managers do exist

This part of the book may sound like a bit of an indictment of the whole active management industry. It is not meant to be. It is just meant to convince you that as an average investor, like me, you are unlikely to have the time, inclination, data or skills to evaluate active managers, or try to invest actively yourself. As a rational investor you need to make decisions based on the likelihood of long-term success, and therefore should adopt a lose-the-fewest points strategy.

There are some exceptional managers in the investment business, some of whom have moved to hedge funds or continue to manage funds or investor portfolios. An example of a long-term outperforming manager in the UK was Anthony Bolton who ran the Special Situations fund at Fidelity – but now you've found him, unfortunately he has retired! Take a look at the box at the end of this chapter to see just what a remarkable job he has done and to see what challenges investors faced sticking through the tougher periods the fund suffered along the way. It took a brave investor to reap the benefits.

4.6 Can you identify them in advance?

At this point you have the answers to the first two questions posed. You know that your mix of investments drives your portfolio returns, and the probability of capturing most of these returns lies in favour of a passive strategy rather than using active managers. You also now know that you cannot use past performance as a guide to picking future winners. As a result, you now have little to go on if you still want to use active managers.

Even if we can find a manager who can demonstrate fifteen years of outper-formance, based on skill, and/or a robust investment process rather than luck, the problem is that it is highly unlikely that they will be around for the next twenty years or more that *you* need them. They will be long gone to their beach houses in the Bahamas. If you can't use something simple such as past performance to choose managers, you have a problem. Waring and Siegel (2003) sum this problem of manager selection up well in a recent paper where they state:

'Each investor has to develop his or her own methodology for forecasting manager alphas ... if you don't think that you can do this, maybe you should not hire active managers.'

Even some of the world's largest and most sophisticated pension plans are index investors for at least some of their assets, such as the California Public Employees' Retirement System (CalPERS), who oversee more than $200 billion of assets. A few successful institutional investors, such as the Yale University Endowment managed by David Swensen and his team, use their proprietary insight, access to information and managers, and evaluation skills (combined with much hard work) to build an entire portfolio of high quality active managers. That may be fine for them, as they are some of the most astute investors around, but for you and me, we should stick where the probabilities favour us, i.e. indexing of long-term investment policy mix and sticking with it.

It is worth remembering the research finding highlighted in the Eye-opener section (Bogle, 2007) that in the US, from 1970 to 2005, of the 355 US equity mutual funds around in 1970 only three (less than 1 per cent) delivered statistically significant and consistent performance through to 2005. The chances of you or even your adviser picking these managers in advance are simply too low. Play the game that loses you the fewest points. Choose a good passive fund instead. As Bogle himself would say:

'Don't search for the needle, buy the haystack.'

4.7 Don't just take my word for it

So, having probably reached the conclusion that a passive index approach rather than an active approach makes most sense in terms of maximising your probability of long-term success, you are now with the 10 per cent of investors that think like you. The other 90 per cent of investors, both individuals and institutions, are still trying to pursue a points-winning strategy. However, you may be surprised by who has advocated the use of index investing as a sensible way to invest for most investors. Let me name a few, all of whom have made reputations for themselves as leading active managers or proponents of active management. You can rest assured that adopting a lose-the-fewest-points strategy is the only way for you to manage your own investing, or for your adviser to do so.

Warren Buffett (the Sage of Omaha), widely regarded as one of the greatest active investors of our time, has been described by John Bogle (Targett, 2001) as follows:

'He thinks like an index investor: he buys a few large stocks, holds them for a good holding period – forever – and it's worked quite brilliantly.'

In further support of index funds, Warren Buffet himself stated in one of the annual letters to shareholders (1997) of the investment firm Berkshire Hathaway that he and Charlie Munger run:

'Most investors, both institutional and individual, will find the best way to own common stocks is through an index fund that charges minimal fees. Those following this path are sure to beat the net results (after fees and expenses) delivered by the great majority of investment professionals.'

Peter Lynch, one-time manager of Fidelity Investment's Magellan Fund, the world's largest actively managed fund, and highly respected active manager states of most investors that (Anon, 1990):

'They'd be better off in an index fund.'

Charles Schwab, the pioneer of online brokerage in the USA, actively supports indexing as the core of an optimal long-term portfolio and states (Schwab, 1999):

'Most of the mutual fund investments I have are in index funds, approximately 75 per cent.'

Fidelity Investments, one of the world's largest active management companies, and familiar to UK investors, implicitly supports the concept of index investing through the addition of an index range of funds to their active fund stable.

What better testimonials could you ask for than those?

Anthony Bolton – the exception that proves the rule

In the introduction, I made an apology to the cohort, be it a small one, of fund managers who truly have something special – the ability consistently to beat the market over long periods of time, either through their exceptional individual skills, a unique investment process, or a combination of the two.

Anthony Bolton was a fund manager at Fidelity, one of the world's largest and most respected active fund management firms. He is an exceptional manager: he has been managing his Special Situations fund for more than 25 years (few others can match his longevity); he is truly dedicated to making money for the investors who place their faith in him; and he is very much a contrarian at heart (unlike some), being prepared to manage his money in quite a different manner from most of his peers and the market benchmark. In his words (Davis, 2004):

'If you want to outperform other people, you have got to hold something different from other people. If you want to outperform the market, as everyone expects you to do, the one thing you mustn't hold is the market itself.'

His UK-focused Special Situations fund has done just that; exhibiting

▶

a focus on smaller to medium-sized companies and value stocks, although that masks the flexibility of his approach to the companies he invests in; and his track record has been exceptional. With his retirement, he has firmly placed himself in the pantheon of active investment greats, alongside the likes of Warren Buffett and Peter Lynch, one of his former colleagues at Fidelity.

For investors who put £1,000 into his fund at its launch in 1979, their money in December 2004 would be worth about £90,000, whereas the market would only have made you just over £20,000. That is 6 per cent every year, on average, better than the market and twice his nearest rival. One of his exceptional feats was to make a positive return of around 4 per cent in the bear market of March 2000 to March 2003, when the market itself was down almost 40 per cent – only a handful of other managers made positive returns in this period. This is a truly remarkable record.

Active management can really pay, if you get it right, because compounding outperformance over time makes a big difference to the money in your pocket. No one in this case would begrudge paying a 1.5 per cent annual fee and all the other associated fund costs! I don't deny the fact; all I am trying to do is help you face the realities when you invest your money and try to make the best decisions you can to increase your chances of success. In that sense, and somewhat disappointingly, going the active route in search of the truly talented is a gamble – a low chance of a high payout, in this case an exceptionally high payout.

Ironically, Anthony Bolton's exceptional track record helps to highlight the very real challenge you are up against. Forgetting the notion that you can invest directly in the markets yourself successfully, finding true talent like Anthony Bolton is not easy and you need to ask yourself if you have the skills and the time to try to do so.

First of all, it is very hard to pick a manager in advance of the twenty to thirty years that you will need them to manage your money. Who in 1979 knew that Anthony Bolton would be one of the best fund managers yet? It's made no easier by the fact that managers hop from job to job so quickly. Bolton is one of only 17 managers who have managed their fund for more than 15 years, out of more than 300 funds.

▶

Here's an illustration of the dilemma you face. Imagine you had £10,000 to invest at the start of 1989. You open the paper and see that his Special Situations fund has beaten the market by a remarkable 8 per cent a year for nine years. You (rightly as it turns out, of course) decide that he is the man to look after your money. You invest. Three years later you find yourself a whopping 45 per cent or so behind the market, turning your £10,000 into £9,700 against the market's £14,300. What do you do? Hold? Sell? The problem is that you simply don't know, at that point in 1991, if he is brilliant or whether his luck has just run out. Even Ned Johnson, the head of Fidelity, seemed to have his doubts, calling him in to talk about the fund's performance.

In 1996 you almost get back in line with the market but 1997 and 1998 see you drop back by about 20 per cent against the market. Still going to hold? In fact, it would have taken you until 2000 to get back ahead of the market. Eleven years of uncertainty – would you really have had the stomach to see this through? I doubt it and I can understand why. If you had, though, you would have ended up with almost twice what the market delivered by the end of 2004! Very few investors have held the fund since inception and over half of today's 250,000 investors have invested in the five years to 2004.

That brings us back to the issue of needing to find a manager now who will be around for the period of time you need them, i.e. from today. New investors in this particular fund won't have Anthony Bolton managing their money. Do you believe his replacement will replicate his unique talent and insight? Who else out there is the next Anthony Bolton? And how can you pick them now, given that past performance is a weak indicator of future success in most cases? That's your dilemma. As a smarter investor you should accept that you may have to give up an outside chance of a very substantial upside of tomorrow's Anthony Bolton and simply accept that the market return, as near as possible, is a worthy ambition, if a somewhat boring one.

Congratulations to Mr Bolton, and to those other managers who in a few years' time we will look back on and say, 'Boy, they were good!' while secretly wishing we had found them today.

4.8 Summarising what you now know

So, given all of the arguments put forward in this chapter, you now need to condense this down into a simple investment philosophy that will provide you with a set of rules to guide you in investment decisions. I am assuming that you have been suitably convinced by the arguments put forward to adopt a lose the fewest points strategy. Let's summarise what you now know:

- Active investors play a less-than-zero sum cost game (after costs and taxes).

- Opportunities may exist for some managers to beat the markets if they have superior skills and/or access to information or ability to interpret information.

- Most professional investors tend to take only small active decisions, such as market timing or security selection, and long-term investment policy thus overrides active strategies as the main contributor to the variation in returns over time. This implies that they believe it is hard to do.

- In fact, professional managers tend marginally to underperform their investment policy portfolio mix due to their active decisions and costs.

- This may be because markets are efficient. Forecasts are hard to make, decisions are in fact two decisions, and markets move very rapidly and with magnitude.

- Even where markets are less efficient, costs tend to be higher and exploiting the inefficiencies that exist after costs remains challenging.

- Logic tells us that as all investors are the market, the average investor will be the market before costs. The average investor after costs will underperform the market by these costs. As index fund costs are lower than active costs, the average index fund will outperform the average active fund.

- That would be fine if the market beaters of the future were easy to identify by their past performance record.

- However, active funds' outperformance does not persist to any degree that is useful. Underperformance may be an indicator of future poor results in some cases. This means you cannot use past performance, profitably, to select managers.

- Some exceptionally skilful managers may out there waiting for your money, but you have a tough job trying to find them in advance. Those few who have already performed through skill are unlikely to be around for the period you will need them, or are inaccessible to you.

■ At least fifteen years of data is generally required to validate statistically that good outperformance is due to skill rather than luck.

■ Most managers have been in their current roles for fewer than three years.

■ If you don't have a proprietary method for selecting these outperforming managers, along with the skill, time, resources and appetite to screen hundreds if not thousands of managers, then don't try to. Your chances of success are very poor.

■ Ask yourself is any adviser is capable of doing so (unlikely).

So, without any hesitation I suggest to you that you choose, as your default, index-replicating products to create your long-term investment policy portfolio. Avoid trying to add returns by moving your mix of investment around or trying to pick winning stocks or managers. The chances are slim that you will be able to do it consistently. I know it's tempting to get swayed by the supposed evidence of short-term performance of markets and managers but you will not be being rational if you are. Play the highest probability game. The rationale for adopting a passive approach to investing is made succinctly by Professor Keane (2000):

'The significance of the empirical evidence is not that passive investment will always outperform active investment, but that, at the time of decision-making, the balance of probabilities is always in favour of passive investment.'

4.9 A personal philosophy

Hopefully at this point you will have a pretty clear picture of what your personal investment philosophy should look like as a rational investor. I will now share with you my personal investment philosophy. Some of the concepts referred to are introduced later in the book.

My philosophy
On goals: I want to achieve my investment goals, which I think of in terms of lifetime purchasing power goals: sending the kids to school, paying off my mortgage and retiring early with a good standard of

▶

living until I die. Success or failure should be measured against these goals.

On being rational: I realise that I do not have a crystal ball that I can foresee the future with and will therefore try and act as rationally as possible to allow myself the greatest chance of achieving these goals, in an environment of uncertainty. If I let emotions sway my reason, I know that it will cost me dearly.

On probabilities: There are many things that I know for sure when I invest. I know that time and compounding are on my side and that inflation and all sorts of costs always work against me. I will maximise the forces that work in my favour and minimise or eliminate those that work against me.

The one thing I don't know for sure is how the markets will perform over my investing lifetime. I therefore need to diversify my portfolio well, and try to make the best estimates that I can that I have a reasonable chance of obtaining an acceptable investment outcome. Research, analysis and empirical evidence provide me with the opportunity to improve my chances of making good investment decisions, and thus reaching my goals.

On my portfolio mix: I understand that choosing and maintaining the long-term structure of my portfolio is the most important decision that I face and all other decisions are secondary to it and revolve around capturing as much of the available return from this mix of portfolio building blocks as is practicably possible.

The choice between holding equities to drive returns from my portfolio and buying 'market trauma protection' by owning bonds is the primary decision I need to make.

I will use the tools that are available to all investors, including diversification, to create the best portfolio that I can within practical reason. I will also seek to add other building blocks to my portfolio, either to increase returns or to diversify my portfolio further in an attempt make my investment journey smoother without giving up too much return potential. I will only use these other portfolio building blocks when I understand and feel happy with the risks that I am taking on by including them.

▶

On costs: Small differences in returns, e.g. caused by bad performance relative to other comparable investment options combined with costs, when compounded over time, can dramatically reduce the effectiveness of my investing and may force me to change my hoped for goals and suffer the consequences that I would rather avoid.

In a practical sense, capturing as much of the market return as possible should be my aim. Index-replicating strategies, with low costs, will be my base position for obtaining these returns, based on the logic, research and evidence that is available. Index (passive) management is the winning strategy because it minimises the risk of losing points. I choose it relative to active strategies for my portfolio.

I will always be alert to the fact that the investment management and brokerage industry, whilst providing me with assistance, is always seeking to maximise its own shareholder value. I understand that there will always be some costs associated with investing but I will ensure that I always fully understand all of the costs involved, that I will not pay for advice that I do not receive or is unnecessary, and will not pay for investment professionals that cannot prove, on terms that I set, that they personally, or the investment process they adopt, can consistently generate long-term value for my portfolio. The onus lies with them to convince me to move away from index products and pay higher costs.

I will always think about the tax consequences of how I invest any funds that I will need to pay tax on. I will look at returns after tax. I will maximise the use of all legal tax shelters and breaks available to me, and will make sure that my investment strategy allows me to maximise the benefit of legitimately paying the tax man later rather than sooner through the reduction of turnover and active efforts to manage my tax position.

On technology: I will use technology to my advantage to monitor, manage and administer my investments, taking advantage of the technology provided at very low costs by some online brokers, banks and investment companies.

On managing my investments over time: As part of the portfolio maintenance process I will rebalance my portfolio regularly, not driven by some hope of benefiting from selling overperforming assets and buying underperforming assets, but driven by the desire to maintain the risk of my portfolio at a level that I can live with, which I worked out upfront before embarking on my investment programme.

On sticking with it: All of these objectives, assumptions, constraints and intentions I will write down in a simple statement of my investment programme. When times get tough, as they inevitably will, I will take out this document and remind myself just why my portfolio is invested the way it is. I will also refresh my memory to the fact that severe bumpiness on the way to meeting my lifetime purchasing power goals is to be expected.

On a personal note: I will try to keep up to date with developments, avoid being tempted into making emotional decisions, which I know can severely damage my wealth accumulation, have the courage to stick to my strategy when times get tough, as they will from time to time, avoid looking at my portfolio too often, avoid listening to financial news programmes and believing what I hear, and try to enjoy my investment responsibilities.

4.10 Your investment philosophy rules

1 *Set an appropriate investment policy mix of assets and stick to it at all times*. This will be the most crucial decision that you will make. How you get to the right mix is explored in Part 3.

2 Remember at all times the wise words of Charles Ellis, particularly if you have any investment decision to make:

'The ultimate outcome is determined by who can lose the fewest points not win them.'

3 A penny saved is a penny earned; become obsessed with reducing the actual or potential loss of points in all aspects of your investing programme, as losing the least number of (return) points is your ultimate philosophical goal. Keep other people's hands out of your investment pie, which includes advisers, active managers, badly structured and managed index funds, brokers and the taxman.

4 Active management is a tough game for all but the few most brilliant or lucky. You have a low chance of winning points and a high chance of losing points if you go this route.

5 Avoid trying to time markets and being tempted to jump between asset classes, countries, sectors or managers. Chasing returns is a road to wealth destruction.

6 Don't try to pick stocks. Too much evidence demonstrates that after all costs, fees and taxes are taken into account it is a game you won't win.

7 You will lose if you try to pick a manager by their performance record. Be sensible and pick a fund that has a 60–80 per cent chance of beating all active funds over the long run, i.e. an index tracker fund.

8 However bright you think you are, or however confident you are, or how convincing a story, sales patter, brochure of performance record is, do not be tempted either to change your investment policy mix or become an active investor yourself.

9 Index all bond and equity market investments wherever possible.

10 Sticking with a passive buy-and-hold index funds approach to investing not only reduces your chances of losing points, but it also provides you with a much more straightforward approach to investing at a number of levels, as you will see.

References

Allan, D., Brailsford, T., Bird, R. and Faff, R. (2002) *A review of research on the past performance of managed funds*, Funds Management Research Centre.

Anon (1990) 'Is there life after Babe Ruth? Peter Lynch talks about why he's quitting Magellan', *Barron's*, April 2, p.15.

Barber, B. M. and Odean, T. (1998) 'Trading is hazardous to your wealth: the common stock investment performance of individuals', *The Journal of Finance*, vol. LV, no. 2, 773–806.

Blake, D., Lehman, B. N. and Timmerman, A. (1999) 'Asset allocation dynamics and pension fund performance', *The Journal of Business*, vol. 72, no.4, 429–461.

Bogle, J. C. (2002), 'The investment dilemma of the philanthropic investor', Bogle Financial Markets Research Center. Available from: http://www.vanguard.com.

Bogle, J. C. (2003) 'The policy portfolio in an era of subdued returns', Bogle Financial Markets Research Center. Available from: http://www.vanguard.com.

Bogle, J. C. (2007) *The Little Book of Common Sense Investing*, John Wiley & Sons.

Brinson, G. P., Hood, L. R. and Beebower G.L. (1986) 'Determinants of portfolio performance', *Financial Analysts Journal*, vol. 42, no. 4, 40–48.

Buffett, W. (1997) *Annual Report 1996: Chairman's Letter*. Berkshire Hathaway Inc. Available from http://www.berkshirehathaway.com/1996ar/1996.html.

Carhart, M. (1997) 'On persistence in Mutual Funds', *Journal of Finance*, 52, pp. 57–82.

Chordia, T., Roll, R. and Subrahmanyan, A. (2003) 'Evidence on the speed of convergence to market efficiency', UCLA Working Paper, November 3.

Cuthbertson, K., Nitzsche, D., O'Sullivan, N. (2006) 'The Market Timing Ability of UK Equity Mutual Funds'. Available at SSRN: http://ssrn.com.

Cuthbertson, K., Nitzsche, D. and O'Sullivan, N. (2008) 'False Discoveries: Winners and Losers in Mutual Fund Performance'. Available at SSRN: http://ssrn.com/abstract=1093624.

Davis, J. (2004) *Investing with Anthony Bolton*. UK: Harriman House, p. 18.

Ellis, C. D. (2002) *Winning the losers game*, 4th ed. New York: McGraw Hill, 3–7.

Ibbotson, R. G. and Kaplan, P. D. (2000) 'Does asset allocation policy explain 40%, 90% or 100% of performance?' *Financial Analysts Journal*, vol. 56, no.1, 26–33.

Keane, S. (2000) *Index funds in a bear market*, a monograph published by Glasgow University in association with Virgin Direct.

Malkiel, B. G. (2000) 'Are markets efficient? Yes even if they make errors', *The Wall Street Journal*, December 28, p. A10.

Malkiel, B. G. (2004) 'Three decades of indexing: What have we learned about indexing and index construction?' In *The handbook of world stock, derivative and commodity exchanges 2004 edition*. London: Mondo Visione. Available from: http://www.exchange-handbook.co.uk.

Rhodes, M. (2000) *Past imperfect? The performance of UK equity managed funds*. London: FSA, FSA Occasional Paper Series 9. Available from: http://www.fas.gov.uk/pubs.occpapers/op09.pdf.

Schwab, C. (1999) *Charles Schwab's guide to financial independence: simple solutions for busy people*. New York: Three Rivers Press, p. 90.

Sharpe, W. F. (1975) 'Are gains likely from market timing?' *The Financial Analysts Journal*, vol. 31, no. 2 (March/April) pp. 60–69.

Sharpe, W. F. (1991) 'The arithmetic of active management'. *The Financial Analysts Journal*, January/February, vol. 47, no. 1, 7–9.

Sinquefield, R. (1995) Opening address: Schwab Institutional Conference, San Francisco, CA, October 12.

Targett, S. (2001) 'Survey – index-based investing: An industry enjoying life in the fast track', *Financial Times*, 18 July.

Waring, M. B. and Siegel, L. B. (2003) 'The dimensions of active management', *The Journal of Portfolio Management*, vol. 29, no 3, 35–51.

WM Company (2001) *A comparison of active and passive management of unit trusts*. A report produced for Virgin Direct Financial Services.

5

Get smart – manage your emotions

While we all like to think that we are capable of making rational decisions, it appears that when it comes to investing, a switch inside even the most sensible person seems to flick and rationality disappears in a cloud of emotion. It is impossible for me simply to tell you to be rational in the decisions that you face, but what I can do is point out the consequences of emotional behaviour on your wealth accumulation and some of the demons that drive it.

5.1 You are your own worst enemy

Being an investor is not easy. You have to contend not only with the erratic and unpredictable nature of markets but also the sometimes erratic and irrational way in which you will be tempted to think and behave. This book encourages you to do your best to make rational decisions and to make your head rule your heart in all matters relating to investing. Yet for most, while understanding that being rational makes sense, putting it into practice can be exceedingly difficult. Benjamin Graham, one of the great investment minds of the twentieth century, famously stated (Graham and Dodd, 1996):

'The investor's chief problem – and even his worst enemy – is likely to be himself.'

Irrational investing manifests itself in many different ways: chopping and changing your investment plan influenced by what has just happened to the markets; trading shares in an online brokerage account; trying to pick market turning points, i.e. when to be in or out of different markets; being tempted into buying flavour of the month investment ideas or products; or chasing performance. The list of irrational decision-making opportunities is long and distinguished. John Bogle summed this up perfectly in an address to the Investment Analysts Society of Chicago (2003):

*'If I have learned anything in my 52 years in this marvellous field, it is that, for
a given individual or institution, the emotions of investing have destroyed far
more potential investment returns than the economics of investing have ever
dreamed of destroying.'*

Reflect on this for a moment

Eye-opener 2 at the start of this book looked at the performance record of
individual investors in the USA over the period from 1984 to 2002. The
staggering results of the study showed that because investors are all
tempted by the media, their own research or their advisers to chop and
change their investment strategy and chase last year's returns, the average
equity investor earned just 2.6 per cent annually over this period, when
inflation was 3.1 per cent. That is a bad result.

The market, as measured by the S&P500 index, a commonly used proxy for
the US market, returned 12.2 per cent a year. If you assume that an investor
could have replicated the market at a 0.2 per cent cost, which is not unreasonable in the USA, you can calculate what the true difference in
purchasing power would have been over this period. Figure 5.1 displays the
results. Remember it every time you make an investment decision. As you
can see from the right-hand chart, investors are their 'own worst enemy'
and cost themselves a lot of money through their decision-making.

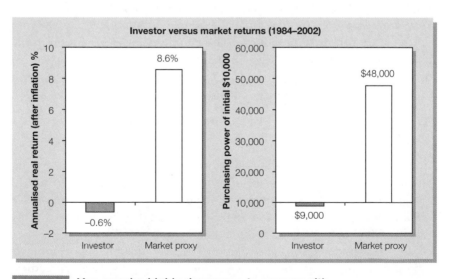

Figure 5.1 You may be highly dangerous to your wealth

Source: Dalbar.

Get a grip on yourself

Unfortunately emotional demons affect the way in which you make your investment decisions. Understanding these demons may help you to identify how you can try to keep them in control. The times when most investors become irrational are generally periods of market trauma or market exuberance. As Warren Buffett said (2001):

'The line separating investment and speculation, which is never bright and clear, becomes blurred still further when most market participants have recently enjoyed triumphs. Nothing sedates rationality like large doses of effortless money.'

Buy high, sell low – a recipe for wealth destruction

Figure 5.2 shows how many people invest, allowing their emotions and lack of market knowledge to drive the type of wealth destruction that you saw in the research above. This is the sort of investing that our hypothetical investor, James, undertook in the previous chapter. While most investors can understand the simple concept of buy low, sell high, the very nature of their behaviour results in exactly the opposite. Investors tend to be influenced by what is going on in the markets over the short term. This makes them vulnerable to what the industry refers to as being 'whip-sawed' as they move from last year's bad performing investment to this year's best performer.

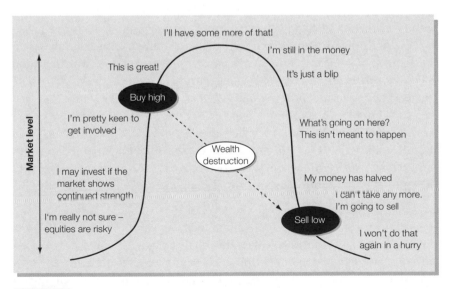

Figure 5.2 Generic wealth-destroying behaviour

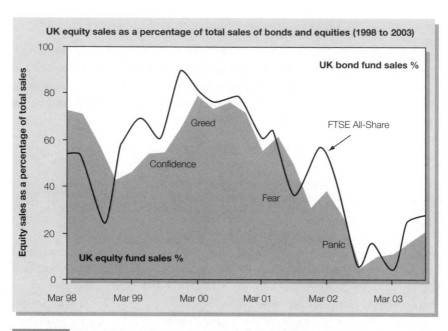

Figure 5.3 Buy high, sell low – the road to wealth destruction

Source: Investment Management Association; Thomson Datastream.

Let's take a look at this behaviour in practice in the UK. Figure 5.3 shows the net retail sales by unit trusts and open-ended investment companies (OEICs) to UK investors. Rationally, you would expect that after the UK equity market had fallen by 40 per cent or so, new fund flows into equities would increase as investors were getting better value for their money than at the start of 2000 when the market was at a high. Yet it is clear that fund sales are driven by short-term market sentiment, where investors become increasingly eager to enter the market when markets have performed well recently, i.e. when they are relatively expensive, and tend to cut back their investment when they fall, i.e. when they are cheaper. This is ironic given that in all other walks of life we have no trouble in being attracted to goods and services which are cheap, yet when it comes to investing we seem to lose not only our rational selves, but also a good deal of common sense.

As you can see from Figure 5.3, the level of sales of equity funds rises and falls almost exactly in line with the market. As equity markets fall, bond sales increase in proportion. Given that the vast majority of sales are made through advisers of some description, it begs the question as to just how valuable and costly this advice is. It appears to constitute selling last quarter's best performer, or am I being too sceptical? Decide for yourself. It is a good illustration of emotions taking over, and bad advice encouraging them.

Ironically, many investors were willing to buy into the equity markets in the late 1990s with 'irrational exuberance' not because it was part of a long-term strategic plan, but because they thought there was a quick buck to be made, as markets powered ahead. When the UK equity market reached its highest point in 2000 where the FTSE 100 Index, which represents the largest one hundred, listed companies, reached almost 7,000, there was an almost hysterical urge to invest in equities. When it fell to 3,500 in mid-2002, few investors wanted to invest money in equities. Corporate bond funds became the flavour of the day as strongly performing havens for investors, or so the salespeople said.

This is perverse and is best described Warren Buffett, who has a habit of speaking common sense (1998). He poses a short quiz to his shareholders:

'If you plan to eat hamburgers throughout your life and are not a cattle producer, should you wish for higher or lower prices for beef? Likewise, if you are going to buy a car from time to time but are not an auto manufacturer, should you prefer higher or lower prices? These questions, of course, answer themselves.'

He follows on with the paradox of investors:

'But now for the final exam: if you expect to be a net saver during the next five years, should you hope for a higher or lower net stock market during that period? Many investors get this one wrong. Even though they are going to be net buyers of stocks for many years to come, they are elated when prices rise and are depressed when they fall. In effect, they rejoice because prices have risen for the "hamburgers" they will soon be buying. This reaction makes no sense. Only those who will be sellers of equities in the near future should be happy at seeing stocks rise. Prospective purchasers should much prefer sinking prices.'

The problem is that these sentiments persuade some investors to change tack when market trauma events occur and often act precisely against their own best interest. To be a good investor at times is a bit like playing a game of poker with yourself, pitching your logical-self against your emotional-self and seeing who blinks first

5.2 Challenges to decision-making

Many investors act irrationally, rather than rationally as economic theory demands; this irrational behaviour is a relatively new and interesting area of academic study. A whole industry has grown up in the past couple of decades studying it called 'behavioural finance'.

The next few pages is not meant to be a review of the psychology of investment decision-making as espoused by these academics, but a practical guide to how you can avoid being tempted into becoming irrational. If you understand a little more about who you are and importantly how, where and when you may be tempted into being irrational then you will have made some useful progress. It is based in part on the general ideas of behavioural economists, in large part on my experience of dealing with a wide number of investors over the past few years, and will probably seem to you like just a dose of common sense.

Making investment decisions

As you make investment decisions, you go through a mental process of trying to evaluate the wealth outcomes that you can expect and trying to assess the likelihood that they will happen. You have a wide choice of options and you need to weigh up one against the other. It is hard trying to process all the information that is available in any ordered and value-added way and in the end you generate some sort of intuitive feel for what the answer is for you.

A lack of knowledge, combined with a number of illusions and biases can lead to errors in making decisions that may damage your chances of making the most from your money. These include: the likelihood that you

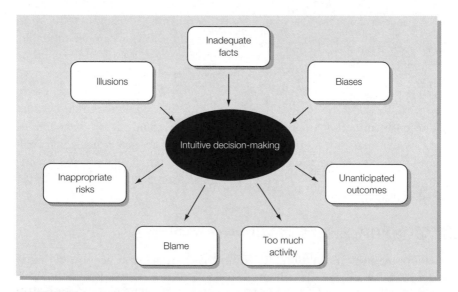

Figure 5.4　Intuitive decision-making can be costly

take on an inappropriate and usually higher level of risk than you might have considered sensible if your assessment of the effect had been more realistic; the possibility that the outcome you get is not one you considered, but should have done; the greater likelihood that you will continue to make decisions rather than leaving your investments alone; and the common and sometimes ugly outcome of blaming your adviser or yourself when your luck runs out (Kahneman et al., 1998).

All in all, not being aware of and not curbing your inner biases and illusions is likely to be painful, upsetting, and from a wealth perspective grossly sub-optimal. Figure 5.4 summarises the decision-making process.

5.3 Thirteen questions for you to answer

A number of emotional demons regularly influence investors, advisers and fund managers; the degree to which they will affect you, only you will know. Think hard about yourself and be honest, because cheating will only lead to bad decisions and cost you money.

1 Are you interested in investing?

I am sure you will have a pretty good feel for this!

No: You probably know that you should be doing something with your money; perhaps improving your retirement planning, sensibly investing the proceeds from the sale of a business, or making provision for education fees, but have little interest in sorting it out yourself. That's understandable. Not everyone needs to have an avid interest in investing, but everyone needs to be an investor. What you probably want is to get everything sorted out, simply and efficiently so you can get on with life. This book will help you to do that. The danger lies in avoiding the issue altogether, because tackle it you must.

Yes: Good for you. Just make sure that your interest and enthusiasm do not cloud your judgement and make you too aggressive with new ideas and overly complex in your portfolio structure.

2 Are you knowledgeable about investing?

This is perhaps a good place to start. By knowledge I mean understanding the basic rules that guide simple, good investing, not how much you know about a certain stock, or economics, bond mathematics or derivative pricing. If you know why these are irrelevant then you have a reasonable knowledge of the basics. Hopefully you will, because they were covered in Chapter 2.

No: Don't worry about it, just don't stay there. Investing is not part of most people's education, even though it inescapably plays a major part in their lives. Picking up this book indicates that you are trying to improve things. You'd be surprised at just how many self-acclaimed knowledgeable investors actually know less than they think. In my experience this group includes many pension fund trustees, private bankers, corporate treasurers and journalists of otherwise respectable papers and journals.

Yes: Extremely knowledgeable investors are few and far between and here sit the likes of Charles Ellis, John Bogle, Burton Malkiel, Warren Buffett and David Swensen, to name a few of the truly inspirational investment minds. Fortunately, we can all exploit their wisdom and knowledge to our own advantage. Most have written books and much of their thinking underpins this book. What they have in common is that they have thought hard about the effects and probabilities of the decisions that they make and the theories of investing that they support. They have established their own consistent philosophy, which they apply ruthlessly to keep them on their rational path, and keep their emotions in control. You too should have put in place a sensible philosophy of losing the fewest points.

3 Are you confident in your investing abilities?

As a general rule, most of us are innately overconfident in our own abilities in most things. Many studies demonstrate this in all sorts of different areas and professions. A classic study is based on giving people a scenario such as 'How high will the FTSE 100 Index (a key UK equity market index) be at the end of the year?' and asking them to set a range that this end point will fall within, which they are 98 per cent confident in but no more. In many studies the surprise rate, i.e. the number of times that the result falls outside the range, is 15–20 per cent, demonstrating considerable overconfidence in our own abilities.

Overconfidence also breeds a state of mind that attributes positive out-comes to skill and poor outcomes to bad luck. I've sat in many meetings with fund managers who have proudly crowed about the great stocks they have picked when they have beaten the markets, yet the next quarter they blame underperformance on unforeseen and random events. Amusingly, every active fund manager is confident of beating the market – a mathematical impossibility but nonetheless a certainty in the minds of all of them. Ask yourself if you are a better than average driver. More than 80 per cent of us think we are, apparently.

No: You may not feel confident that you have the appropriate understanding or knowledge to make investment decisions for yourself, but don't worry. The danger for you is that you turn to industry professionals for advice and abrogate almost the entire decision-making process to them. Advice is frequently costly and, even if it is good advice, may strip away too much of your wealth. With a little time spent understanding the fundamentals, you can quickly build your confidence level to allow you to discuss what you want from your investments sensibly and rationally with an adviser, if you choose to hire one.

Yes: Take care, as this is one of the main danger areas for you. Overconfidence can tempt you to make ill-judged decisions, often based on a lack of hard facts, hearsay, or simply a lack of thought. Overconfidence can manifest itself in a number of many ways. You may believe that you can pick outperforming managers, pick market-turning points, or believe that you understand a company stock well enough to own it, to name a few. The major detrimental consequence is usually excessive trading of the investments in your portfolio.

4 Do you have trouble controlling your emotions?

Investors often have trouble keeping a grip on their emotions, resulting in overly optimistic or pessimistic outlooks relative to reality. Emotions nearly always affect wealth creation, driving a buy-high-sell-low strategy, illustrated earlier.

No: You are one of the lucky few. As an investor you are playing a probability game, trying to maximise the chances of success by looking at the evidence that you have, evaluating it in realistic and unemotional terms and acting upon it. Taking emotion out of investing is the best, yet probably hardest, thing to do. Being a stoic, getting neither too optimistic nor too pessimistic about what is happening to the markets, is a significant plus. The chances that you will be a successful and astute investor are high.

Yes: Beware. Emotional investors tend to become overly optimistic in good times and overly pessimistic in bad times leading to a 'fear and greed' syndrome, synonymous with a buy-high-sell-low strategy. The difficulty for you is that you may feel rational when sitting in the calm oak-panelled offices of your private banker or fund manager, and agree wholeheartedly with the rational investment plan you draw up. However, when the markets begin to tumble, as they inevitably will from time to time, or rise dramatically, the emotions take over and rash heart-driven decisions overrule the head. These emotions tend to drive panic decisions such as 'I need to get out of equities' or 'I want to be in cash' with serious consequences for your long-term wealth. Optimism combined with overconfidence can lead to poor decisions.

5 Do you see patterns in things?

The human mind tends to seek order in the world around it, and the search for patterns in investment data is an example. Acting on these so-called patterns seems to be a common human weakness.

Imagine the outcomes from two sequences of dice throws being 6,6,6,6,6,6, and 2,2,6,1,4,3. From a gut-feel perspective, the second sequence seems the one that is more likely to occur, although rationally we know that they both have the same chance of being rolled. If we rolled again for the first sequence, do you feel that there is a good chance of a 6? Some gamblers would; see how many double up on the roulette table the spin of the wheel after 'red 9' comes up, or track the patterns of results on different tables. Short-term random sequences are relatively common in investing but rarely warrant any attention. Some investors see patterns everywhere. Technical analysis, a practice that looks at charts of market movements, seeks to find meaning in them. This 'art' is sometimes referred to as 'reading the tea leaves' by some in the industry!

No: The ability not to get tempted into seeing patterns in random numbers is a bonus. Broker-inspired lines such as 'the trend is your friend' should be taken with a large handful of salt.

Yes: The danger is that you see signs everywhere, which if combined with overconfidence and optimism can result in damaging levels of investment activity and decision-making in your portfolio, ultimately leading to suboptimal investment performance. An example would be the temptation to sell a fund you own because another fund has done better over the past couple of years, extrapolating what is in all likelihood a chance event into a basis for judging future long-term outperformance.

6 Are you prone to being a hindsight expert?

It is tempting to try to make sense of events that have occurred and post-rationalise that there was some rhyme or reason to them. This behaviour may lead you to believe that events are more predictable than they actually are and may lead you to regret not taking appropriate action sooner. It is difficult to remember how you felt before a market event happened; after the event you may have conveniently forgotten your exuberance, for example for technology stocks in 1999!

Behavioural economist Robert Shiller undertook some research (1997) relating to the Japanese stock market crash in 1989. It showed that before the peak of the market, 14 per cent of people thought the market was over-valued. Afterwards, 32 per cent said they had thought the market to be overvalued at the time of the crash.

This trait frequently manifests itself in blaming advisers for missing what was, now in their minds, a perfectly predictable event: 'Why didn't you spot that commodity stocks were overvalued? Anyone could have seen that.' This is probably a common comment to advisers in 2008.

No: If you can accept that professionals' crystal balls are just as clouded as your own and that things always seem easier to make meaning of after-wards than at the time, then you will have considerably less angst in your life. Knowing that markets are not predictable in the short term reduces feelings of regret and blame and allows you to make decisions that are not clouded by these emotions.

Yes: The danger is that you blame your advisers or investment managers for decisions that they did or did not make. By all means talk through past events with your manager but don't blame them for events that you should have anticipated when establishing your portfolio in the first place. You may also fall into the trap that decisions are easier to make than they actu-ally are.

7 Do you regret decisions that you make?

All the investment decisions that you make will have consequences for your wealth in the short term as well as the long term. However, some investors regret sensible long-term decisions when in the short term the markets seem to be working against them. Your ability to avoid regret in the short term in order to achieve your long-term purchasing power goals is critical.

No: If you can accept the consequences of decisions, you are in a good pos-ition to stay the course.

Yes: If you are prone to suffering regret over decisions in your life, then you are vulnerable to making decisions that can seriously jeopardise your wealth. If you establish a rationally structured portfolio and understand why it is structured as it is, then times when you may feel it was the wrong thing to do may arise. The classic case is investing part of your portfolio in bonds for downside protection and then regretting that you are not 100 per cent in equities when the market soars.

8 Do your losses hurt more than gains please you?

You may feel a greater degree of pain from losses on your portfolios when markets fall than the pleasure you feel when markets rise. Studies have shown that this ratio of pain-to-gain may be more than 2:1 for many investors (Kahneman and Tversky, 1979).

No: You are lucky because you will be able to accept the overriding reality of investing that in order to achieve higher long-term investment returns, a greater tolerance for short-term market trauma will be required. You may feel uncomfortable and disappointed when markets fall but not to the degree that it makes you panic and sell out.

Yes: Unfortunately you are in a delicate position as you feel more pain when things go wrong than pleasure when things go right. That is fine. Feeling comfortable in your investing is important provided that is within sensible bounds. The danger for you is that when markets are rising you would like to participate in the returns on offer, but the pain you suffer when they sell-off frightens you away from these investments. You sell at the bottom and then become overly conservative in how you invest, focusing on avoiding further losses and sacrificing longer-term purchasing power potential.

Some investors have the unrealistic expectation that you can have the upside without the downside – sorry but that's not possible. Avoid any products or managers that purport to create this elusive asymmetry. The only way you can improve this trade-off is by structuring a highly diversified portfolio with several investment building blocks.

9 Do you like long shots and insurance?

On the surface this is less intuitive than the previous questions. In general people have a preference for gambles, i.e. low probabilities of high value outcomes, and insurance, i.e. greater certainty of outcomes with lower pay-offs. In other words, people like gambling and insurance.

Some people are more than willing to pay more than £1 for a 1 per cent chance of winning £100, or more than £1 for raising a 99 per cent chance of maintaining £100 to 100 per cent certainty. Yet few are willing to pay £1 to raise the chance of maintaining £100 from 65 per cent to 66 per cent, even though it has the same utility as the other two options. Some products on the market prey on investors' desires to satisfy their irrational preference for long shots and insurance.

No: If you are able to understand and accept that investing is about trying to get the chances of a favourable outcome as high as you can in your favour then you are well on the way to becoming an astute investor.

Yes: Paying over the odds for products that incorporate gambling and insurance characteristics is poor investing. Favour investing in portfolios that have reasonable probabilities of survivable outcomes to you over gambles and insurance. Any products made up of the two should be avoided, e.g. structured notes, including equity-participation notes, where you invest your money for a set period, get a share of the market upside, or your money back, before inflation, if markets fall (except in the circumstances covered later in the book).

10 Do you have difficulty seeing beyond the short term?

Many investors find it difficult to see the long-term wood for the short-term trees. Their focus tends to be on the effects of recent market conditions on their wealth and this affects their ability to make good decisions for the long-term success in meeting their lifetime purchasing power needs.

The advent of online accounts and investment tracking software has made this a lot worse and too many investors now look at their investments too frequently, getting highly excited as the markets rise and desperately disappointed as they fall. On any day, the chance of seeing a loss on your equity investments is around 50:50 (Swedroe, 2002). Even once a year you have around a 30 per cent chance or more that you will see a loss. Given the ratio of pain to gain, the longer the period between peeks the better!

No: You are in a good position. You can control the pain that accompanies short-term losses because you can see beyond the short-term volatility, encouraging you to stick to your long-term plan.

Yes: The danger is that the losses you see regularly give you unnecessary pain, blinding you to the gains you will make in the long term. It may tempt you into changing your strategy, as the short-term pain seems too

much to bear. The answer is not to look at your portfolio too often. Time smoothes out return volatility. If you look at your portfolio every day you will think you are riding a bucking bronco. Look at it yearly as a whole and you will be trotting along comfortably most of the time.

What the eye doesn't see . . .

11 Do you have trouble seeing the big picture?

Some investors tend to look at their investment portfolio, or for that matter other issues in their lives, from a big picture perspective, while others tend to focus on minutiae.

No: Looking at the big picture is a great asset as an investor. What you should be interested in is how your portfolio as a whole is progressing relative to the purchasing power targets you have set, not dissecting and feeling anxious about how each component has performed. The danger for holistic thinkers is that any rotten apples in the portfolio, perhaps a badly managed fund, may be jeopardising the portfolio goals as a whole. Just make sure that each component of your portfolio is doing the job you ask of it.

Yes: Looking at each separate component of a portfolio in isolation from the other pieces and the overall picture has the danger of making you focus on the wrong things. As an example, if your equity holdings do really well you may be tempted to sell some of your other investments, e.g. bonds that were not performing as well, and buy more equity. The problem is twofold: timing markets is very difficult but, just as importantly, you have sold bonds that were part of the portfolio to protect you when equities suffer a severe reversal, which is almost inevitable at some point. Remember the big picture and keep your long-term goals in mind.

12 Do you prefer action to planning?

Time spent planning is a crucial step in successful investing: defining what your lifetime purchasing power goals are; working out what mix of portfolio building blocks has the greatest chance of attaining them; and pre-testing your emotions against this mix is critical to good investing and controlling your emotions.

No: If you enjoy the planning process and derive comfort from its thoroughness or if you merely acknowledge that it is a necessary evil, then that is a bonus. Whether you enjoy it or merely tolerate it, you are at the better end of the spectrum and are likely to end up with a workable and successful investment strategy.

Yes: Here lies danger. Whilst being action-orientated is not in itself a problem, action at the expense of planning is. For some of you, planning may seem mundane and boring compared with the excitement of the markets. However, counting the cost of a poorly thought out investment strategy is more painful. An action-orientation combined with overconfidence and insufficient knowledge is a volatile cocktail. Simple, good investing, as you will see, requires relatively little action.

13 Are you more trusting than sceptical?

As you will see as this book moves along, a healthy dose of scepticism is a good thing.

No: Excellent. If you are a bit of a sceptic you are likely to make a good investor. Treat everything that you see or hear with an element of suspicion. If you ask yourself questions like: Where are the vested interests? Are the fees reasonable? Why is this supposedly such a good investment? Where's the catch? You will be rewarded in the long run. Starting from the premise that many advisers and much of the industry are working, at the margin, against your best interests, it sets up your defences for the conflicts of interest that you will encounter.

Yes: If you do not have much interest in or knowledge about investing, or are merely a trusting soul, you may unfortunately believe that professionals must know what they are talking about and, worse than that, believe that they have a superior insight and understanding that allows them to outperform the market by stock-picking and timing markets. As you have seen, the evidence shows quite categorically that it is highly unlikely. Try to develop a healthy level of scepticism when making investment decisions. Remember three things:

- There are no free lunches in investing, except perhaps for diversification.

- If it looks too good to be true, it is too good to be true.

- Everyone is trying to make his or her bonus from your money in one way or another.

5.4 Ms Rational versus Mr Irrational

As a summary of these behaviours that blur the edges between rational and irrational decision-making, let's take a look at caricatures of two investors: Ms Rational Investor and Mr Irrational Investor. I have made them female and male deliberately, because research shows that men have significantly worse investment track records than women – they are more overconfident and overly optimistic about their investing, which leads to higher level ultimately irrational investment behaviour, over-trading.

Ms Rational Investor

Ms Rational Investor may or may not understand the fundamentals of investing at this point, but she knows that she needs to. She may not be particularly interested in investing, but knows that whether she is or not, she has to face the fact that she must take it seriously as being integral to her financial well-being. Even if she decides to use professional advisers, she knows that she needs a good grasp of the basics of investing so she can evaluate the advice that she is given: in the end, she has to carry the responsibility for the investment decisions taken.

She is realistic about her abilities and that any overconfidence in her ability to make better decisions than others is delusional and likely to be detrimental to her long-term wealth. She uses her head rather than her heart to make decisions based on research and facts, not gut-feel and hearsay. She tries to remain stoical about the market's ups and downs and avoid getting sucked into the emotion accompanying these short-term situations, merely rationalising that that is how markets are. She avoids being influenced by any newspaper articles that start with the words 'Is now the time to be investing in ...?'

When times get tough she remains calm and reviews where recent events fall in the range of expectations that she established when she first sat down with her adviser and carefully planned her investments.

She avoids being influenced by the wisdom of hindsight, knowing that in reality the evidence shows that virtually no one can consistently guess the markets right, and as a consequence won't take out any short-term disappointment on herself or others.

In establishing her investment plan, she realises that she needs to seek investment options that provide a reasonably high chance of a satisfactory outcome. She understands the chances that the outcome may be unsatisfactory and this disappointing scenario's consequences for her. Taking long shots to try and reach her goals are resisted because this is gambling not investing, irrespective of how attractive these opportunities appear to be. Insuring the short-term downside may feel attractive but she knows that the premium paid, in terms of significantly reduced future purchasing power, is not a trade-off worth making long term.

She also understands that she may well feel more pain from short-term losses than short-term gains but fights hard to make sure that this asymmetrical short-term pay-off is balanced by the potential rewards of long-term wealth accumulation that comes with bearing the pain. She understands that you cannot have your cake and eat it and understands that anyone, or any product that aspires to do so, is not what it appears. If she needs greater comfort in short-term down markets, she accepts that she needs to be prepared to give up some of her long-term potential upside. To be overly influenced by short-term pain will be detrimental, long term, to her purchasing power.

She is wise enough to understand that as long as she has taken the time and planned her investment programme sensibly and put her plan into action sensibly, it is more important to focus on the total portfolio performance against her long-term goals, than on the individual components.

Ms Rational employs a healthy dose of scepticism whenever she meets with her private bankers, fund managers, or reads her unit trust investment reports. She reserves a large dose of scepticism for anyone who claims to be able to outperform the market consistently, or to provide upside returns while at the same time protecting her downside. She reviews, with care, all claims made in investment product marketing brochures and advertisements. She is also aware that most advisers, while being people of integrity, have vested interests in the advice they give in one form or another.

She avoids looking at her portfolio too frequently, comfortable that in the long run it has a good chance of delivering what is asked of it.

Mr Irrational Investor

He is a surprisingly common species, often spotted at parties bragging about the great investments he has made. He often knows less than he thinks he knows, and what he does know is often way off the mark in terms of simple, sensible investing.

Nevertheless, he is confident in his own abilities and believes that he and a few others out there can outperform all the other dozy suckers in the market. Not only does he feel he has a greater insight into individual companies, and valuations of markets, than most, but when he does use professionals, he is confident that he can pick those who will be future winners. He feels that he has control of the situation and understands the markets and has an insight that allows him to beat it. Good investments are down to his skill. Bad trades are due to bad luck. He has a few dog stocks in his portfolio that he doesn't want to sell because he will have to realise his losses on them as well as recognise his poor decision-making. They'll come back in any case as he chose them for a reason that is still valid in his mind.

He doesn't want to waste his time with some private banker or adviser carefully planning what he should be doing but wants to get into the fray and start investing as soon as possible and tells them not to bother to ring him unless they have a good investment idea to talk to him about. However, he has confidence in his broker, trusting him implicitly, having been shown a couple of interesting 'deals' in the past.

When the market is bullish, he gets caught up in the excitement of the stampede, becoming overconfident in where the market is going and his ability to outperform it through his own superior skills. He tends to end up taking bigger risks than he should.

However, when markets correct, he becomes overly pessimistic, sells his equities at the bottom, moves into bonds, bawls out his adviser and tells him that his blind grandmother could have seen a bear that size coming. He blames others for being incompetent and not protecting his assets from the downturn, in turn firing his broker. He doesn't regret the fact that last year he sold his conservative bonds, because they were only making 6 per cent a year in any case, because that would be apportioning blame to himself. But he'll crawl back once the bull returns.

This caricature is not too far away from the sad truth about how many people go about their investing.

Whilst these two examples may be extremes, they do make a point.

Recognising the degree to which you exhibit these emotional demons is a step towards getting them in control. While you may think Ms Rational Investor is a bit dull, it is better to be dull and successful than exciting and almost inevitably doomed to miss your investment goal. The choice, as they say, is yours. This book focuses on why being rational is the only rational choice that you have.

Interesting research to mull over

Take a look at the research below. It provides a good insight into the behaviour that many investors portray, to their great cost.

Investor behaviour destroys wealth

Research undertaken by Brad Barber and Terrence Odean (2000), which looked at over 60,000 household accounts of a discount brokerage firm in the USA, from February 1991 to December 1996, analysed the investment performance for equities held by these individuals. It revealed some interesting facts: average turnover, i.e. the percentage of the portfolio value bought and sold, was very high at 80 per cent a year and average net returns, after transaction costs, were 15.2 per cent compared with 17.1 per cent for the market, calculated on an annualised basis; most shockingly, the top 20 per cent of households with the highest turnover, of approximately 10 per cent per month, generated an annualised net return of only 10 per cent, being a full 7 per cent lower than the market.

The central message from this research is that trading is hazardous to your wealth, largely due to costs. Putting a monetary value on this is revealing. A $100,000 portfolio invested in an index (tracker) fund, assumed reasonably to return the benchmark less 0.5 per cent costs, or 16.6 per cent per year, would have grown to $250,000 during this period whereas the individuals with high turnover would have returned only $175,000. Being overconfident in their own perceived skills cost these people a staggering $75,000. A sobering thought.

Overconfidence destroys wealth

The same researchers also looked at 35,000 household accounts from a large brokerage firm from February 1991 to January 1997 (Barber and Odean, 2001). They found that, consistent with other research that shows that men tend to be more overconfident than women (although both are overconfident), men trade 45 per cent more than women. This is reflected in risk-adjusted returns 1.4 per cent a year lower than women. Looking at single women and men, single men trade 67 per cent more than women and generate annual risk-adjusted net returns 2.3 per cent less than single women. Given that by and large self-invested investors, i.e. those that buy and sell shares and other investments themselves through a brokerage account, underperform the markets, as we saw above, this is bad news for wealth accumulation for either sex.

5.5 Wise words to leave you with

Perhaps reflect a while on these wise words written by Charles D. Ellis in his excellent book *Winning the Loser's Game*:

'The hardest work in investing is not intellectual, it's emotional. Being rational in an emotional environment is not easy. The hardest work is not figuring out the optimal investment policy; it's sustaining a long-term focus at market highs or market lows and staying committed to a sound investment policy. Holding on to sound investment policy at market highs and market lows in notoriously hard and important work, particularly when Mr Market always tries to trick you into making changes.'

He shares more wisdom with us:

'Don't trust your emotions. When you feel euphoric you're probably in for a bruising. When you feel down, remember that it's darkest just before dawn and take no action. Activity in investing is almost always in surplus.'

5.6 Behavioural rules and tips

Try to be rational about your investing, from planning how you will invest to how you will respond when times get tough, as they will at some point. It's hard when markets are painful. But the costs of being irrational are far higher, as we have seen.

- Take time planning your investment strategy.
- Form an understanding of the chances you have of achieving the long-term outcome you want and the chances that you may not achieve it.
- Consider the ranges of returns that your portfolio will, in all likelihood, exhibit during the time you are investing, however unpalatable they may seem. Forewarned is forearmed.
- Put a plan in place, for when times get tough, that details how you should respond, based around: 'Don't panic, be brave, do nothing'!

- Stick to your long-term plan unless personal circumstances unexpectedly change significantly and you need to reassess your goals. Never change a plan because of what markets are doing today, or how a fund you don't own has done.

- Do not look at your portfolio too often; it will only make you feel overly euphoric or miserable. Think long term.

- When you do, look at your whole portfolio and judge how it is doing relative to your long-term purchasing power goals. Don't get over-anxious about short-term weak performance in a single element, or even your portfolio as a whole. That's the markets for you.

- Don't believe that you can outsmart the market – you are probably being overconfident, seeing patterns where none exist, being over-optimistic, or have an unrealistic hindsight view of events.

- Don't therefore try to own individual stocks yourself through a brokerage account. There are far better ways of doing things.

- Avoid the temptation of gambles and insurance, however tempting they may be. These products play on your emotions and you often pay usurious costs that are hidden in the structure (unless you understand the Black & Scholes option pricing model – No? Then avoid these products).

- Maintain a healthy level of scepticism about all products and advice.

References

Barber, B. M. and Odean, T. (2000) 'Trading is hazardous to your wealth: the common stock investment performance of individuals', *The Journal of Finance*, vol. LV, no. 2 April, 773–806.

Barber, B. M. and Odean, T. (2002) 'Boys will be boys: Gender, overconfidence, and common stock investment', *Quarterly Journal of Economics*, vol. 116, no. 1, February, 261–292.

Bogle, J. C. (2003) 'The policy portfolio in an era of subdued returns', Bogle Financial Markets Research Center. Available from: http://www.vanguard.com.

Buffett, W. (1998) *Chairman's letter to shareholders 1997*. Berkshire Hathaway Inc.

Buffett, W. (2001) *Chairman's letter to shareholders 2000*. Berkshire Hathaway Inc.

Ellis, C. D. (2002) *Winning the losers game*, 4th ed. New York: McGraw Hill.

Graham, B. and Dodd, D. (1996) *Security analysis: the classic 1934 edition*. New York: McGraw Hill.

Kahneman, D. and Tversky, A. (1979) 'Prospect Theory: An analysis of decision under risk', *Econometrica*, 47, 263–291.

Kahneman, D., Higgens, E. and Riepe, W. (1998) 'Aspects of investor psychology', *Journal of Portfolio Management*, vol. 24, no. 4, 52–65.

Shiller, R. (1997) *The Wall Street Journal*, June 13. As quoted on: http://www.investorhome.com/psych.htm. See also: http://www.econ.yale.edu/~shiller.

Swedroe, L. (2002) *Frequent monitoring of your portfolio can be injurious to your financial health* [online]. Available from: http://www.indexfunds.com.

part

3

Building smarter portfolios

Now that you are a convert to the lose-the-fewest-points philosophy and you have your emotions in control, you can begin the process of defining your investment goals and building a portfolio that makes sense for you, providing you with a reasonable chance of success and survivability – about as much as you can ask for as an investor.

Chapter 6: Understanding your emotional risk tolerance

The challenges that you face controlling your emotions were covered in the previous chapter. Here we will explore your emotional risk profile, i.e. the degree to which you are willing to accept less favourable outcomes (weak performance) in your pursuit of the favourable outcomes that you hope to achieve (e.g. retiring at 55). At the end of the day, it is simply not going to work if you end up in a portfolio that keeps you awake at night, or does not have any real chance of delivering your goals.

Chapter 7: Sorting out your goals

Whilst Chapter 6 addresses your emotional tolerance for risk, this chapter helps you to sort out your lifestyle and expenditure goals and narrow these down into investment goals, including the important issue of how much investment risk you need to take and can afford to take. The process of reconciling these with your emotional risk profile is addressed. It's no good having financial need to take investment risk that is simply too much for you to handle emotionally (and vice versa).

Chapter 8: Smarter risk taking

The reality of being an investor is that you have to take some risks. While lending your money out in the short term to the government or to a good bank (by placing a deposit) may feel safe, it is unlikely to allow you to meet your goals, particularly when inflation and tax are taken into account. The key is to work out what risks are out there when you step away from this 'safe' position, identify those that you understand and reward you sufficiently, and studiously avoiding those that you do not understand or do not compensate you adequately. This chapter shows you that it is not that difficult to do and once you have, constructing portfolios becomes far simpler.

Chapter 9: Smarter portfolio construction

The challenge and ultimate goal of smarter portfolio construction is to create a robust and stable 'portfolio for all seasons' that is likely to do a reasonable job of weathering the storms that the markets will inevitably test you with over your investment lifetime. Doing so requires an understanding of what risks to take, which to avoid and what each asset class contributes at the portfolio level. This chapter explores how sensible portfolios can be constructed from a short, yet robust, menu of assets.

Chapter 10: Smarter portfolio choice

Having established the structure of six portfolios along the risk spectrum, which should cater for most investors, from 100 per cent defensive to 100 per cent growth-oriented, it is important to explore the characteristics of each. In this chapter each portfolio is explored in depth and linked into the emotional risk tolerance and financial need to take risk explored in Chapters 6 and 7.

Chapter 11: An insight into key asset classes

This chapter provides a high-level look at each of the asset classes that you should consider including in your portfolio and a paragraph or two on a couple that are probably best avoided. It makes sense only to include asset classes in your portfolio that you feel entirely comfortable with. Otherwise, you won't have the conviction to keep the faith, particularly if it is this specific asset class that is performing poorly, as every one will do from time to time.

6

Understanding your emotional risk tolerance

As you have already discovered, emotions have the capacity to destroy hard won investment returns as they tend to lead you astray; they tempt to get into things that perhaps you should not at the peak and make you exit otherwise sensible long-term investments at the lows. While we would all like to think that we are capable of rational behaviour and avoid such obvious wealth destroying strategies, the empirical evidence is that most investors do not. What we can do though is to identify portfolios that sit within our risk comfort zone, where we have a greater chance of standing firm. This chapter helps you to understand how you can identify your risk comfort zone.

As investors, we all need to understand and feel comfortable with where we sit emotionally with the favourable outcomes we desire (such as retiring early, being able to fund a stable and enjoyable lifestyle in retirement etc.) against the less favourable outcomes that we may experience along the way in terms of weak performance, potential losses, and possibly not even reaching our goals at all. This personal emotional stance is what is generally referred to as your 'risk profile'.

6.1 What is your risk profile?

In its broadest sense, your risk profile relates to your personal tolerance for accepting risks in your life. These fall into four main categories: physical risks, e.g. rock climbing and parachuting, ethical risks, social risks and financial risks, each of which are distinct; just because you like driving fast cars on track days does not mean that you will be comfortable taking high levels of financial risk.

We will focus on your financial risk profile, which is a psychological trait that is a consequence of your genetics, as well as your own learned values, motivations and attitudes towards financial risks. Interestingly, it appears that there is some positive correlation with the level of your income, your wealth and your education (i.e. the higher they are, the higher your risk tolerance is likely to be) and negatively with being in a partnership and the number of people that rely on you. This is perhaps intuitive. The definition below of what a trait is provides more insight:

Trait n. *A characteristic or quality distinguishing a person … especially a more or less consistent pattern of behaviour that a person possessing the characteristic would be likely to display in relevant circumstances, typical examples being shyness, honesty, tidiness, and stupidity.*
Source: Coleman, M. (2001) © *A Dictionary of Psychology,* 2001, Oxford University Press.

Given this definition, you would expect an investor's risk profile to be pretty consistent over time in the same way that a relatively shy person is likely to be consistently shy compared to others.

Whilst an investor's risk profile remains largely consistent across time (see Figure 6.1), it may change slowly over time through increased education, experience and changing circumstances, although the influence of these are somewhat uncertain and unresearched. It probably makes sense to test your risk profile over time, but it is unlikely to change that much, even if markets are volatile and performing poorly. More likely in these circumstances is an investor's awareness of risk that changes rather than their tolerance of it. The key is that if you know what to expect from your portfolio, the emotional impact of the less favourable outcomes will be reduced. Educating yourself on the characteristics of your portfolio is critical and each portfolio choice is explored in some detail later in this part of the book. Granted, when markets actually fall, as opposed to looking at a chart on paper, we all feel a greater emotional impact, but at least we can resign ourselves to a 'well I knew it could happen' attitude. Forewarned is always forearmed in smarter investing.

Take a look at Figure 6.1. It illustrates some research work that was undertaken using the period between May 1999 and December 2008 (Davey, 2009), which captures the last desperate moments of the technology boom and subsequent bust, the rise in the markets from 2003 to 2007 and the slump from the end of 2007. The global equity markets are overlaid on top of the average risk profile from the UK, US, Australia and New Zealand. The conclusion is obvious: risk tolerance is a pretty stable trait.

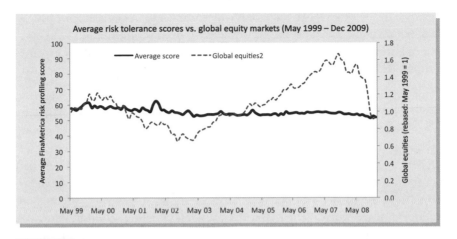

6.2 Why is it so important?

Choosing the right portfolio comes down to matching your emotional risk profile with your financial need to take risk and your capacity to suffer losses. Only then can you sensibly decide what type of portfolio or investments make sense for you. You can create the best looking diversified portfolio possible and implement it using the best funds available, but if you

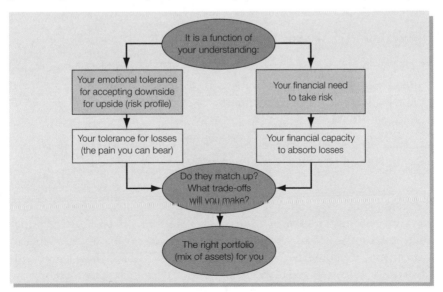

Figure 6.2 Choosing the right portfolio for you

cannot live with it emotionally or it will not meet your goals, it is worthless. So, before you can decide on a portfolio you need to understand your emotional capacity to trade off unfavourable outcomes for favourable outcomes and your financial need to take risk to achieve your goals (see Figure 6.2).

Our financial need to take risk relates to the financial goals that we wish to achieve which describe our lifestyle goals such as retiring on a good income at 55 or making sure our wealth will last as long as we do. Imagine someone who has a low tolerance to risk (i.e. they are unwilling to choose to risk suffering a less favourable outcome in pursuit of their goals) but, given their current level of wealth and future lifestyle dreams, they will be forced to invest in a 'risky' portfolio, which could suffer large losses, in order to achieve their goals. Their emotional goals (feeling comfortable) and financial goals (their dreamed of lifestyle) are at significant odds. Stress, anxiety and irrational and detrimental decision-making are an inevitable outcome. Conversely, an investor with a high risk profile may not actually need to take much investment risk as the magnitude of their assets can easily support their anticipated lifestyle.

What is plainly evident is that it is important to make sure that you understand, think hard about and resolve any mismatch that may occur in your own circumstances. That is what this and the next chapter seek to help you to do. At that point, you are in a position to choose what portfolio makes most sense for you, which we will cover in Chapter 8.

6.3 Exploring your risk profile

If you have ever used an adviser then you will no doubt have been subjected to some form of questionnaire or discussion about your 'attitude to risk'. Not surprising given its importance and the regulator's requirement for advisers to do so:

'Ascertaining a private customer's true attitude to risk is critical for any adviser in assessing suitability and making an investment recommendation.'

FSA 2008

Unfortunately, little guidance exists as to what the standards of care and professionalism should be in assessing an investor's risk profile. Given that your risk profile is a psychological trait, it would not be unreasonable to expect that it should be tested by way of a psychology-based test, constructed in a rigorous and disciplined manner. It rarely is, except among the more astute firms at the professional end of the industry.

Industry amateurism is dangerous to your wealth

In fact, much of the industry seems to operate on a self-assessment basis, asking nonsensical questions such as *'what would you say your attitude to risk is?'* or *'do you like to jump out of aeroplanes?'* to arrive at a score or statement such as 'low risk taker', or 'moderate risk taker' – whatever that means – that is usually ringed by the adviser and placed on the compliance file to create the appropriate paper trail linking the client score directly to the portfolio chosen.

The true paper trail really points towards a lack of thought, open-mindedness and care for their clients. If you meet with an adviser who presents you with such an approach, stand up and walk away.

The problem here is that many of the questions end up confusing the two areas that need to be understood: your emotional tolerance for risk and the risk you need to take to reach your financial goals. What you get is an unscientific and confused approach to assessing your risk profile that risks failing to resolve any differences that might exist between the two, storing up big trouble between you and your adviser, as well as affecting your ability to see your investment strategy through or even achieve your goals.

Taking a professional approach

Is it then unreasonable to expect that a sensible way to test your risk profile should be via a psychometric test? If an adviser does not use one, or attempts to rubbish their use, perhaps you should think twice about what else they are dismissing that may be to your advantage and the quality of the advice you are likely to receive.

Psychometrics is the field of study concerned with the theory and technique of educational and psychological measurement, which includes the measurement of knowledge, abilities, attitudes and personality traits. The field is primarily concerned with the study of measurement instruments such as questionnaires and tests[1]. Psychometrics helps in the construction of tests that effectively measure what they are asked to measure, i.e. they have validity, and ensures that they do so consistently and accurately, i.e. they are reliable.

You may well be familiar with psychometric tests and may have even undertaken some yourself; in fact, over 95 per cent of the FTSE 100 companies use psychometric testing to select their staff, as do the police,

[1]Definition given by Wikipedia (http://en.wikipedia.org/wiki/Psychometrics)

the civil service, airlines and even football clubs such as AC Milan (*Guardian*, 2002). Basic psychometric testing was developed during the Second World War to try to identify the jobs that would best suit different women entering the workforce in support of the war effort and the resulting Myers-Briggs test is still widely in use today.

While many people are wary of such testing, I for one am a big convert. When I went to business school we all completed a psychometric personality test shortly after we arrived, with much harrumphing about the questions and a high degree of scepticism. A few weeks later we were split into small groups and sent out of the lecture hall with the task to plan a holiday together in 15 minutes. My group ambled into one of the study group rooms and decided on a backpacking trip to South America, where we would head off individually and then meet up in Rio for Carnival – job done. We spent the next 10 minutes talking about the rugby; the next group came armed with their detailed presentation of the *'we'll catch the 10:31 from Paddington and John will pre-book the tickets'* variety; and the third group hadn't reached a conclusion and so on. The remarkable thing was that the psychometric test had very neatly identified each group's dominant personality traits. It was a revelationary moment for me.

The construction of a risk profile test – let's call it a questionnaire, as it sounds less intimidating – therefore requires far more than a financial planning firm putting together a list of ten questions to score. In the same way you would not ask an adviser to service your car, don't ask them to create a psychometric test themselves! The same applies if you are not intending to use an adviser – seek out a professional psychometric risk profiling tool – they do exist.

When I work with my clients (leading firms who manage the wealth of individuals and families) they occasionally say that some clients have a reluctance to undertake the tests at first, worrying that there are right and wrong answers or that they will be judged on the results in some way. In fact (and perhaps unlike doing a psychometric test for a job interview where the outcome may be detrimental to your chances), undertaking a risk profiling test can only be beneficial. If you have a 'low' risk profile score, that is no better or worse than having a 'high' risk profile score – you will simply be in a position to make better, more informed choices. That is the secret to successful investing and what this book is all about. Almost without fail, all of their clients who take these psychometric risk profiling tests and talk through the implications find them to be an exceptionally valuable part of the investment process.

With or without an adviser, psychometric risk profiling should be part of your own process for building a suitable portfolio.

Completing a psychometric risk profiling questionnaire

Fortunately a number of psychometric risk profiling tests are available online. Broadly, you pay a small fee and complete the questionnaire, which should be in plain English and very straightforward, and will most likely consist of 25–30 multiple choice questions and answers as the accuracy increases with the greater number of questions asked (Krus and Helmstader, 1987). Once complete, most will provide a detailed written report that relates specifically to your profile and explores the implications of your answers. The better ones will provide a suggestion as to the appropriate level of 'risky' assets (which you can generally read as equities at this point) that you can emotionally tolerate.

The results provide a catalyst for thinking hard about your risk profile within a framework that makes sense; it does not provide the 'right' answer; it does not mean that you should invest in a portfolio with this level of 'risky' assets; but it does provide the start to useful thinking and dialogue. The next step is to work out how much risk you need to take to reach your financial goals and then see if the two match. If they don't then you will either need to adjust the level of risk you are willing to take emotionally (not that easy given that your risk tolerance is a psychological trait) or to adjust your financial goals: contribute more, retire later or spend less in retirement, for example.

Use this useful tool, not to think for you, but to help you think.

When it comes to deciding which tool to use, your choice is limited, which is a good thing, particularly if within that choice strong solutions exist. Fortunately that is the case. One of the most highly regarded, long standing and widely used is FinaMetrica (www.MyRiskTolerance.com). This tool was developed in conjunction with the University of New South Wales Applied Psychology Unit and has been available since 1998. It exceeds international standards for psychometric tests of this kind and is widely used by leading advisers around the world including the US, Australia and the UK (Davey and Resnik, 2008). The answers to the questionnaire are scored and the outcome is a risk tolerance score that translates into a comfort/discomfort range for 'risky' (equity-like) assets. To date around 250,000 investors have used this questionnaire. In fact, the vast majority of my innovative and proactive clients use FinaMetrica with their clients and were doing so long before I worked with them.

Take a look at the website and read some of the interesting background comments and articles and consider completing the questionnaire – it may be some of the best money you spend.

Others exist too, although I have no first-hand knowledge of their efficacy or methodology, and they are often embedded in the software used by advisers and are not available to those investing directly themselves. Examples would include Distribution Technology's Dynamic Risk Profiler, quite widely used in the UK.

6.4 The process from here

As we work our way towards building a portfolio that is suitable for you, there are a number of steps that you need to cover to get there.

1 Complete a psychometric risk profiling questionnaire. This will provide you with a quantified sense of the level of risky assets that you can tolerate in a portfolio. If you decide not to do this, you will have to take a calculated intuitive guess. By studying Table 10.1 (see p. 184) you can try to gauge how you feel about the potential outcomes, both good and bad of different levels of 'risky' assets in a range of portfolios from high risk to low risk. Not ideal, but better than nothing.

2 Quantify your financial goals. This is covered in some depth in the next chapter. You should be able to identify broadly the rate of return that you require from the process and tables provided. That in turn will provide a sense of the level of 'risky' assets that you need to hold to have a reasonable chance of meeting your financial goals.

3 Compare the two. One of three outcomes will present itself: they are the same; your risk tolerance is lower than your financial need to take risk; or your risk tolerance is higher than your need to take risk. You will need to resolve any differences by either altering your goals or accepting that you will have to emotionally bear risks that are not naturally in your comfort zone but not to the extent that you will be panicked out of the markets if (and when) they fall.

4 Study, understand and commit to an appropriate portfolio strategy. At the end of the day, you need to reconcile with yourself the portfolio strategy that you choose and be prepared to commit to it, through thick or thin. A number of tools are provided that allow you to explore your portfolio choice in Chapter 10.

5 Decide how you are going to implement your strategy. While the passive product route should now be your default option, you need to decide whether you have the time, inclination and discipline to do this yourself on an ongoing basis or whether you want to employ someone to act on your behalf and do it for you, working as a partner over time to guide you through the journey. Engaging an adviser is covered in Part 4 Chapter 12, as is the process for identifying strong passive product choices.

References

Guardian, http://jobs.guardian.co.uk/careers/200256/356292/psychometric-testing-podcast.

Krus, D. J. and Helmstader, G. C. (1987) 'The relationship between correlation and internal consistency notions of test reliability', *Educational and Psychological Measurement.*

Davey, G. (2009) 'Risk Tolerance Revisited', FinaMetrica Pty Limited (www.riskprofiling.com), p.1.

Davey, G. and Resnik, P. (2008) 'Risk Tolerance, Risk Profiling and the Financial Planning Process', FinaMetrica Pty Limited (www.riskprofiling.com), p.3.

FSA (2008) www.fsa.gov.uk.

7

Sorting out your goals

Let's spend a little time thinking about how to turn the question 'Where do I start?' into a definite plan of action.

A good friend of mine, who is a businesswoman in Melbourne, once announced to her long-suffering accountant that she had started investing her money seriously. Her much-relieved accountant asked her what she was investing in, only to get the simple response 'Me'. Unlike her, your challenge is to think ahead about your future purchasing power needs, rather than today's gratuitous consumption; while most of us understand that, we suffer a sort of fatal inertia, caused by the apparent complexity of the decisions (and maths) that we face.

Another friend of mine, in his early forties, recently that told me that he knows he needs to start thinking about what he should do about his pension, as his existing pension will only deliver around £10,000 a year. He knows he desperately needs to do something, but simply does not know where to start or who to ask. Familiar story? He is not alone by any means, and nor are you if you are struggling to get a handle on what you need to do to put things right, whether for your retirement or other investment goals you may have.

The answer is that you start right here; in the next few minutes you should have a pretty fair idea of what you should be doing.

7.1 Well thought-out goals underpin success

Understanding what you want from your investing is the critical starting point of any investment programme; being able clearly to articulate these goals will help you and any one else assisting you, to tackle the issues you face. One of the constants that I found in my discussions with clients over the years is that many of them have only vague notions about what they want to achieve with their money and relatively few have a precise set of articulated goals.

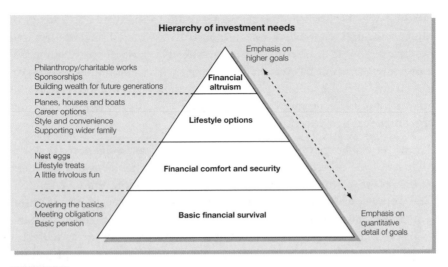

Figure 7.1 **Different levels of needs**   *Source: Maslow (1970).*

In many ways that's not really very surprising. We find it easy to think emotionally about our vision: 'I want to be comfortable in my retirement'; 'I want to be involved in more philanthropic works'; or 'I want to provide my children with financial security', but find it harder to articulate in much more detail what we really want our money to do for us, such as 'I need a £1.2 million pool when I retire to generate an income equivalent to £50,000 in today's money (before tax) giving me a standard of living that is comfortable, without having to worry about running out of money before I die'.

Investment needs can be viewed as a hierarchy, with those at the bottom being essential to achieve because life will be difficult if you fail to meet them, e.g. not having any income in retirement, to those that are nice to achieve but perhaps less critical, such as lifestyle choices. This is similar to a behavioural scientist's hierarchy of human needs (Maslow, 1970), which I have bastardised in Figure 7.1.

Looking at your own goals in this way may help you to understand them a little better. Your focus may be on investment goals towards the top of the pyramid, if you are already financially secure, or your focus may be towards the bottom of the pyramid, as you strive to put in place some financial security for yourself and your family. Most institutional investors such as pension plans, endowments, foundations and corporate treasurers have basic financial survival goals.

At the lower levels of the hierarchy, attention to the nitty-gritty detail of time, contributions, rates of return (and their associated uncertainty) and the size of your investment pot is more critical because the consequence of not being successful has serious repercussions. Those at higher levels have the luxury of being able to concentrate on higher-level objectives such as maintaining or increasing their purchasing power over the long run, and may need less detail in their planning.

I have not split investors down into the broad classifications that the industry uses of retail (up to £100,000 of investable assets), affluent (£100,000 to £1 million), high net worth (usually more than £1 million) and ultra-high-net-worth (£20 million upwards), to make a point. An 'affluent' individual with £200,000 of investments may have a good company pension to live on and may want to use this money to set up a small trust to benefit a pet cause in perpetuity – an example of financial altruism at the top of the pyramid. On the other hand, an individual with £3 million to invest critically needs these assets to generate income to live on and to avoid having to go back into the City everyday. This may be basic financial survival. You will know where you stand. Let's take a quick look at some of the goals that investors have.

General goals for individuals

As you read through each of the generic goals below, think hard about those that are relevant to you.

Basic financial survival – retirement

Increasingly, people are having to plan and invest for their own retirement as traditional defined benefit (final salary) schemes, where your benefits are defined as a function of your time with the company and your final salary, become unavailable to employees. Many are rightly concerned with being able to generate an acceptable level of income for their retirement. Common goals may be to 'avoid being poor' or 'to be able to enjoy ourselves in our retirement' or to 'feel comfortable that we can live how we do now, for the rest of our lives'.

Today, with the ever-growing influence of defined contribution pension plans (where a set monthly contribution is made by an employer, into an employee's individual pension pot), you alone are responsible for investing to satisfy your basic financial survival. All of the investment responsibility and investment risk is on your shoulders, and getting your investing programme right, i.e. giving yourself the greatest chance of having the right level of purchasing power available at the right time, is critical.

Basic financial survival – school/university fee

'I want to be able to give my children the best education I can,' is a common goal for some parents, which is often achieved by building reserves to meet school and university fees, through regular savings plans as the children grow up. Fortunately, many schools provide indications of future expected fees; the downside is that these seem to be growing faster than inflation. How important this is to you, only you will know.

Nest eggs

'I want to put something aside for a rainy day', 'We want to be able to afford a few small luxuries in our retirement', or 'It's good knowing that there is a little extra' are all familiar investment visions. These types of goals often apply to investors who have sufficient sources of income to take care of their basic financial survival and represent funds to provide an additional layer of security.

Lifestyle options

'I want to be free to pursue the things that I want to do' and 'I want to be able to have some fun with my wider family' are examples of higher-level goals. No one is at risk of being hungry or not being able to afford their heating bills, but these goals are as important to those fortunate enough to be in this position as any other investor's goals, even if they are not, in an absolute sense, as critical.

Philanthropic works

Fortunately for society, there are many investors who use their wealth for philanthropic purposes. 'I would like to set up a foundation to provide annual scholarships . . .' and 'We would like to provide a trust to maintain . . .' are philanthropic objectives, for investors who feel that their other financial needs have been taken care of and they would like to put their wealth to good use within society or their local community.

7.2 Five steps in defining your goals

Sitting down and thinking hard about what you want your wealth to achieve may feel like a daunting and tiresome proposition. But a little time spent thinking about and planning what you want to achieve is time well spent. This task is made easier by dividing it into five manageable steps.

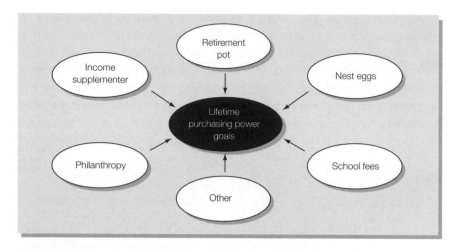

Figure 7.2 **Identifying each of your purchasing power goals**

Step 1: Divide your plan into appropriate pools

The first easy step is to divide up your money into different goals. These can usually be defined by the function that they will serve: retirement funds; school fees; future gifts; house purchase, etc., and Figure 7.2 provides some examples of some common pools of investment funds. Identifying them allows you to set clear and relevant objectives for each pool. Lumping all your money together and managing it as one pool is possible, but most investors tend to segregate their wealth into different pools – a form of mental accounting – even though, at the end of the day it is an aggregated pool of money that is meeting a series of lifetime purchasing power needs.

Step 2: State your vision for each pool

Express the ultimate outcome that you want to achieve and which would make you content, within the bounds of realism. Usually your vision is relatively easy to state and understand. Examples include: 'I want to lead a comfortable life throughout my retirement'; 'I want to establish a charity that provides money for malaria research'; 'I want my children to be financially secure when I am no longer around'.

Step 3: Define your investment horizon for each pool

Your investment horizon is the amount of time that your money can remain invested for and largely defines the mix of portfolio building blocks that you should use. The longer your investment horizon is, the greater the chance that your investments will act like their generalisations, rather than their exceptions. Longer-term investors can afford to have more of their money invested in building blocks that have the potential to generate higher returns, but will suffer periods when returns can be painful. The link between your investment horizon and your portfolio of investments is explored in depth in Chapter 9.

The horizon should be as long as possible to allow you to maximise the use of your money through time and compounding. Build a small pot of cash to cover contingencies or arrange overdraft facilities to allow you to get through temporary liquidity needs, say six months' salary. Mismatching your investment horizon with your portfolio mix can be costly.

Choosing a portfolio that is too conservative

Your portfolio mix should match your investment horizon. If you choose too conservative a portfolio for a long-term horizon you will generate lower returns. Compounding lower returns over time cuts your future purchasing power and may require you to scale back your goals. This is illustrated in Figure 7.3.

Choosing a portfolio that is too aggressive

On the other hand, if a portfolio is too aggressive for your investment horizon, purchasing power may be at risk just at the time you need it. If

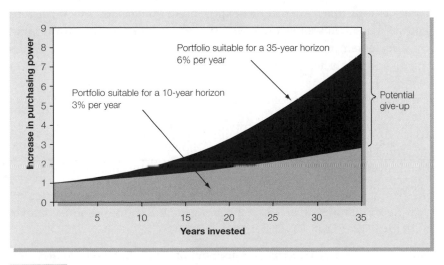

Figure 7.3 Your opportunity cost is high

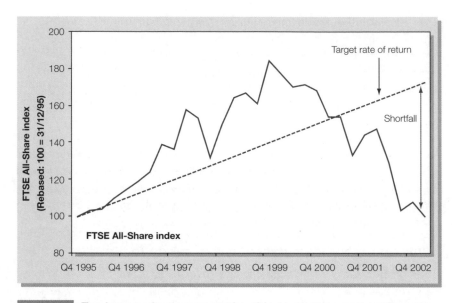

FTSE All-Share index
(Rebased: 100 = 31/12/95)

Figure 7.4 **Too long and you may not be able to meet your commitments**

Source: Thomson Datastream.

markets fall and do not recover before you need the cash, you will have a shortfall between what you hoped for and what you end up with.

A sobering example of this occurred at the end of the 1990s. Some investors, with only a handful of years to go in the accumulation phase, were tempted into holding too great an exposure to equities, lured by high equity returns that they had just experienced. Markets fell by 40 per cent and still remained well below the high five years later. The wealth to fund their retirement dreams was irreparably damaged; for some, their retirements have been delayed or their plans scaled back. This is illustrated in Figure 7.4.

Remember that the accumulation phase reaches a point at which your accumulation ends and your distribution phase begins, e.g. the start of your child going to school or the day you retire and need to begin drawing a pension from your pool of assets. You need to determine how long each phase is likely to be. This may be from three years to beyond your mortal lifespan; anything less than three years and you are probably better off putting your money in an interest-bearing bank account or money market fund.

Getting it right and matching a sensible portfolio to it is key to successful investing.

Step 4: Consider the consequences of failure

Each of your goals will have consequences for you if they are not met and some of these goals might be more important to you than others. Being able to afford to send your child to the university of his or her choice or not having to worry about how you will pay the bills in your retirement may be critical; however, passing on assets to future generations may not be a life-and-death consequence. Only you can decide. You need to work out what represents a survivable outcome and what does not. There are three stages to working this out: the first is to define what the worst case would be for you; the second is to understand how likely it is to occur; and the third is to understand how you would respond if it did occur.

An example may help. Imagine that you are planning a party in your garden in the summer and will invite one hundred friends. The worst-case scenario is that it pours with rain and it is a complete washout. We all know that that is a possibility, but that does not help you to decide whether to go ahead or not. This alone is insufficient to base a decision on. However, if I tell you that the chances of a torrential downpour are less than 5 per cent you would probably go ahead. If on the other hand I tell you there is a 50 per cent chance of rain, that might result in a different decision. If you are conse-quence-orientated, the thought of mud in the house and disgruntled friends is too great. If you are possibility-orientated, the opportunity of catching up and having a few drinks with your friends will be worth it, despite the mud. The outcome of rain and mud is the same, yet your response to it may well differ from someone else's. Only you will know which you are.

You need to understand the equivalent as it relates to each of your invest-ment goals: what would happen if your portfolio were ultimately only £500,000 instead of £1 million when you retire? What are the chances of this outcome happening? Can you live with this outcome? Answer these questions and you will be well on the way to setting the parameters for a successful investing programme. Figure 7.5 illustrates the mental process you need to go through for each pool of money.

For the moment, try to define for yourself what you think the worst case would be for each of your pools of money. Decide what is an acceptable probability (that you can live with) that it happens, e.g. 5 per cent chance, 20 per cent chance, etc., and designate yourself either possibility- or conse-quence-orientated decisions for each.

We will look at worst-case scenarios and the chances of success or failure for different portfolio structures in Chapter 10, depending on your investment

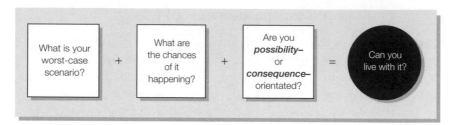

Figure 7.5 **Evaluating the consequences of investing**

Table 7.1 **How bad does it get?**

Pool	Examples of possible worst-case outcomes
Pension	▪ Ending up with less than half of your current salary ▪ Running out of money before you die ▪ It's a bonus – you have other income to fall back on
School fees	▪ Having to pay more than 30 per cent of the fees due to a shortfall ▪ The kids have to go elsewhere
Nest egg	▪ Without this nest egg, life will be spartan ▪ Pity, but you can get by without it
Lifestyle	▪ You really don't want to have to go back into the City ▪ You need this for your sanity
Philanthropy	▪ This is the culmination of your life's work. It's critical ▪ Disappointing, but life goes on

horizon. This will allow you to work out which portfolio structure makes most sense for you. Table 7.1 sets out some examples of possible worst-case situations.

Step 5: Explain your goals in financial terms

At some point you need to translate your vision in Step 2 into hard numbers.

Defining higher-level financial goals

If you are describing higher-level goals that are over and above basic financial survival goals, translating them into financial terms is a little easier because you can afford your objectives to be a little looser. Table 7.2

Table 7.2	Common financial goals – filling in the gaps

Criteria	Requirement	Financial terms used
Returns	Absolute (nominal or real)	I expect to make [ ]% a year
	Relative to cash	I want to beat cash by [ ]% a year
	Relative to something else	I want to beat [ ] by [ ]% a year
Inflation	Increase purchasing power	I want to beat inflation by [ ]% a year on average
	Maintain purchasing power	I want to at least maintain my purchasing power
Assets	Amount (nominal or real)	I want my assets to grow to £[ ] over [ ] years
	Doubling (nominal or real)	I want to double my money in [ ] years
Income	Withdraw income as %	I want to withdraw [ ]% of the value of the portfolio a year
	Withdraw income £ amount	I want to take an income in today's money of £[ ]
	Withdraw income and capital	I want to take £[ ] from my portfolio over [ ] years
Chances	Good chance	I want to be pretty sure I will achieve my goal
	Reasonable chance	I want a fair chance of being successful
	Gamble	I will try to shoot the lights out on this
Constraints	Annual losses	I can accept losses of [ ]% in any 1 year
	Over [ ] years	I can accept losses of [ ]% in any [ ] year period
	Over economic cycle	I expect real gains over an economic cycle
Attitude	Possibility-oriented	I am looking for the upside and can live with the downside
	Consequence-oriented	I need to make sure that I succeed

provides an example of some of the goals that investors often state when they set up their investment portfolios. Few, though, ever have much of a feel for how likely they are to succeed – something that we will try to put right.

Defining basic financial survival goals

If, on the other hand, your investment goals are of the basic financial survival variety, such as planning your retirement income, it becomes critical
that you define what it is you are hoping to achieve in tight financial
terms, as the consequences of not meeting them will affect your life significantly.

7.3 Basic financial survival goals

You need to work out what the nitty-gritty numbers that underlie your
emotional investment goals are, however boring that may sound. This is
not difficult if you think about it logically.

At this point, some people throw their arms up in horror. Don't panic! With
a few simple calculations you can begin to get a rough idea of what you
should be aiming for. Most of the maths is done and the results are set out
in the tables that follow. These provide estimates to help you to understand
the task in hand and some of the challenges that you face. Don't switch off
at this point, however tempted you are!

Essentially, investing is about growing a pool of money (which may start at
zero), over time, through the returns that your asset mix delivers and
additions that you make to the pool, in order to allow you to do something
at the end of the accumulation phase. This may be either to meet a capital
commitment, or to provide an income over time, such as a retirement plan.
Figure 7.6 illustrates this process.

For many, investing for retirement is the main investing challenge that
they face and it may be for you too. Therefore this section is structured to

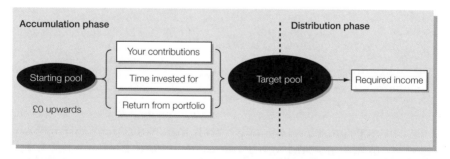

Figure 7.6   **The process and goals of an investment programme are
simple**

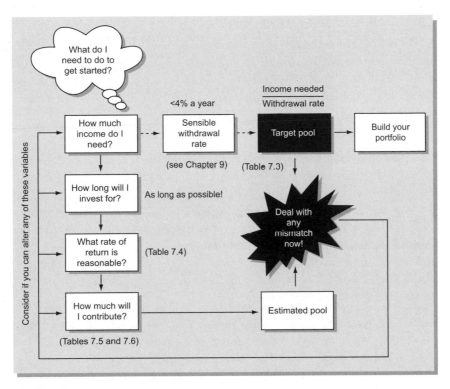

Figure 7.7   **The road map to your financial goals**

help you explore how you can define your goals in financial terms where you are looking eventually to take an income from your portfolio (the *distribution phase*) and will make regular contributions into the pool up to this point (the *accumulation phase*). You will be able to see the effect that changing time, contributions, the returns from your portfolio and the level of income you withdraw will have on the overall programme.

What do you need to do to start?

Getting started is straightforward, and simply looks at Figure 7.6 in a different order. Take a minute to study Figure 7.7, above.

One of the biggest problems in saving for retirement is that while people may have a picture of a comfortable retirement, they have no real idea just how big their target pool needs to be to deliver the level of income they would wish for. In addition, they have little idea whether the contributions they or their employer are making into their pension plan (if they have one) and the way it is invested is going to deliver what they need. A mismatch often exists between dream and reality. You may be surprised just how much you need to accumulate and how much you will need to save regularly to get there – but get there you will, with a little planning and a sensible portfolio. You need to answer the following questions for yourself.

Question 1: How much income do I need?

The goal of investing for retirement is to be pretty sure that you will be able to pay yourself an acceptable level of income that keeps pace with inflation throughout your retirement, so the first thing is to decide how much income you will require. Thinking in terms of the income you require in terms of today's money is the easiest way to look at things: 'I need 75 per cent of my salary today to live comfortably'.

This is a good way to think because it allows you to talk about things in today's money terms and know what your income will buy you. It's hard to conceive how comfortable your retirement will be unless you factor in the effects of inflation. Will an income of £80,000 a year in tomorrow's devalued money provide a comfortable retirement? Not if a loaf of bread costs £15 and a pint of beer £35! To allow yourself the ability to talk about things you want in the future, in today's money terms, you must always use real, i.e. post-inflation, returns in any calculations you make. Using real returns on the asset side of your personal balance sheet allows you to ignore inflation on the liability side. Throughout the rest of this book, we will use real returns.

Sit down with a piece of paper and decide what level of income you need. Remember to allow for any state or other pensions or sources of income that you will have. Use the level of income you decide for the remainder of this section. I leave it to you to work out how much this represents!

Question 2: How large does my target pool need to be?

A significant challenge is that we do not know how long we will live and therefore cannot be certain how quickly we can spend the capital. Obviously, if you spend your capital over time, your target pool size does not need to be as large as if you wish preserve the purchasing power of your capital pool. You have three options on retirement:

- Maintain the purchasing power of your portfolio and your income. This implies that you withdraw an income that is equal to or less than

Table 7.3 How large does your target pool need to be?

Withdrawal rate p.a.	Income required							
	£10,000	£20,000	£30,000	£40,000	£50,000	£60,000	£70,000	£80,000
2%	£500,000	£1,000,000	£1,500,000	£2,000,000	£2,500,000	£3,000,000	£3,500,000	£4,000,000
3%	£333,333	£666,667	£1,000,000	£1,333,333	£1,666,667	£2,000,000	£2,333,333	£2,666,667
4%	£250,000	£500,000	£750,000	£1,000,000	£1,250,000	£1,500,000	£1,750,000	£2,000,000
5%	£200,000	£400,000	£600,000	£800,000	£1,000,000	£1,200,000	£1,400,000	£1,600,000
6%	£166,667	£333,333	£500,000	£666,667	£833,333	£1,000,000	£1,166,667	£1,333,333

= You have a serious danger of running out of money (see Chapter 10)

the real return generated by your portfolio. Given that we are living longer, perhaps into our nineties, this is a sensible approach, particularly if it represents the bulk of your retirement income. Although as the US comedian Henny Youngman once said:

> 'I went to the bank today and I have all the money I need . . . if I die tomorrow.'

■ Pay yourself an income that includes capital, using up the capital over a designated period of time. This is an option suitable for some. However, trying to predict when exactly you might run out of money is not easy with unpredictable markets and longevity.

■ Use some or all of the accumulated pool to buy an income from an insurance company in the form of an annuity. Basically, you hand over your money in return for an income for the remainder of your life. They now hold the risk of you outliving the standard mortality tables and you take the risk that you die sooner and your estate loses monies that would have existed by controlling these assets yourself.

As a general rule of thumb, you should withdraw 4 per cent or less from your portfolio (well balanced between equities and bonds), if you want to avoid the possibility you will run out of money before you die, as this represents the level of real returns that such a mix of investments would hope (but is not certain) to achieve.

The level of income required divided by the withdrawal rate defines how much money needs to be in your target pool at the end of your accumulation period. Table 7.3 provides an indication of the size of pool you require at different rates of withdrawal, to generate your required annual, pre-tax income. You can see that in real terms these pool sizes can be frighteningly large (and appear even bigger in before-inflation terms) and just how valuable non-contributory final salary schemes really are. We will explore the chances of you running out of money for different withdrawal rates and portfolio mixes in Chapter 10.

Don't be discouraged by the magnitude of the task. As you will see from later tables, the combined effect of compounding of moderate returns over time and regular drip feeding of contributions into your pot have the ability to create substantial wealth.

Question 3: How long will I invest for?

At first glance that appears an easy question to answer, perhaps picking your sixty-fifth birthday, the normal 'retirement' age in the UK, as the end of your accumulation phase (unless of course the Chancellor decides we all need to work longer). In reality, as organisations narrow rapidly near the top, and loyalty to long-serving employees fails, you should perhaps consider that being in gainful, full employment at sixty, let alone sixty-seven, is no longer going to be the norm. Perhaps you should consider having more in your pot at an earlier stage (say fifty-five perhaps), which means investing higher, regular contributions, to provide security and flexibility in your later working years; working if you choose, or when you can.

Question 4: What portfolio returns are reasonable to use?

This is probably the most used, abused and misunderstood area of investing. Overly optimistic estimates of return will always come back to haunt you, as they did the endowment mortgage sales industry. You may be lucky and get higher returns or unlucky and get lower returns than you expect from your portfolio; even over long periods of time, returns can vary significantly from their averages. Understanding your chances of achieving an acceptable rate of return from your portfolio is therefore critical.

You face a trade-off between choosing a higher rate of return, with less chance of success but with lower contributions, or a lower rate that you have a good chance of achieving but with higher contributions. If your goals are critical to you, err on the side of caution. Too many investors ask too much of their portfolios – markets don't deliver just because you hope they will! If your expectations are unrealistic, given long-term and recent history, they will probably catch up with you later.

As you embark on your investing programme, there are many possible investment outcomes that your portfolio may deliver, depending on what happens to the markets. The problem is that you do not know what your investment life will look like until it has happened. Fortunately, these days, with the help of multiple life simulations of portfolios, we can at least get a sense of what the chances are that we will achieve a certain level of return – a very useful piece of information. (The process used is called Monte Carlo simulation.)

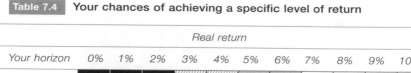

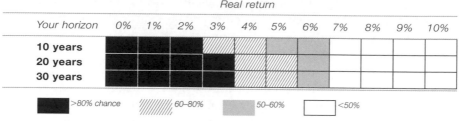

Table 7.4 shows the chances of achieving a specific rate of real return, or better, over different investment horizons. It is based on the Smarter Portfolios that are constructed in Chapter 9 and the expected rate of return and risk parameters of each. While a portfolio may exist that delivers a high chance of delivering a specific rate of return, it is important to remember that you may not be able to stomach the ride of that portfolio. In that case you will need to accept that you may need to scale down the returns that you can realistically expect your portfolio to deliver for you. Tables 10.1 to 10.6 provide a more detailed insight into what each Smarter Portfolio could deliver and should ultimately form the basis on which you should decide what rate of return is reasonable and what portfolio structure you can live with.

As an example, over thirty years, you have a chance of better than 50 per cent of achieving an annualised return of 6 per cent or better, but a pretty good chance, 60–80 per cent or more, of generating a real return of 5 per cent. You can look at what the consequences are if you change the rate of return that you use on both target pool size and contribution level, using other tables in this chapter. Used sensibly, you should be able to arrive at reasonably detailed financial objectives for your investing programme, which, if you are consequence-orientated, will err towards more cautious return expectations, higher contributions and the longest investment horizon you can stretch to.

Question 5: What contributions will I need to make?

At this point, you know what income you need, have worked out what target pool size you are aiming for with a given withdrawal rate, and have

Table 7.5	Approximate monthly contributions to build £1,000,000

				Real rate of return				
Years	1%	2%	3%	4%	5%	6%	7%	8%
10	£8,000	£7,600	£7,300	£6,900	£6,600	£6,300	£6,000	£5,800
20	£3,800	£3,400	£3,100	£2,800	£2,500	£2,300	£2,000	£1,800
30	£2,400	£2,100	£1,800	£1,500	£1,300	£1,100	£900	£800

chosen a rate of return that has a reasonable chance of being achieved over the time that you will be investing for. You now need to work out how much you should contribute every month.

As you saw in Figure 7.6, the pot of money you end up with is a function of the regular contributions you make, the time over which you make them and the real return that your portfolio generates. Many would-be investors become too focused on the rate of return that their portfolio will achieve, even though you cannot control this with any certainty – the best you can do is to choose a rate that gives you a reasonable chance of success, but with no guarantees. On the other hand, time (in some cases) and the contributions you make may well be variable and can play a significant role in increasing the chances of a successful outcome. As they are in your control, they are all the more valuable.

There are two approaches tackling the question of contributions.

Approach 1: Contributions to build £1,000,000

This first approach calculates the monthly contributions that you would need to make to accumulate £1,000,000 of purchasing power, depending on your investment horizon and the real rates of return you expect from your portfolio. You can scale the contributions up or down depending on your target pool size. For example, to accumulate £1 million at 4 per cent over thirty years you would have to contribute approximately £1,500 a month. To build £300,000, then multiply £1,500 by £300,000/£1,000,000 or 30 per cent, to give £450 a month. Take a look back at Table 7.4 before you choose a rate in Table 7.5 above.

Approach 2: Pool size based on monthly contributions

The second approach estimates how large the target pool will be depending on the level of monthly contributions that you make at different rates of expected real returns and the investment period (Table 7.6). Again, see what

Table 7.6	How large will your target pool be?

Real return				Monthly contribution				
2%	£100	£200	£400	£600	£800	£1,000	£1,500	£2,000
10 years	£15,000	£25,000	£55,000	£80,000	£105,000	£130,000	£195,000	£265,000
20 years	£30,000	£60,000	£115,000	£175,000	£235,000	£290,000	£435,000	£585,000
30 years	£50,000	£95,000	£195,000	£290,000	£390,000	£485,000	£730,000	£975,000
3%	£100	£200	£400	£600	£800	£1,000	£1,500	£2,000
10 years	£15,000	£30,000	£55,000	£85,000	£110,000	£140,000	£205,000	£275,000
20 years	£30,000	£65,000	£130,000	£195,000	£260,000	£320,000	£485,000	£645,000
30 years	£55,000	£115,000	£230,000	£345,000	£455,000	£570,000	£855,000	£1,140,000
4%	£100	£200	£400	£600	£800	£1,000	£1,500	£2,000
10 years	£15,000	£30,000	£60,000	£85,000	£115,000	£145,000	£215,000	£290,000
20 years	£35,000	£70,000	£145,000	£215,000	£285,000	£355,000	£535,000	£715,000
30 years	£65,000	£135,000	£270,000	£405,000	£540,000	£675,000	£1,010,000	£1,345,000
5%	£100	£200	£400	£600	£800	£1,000	£1,500	£2,000
10 years	£15,000	£30,000	£60,000	£90,000	£120,000	£150,000	£225,000	£300,000
20 years	£40,000	£80,000	£160,000	£240,000	£315,000	£395,000	£595,000	£795,000
30 years	£80,000	£160,000	£320,000	£480,000	£640,000	£795,000	£1,195,000	£1,595,000
6%	£100	£200	£400	£600	£800	£1,000	£1,500	£2,000
10 years	£15,000	£30,000	£65,000	£95,000	£125,000	£160,000	£235,000	£315,000
20 years	£45,000	£90,000	£175,000	£265,000	£355,000	£440,000	£660,000	£880,000
30 years	£95,000	£190,000	£380,000	£570,000	£760,000	£950,000	£1,425,000	£1,900,000
7%	£100	£200	£400	£600	£800	£1,000	£1,500	£2,000
10 years	£15,000	£35,000	£65,000	£100,000	£135,000	£165,000	£250,000	£330,000
20 years	£50,000	£100,000	£195,000	£295,000	£395,000	£490,000	£740,000	£985,000
39 years	£115,000	£225,000	£455,000	£680,000	£905,000	£1,135,000	£1,700,000	£2,265,000

the effect is on your potential pool if returns are worse than you expect. Remember to take into account any tax relief on the contributions you make. Running a few 'what if?' scenarios using these tables will be time well spent.

Growth of £1				Expected real return				
Years	1%	2%	3%	4%	5%	6%	7%	8%
10	£1.10	£1.20	£1.30	£1.50	£1.60	£1.80	£2.00	£2.20
20	£1.20	£1.50	£1.80	£2.20	£2.70	£3.20	£3.90	£4.70
30	£1.30	£1.80	£2.40	£3.20	£4.30	£5.70	£7.60	£10.10

Table 7.7 The effect of time and return on lump-sum investments

Increasing your chances of success

At the end of the day, there will always be some uncertainty. However, you can control most of the elements involved: you can choose a rate of return that has a high chance of being achieved; pay in higher contributions to compensate for this lower rate of return; and if necessary either scale back your goals or extend the investment period. Perhaps these are unpalatable actions, but all are preferable to a long retirement spent scrimping and saving to meet basic needs. I leave it up to you at this point to decide.

Lump-sum investing

Your investment programme may consist of making a lump-sum investment, perhaps due to monies acquired through the sale of a business, an inheritance, work related bonuses, or the sale of a property. In this case, the end value of an investment pool is based on three things: the amount you invest as a lump sum, the time it is invested for, and the real rate of return from the mix of portfolio building blocks used. This would also apply to any capital you already have in your investment pool, and to which you will make additional regular contributions.

You can see the effect of time and return on the purchasing power of £1 in Table 7.7. You can multiply any lump sum investment that you plan to make by this number. Choose your investment horizon and the real rate of return that gives a suitable chance of success.

A caveat to using the numbers

Always bear in mind that using these outputs only provide rough figures and cannot fully describe the uncertainty of the markets that you face. You can never be certain of the returns in advance, although by choosing a rate of return that has a good chance of being achieved over your investment horizon using Table 7.4 is a start. You can hope that your investments achieve such returns and, if they do, then these numbers will give you an indication of what to expect.

Even if you receive your expected return, this will in all likelihood be made up of negative as well as positive periods and the interim value of your portfolio will be out of line with the straight-line projections. This means that you need to think carefully about how you monitor your portfolio and judge how it is doing against your long-term goals (Chapter 12). The actual value of your portfolio will be different from this in tomorrow's debased money: don't worry, so too will the income you withdraw from it later. Just remember that if you use real return numbers, as you have, this does not matter.

Remember, too, that any contributions that you make need, in real life, to be scaled up to reflect the nominal amount you need to invest. You can use an inflation index to do this simply. Finally, remember that investing will cost you. Build in investing costs into your expected returns. If you use index funds, then 0.5 per cent a year in costs is a reasonably conservative deduction.

The danger of using simplistic models like the ones above is that they can lull you into a false sense of security. Be smart and think about some of their limitations. At this point you at least have a reasonable chance of finding the right ballpark for your financial targets.

7.4 A working example

Imagine a professional couple, both in their mid-thirties, with a gross annual combined income of £100,000. They have a daughter, who is three years old. They have two main investment goals: the first is to be able to retire on a similar standard of living to that they have today; the second is to buy a property for their daughter for her twenty-first birthday. With this gift, they won't feel so bad about spending the rest of their capital.

The retirement pool (basic financial survival)

The couple want to make sure that they have £70,000 of purchasing power available in total when they retire. Part of this income will come from company pension plans, which they estimate will bring in £40,000 (in real terms) a year. The remaining £30,000 needs to come from an investment programme. The current balance of their savings is £50,000 from a recent inheritance. If they fail to generate at least £15,000 additional income a

Table 7.8	**Work out your five-step plan**	

Step	Pot 1	Pot 2
Step 1: Investment pools	Retirement income	Property purchase
Step 2: Vision	Comfortable retirement	Foot-up on the property ladder at 21 for daughter
Step 3: Horizon	30 years to retirement at 65 Live until at least 90	18 years
Step 4: Consequences	Critical. Need at least half the income target (£15,000)	Non-critical. Something is better than nothing
Step 5: Goals in financial terms	Nitty-gritty calculations required. Need £30,000 income	Nitty-gritty calculations not essential but useful

year then this will severely hamper some of their plans for travelling in their retirement, which they would be pretty upset about. They have thirty years to accumulate the assets and intend to live well into their nineties.

The flat purchase (nest egg)

While this goal is a nice altruistic gesture, they are not that fussed if the amount that they end up with is less than the price of a one-bedroom flat in a reasonable area, which they estimate to be about £150,000 in real terms. After all, a small mortgage never hurt anyone and might instil some financial discipline in their daughter. They currently have nothing put aside. They want to try and keep the contributions into this pool at a reasonably low level, given the investment they are going to have to make to generate the retirement income they need. As a consequence, they may ask a bit more from the investment portfolio they choose, i.e. more aggressive with a higher expected return, because failing to meet their target is not so important. Something above the level of their contributions, after inflation, is better than nothing.

Five steps to building the plan

They scribble down the five steps that this book suggests they should take to unravel their goals. They come up with Table 7.8.

As you can see, retirement income is their main concern and they need to be pretty sure that they will be able to generate at least half of what they are hoping for.

The nitty-gritty of the plan

The calculations they need to make are based on the step-by-step approach of Figure 7.8.

To generate an income of £30,000 a year without eroding their pool of capital in retirement, they need a target pool of £750,000, if they are comfortable with an annual withdrawal rate of 4 per cent. This target pool figure is obtained from Table 7.3. From Table 7.4, you can see that there appears to be a 'good chance' of 60–80 per cent that a real rate of return can be achieved of 4 per cent over the period they expect to be retired (thirty years or more), which should allow them to protect the purchasing power of their capital and the income derived from it.

The £50,000 in savings they have will grow and cover some of the capital they require. In the thirty years over which they will be accumulating assets, there is a 'good chance' that 4 per cent real returns will be achieved

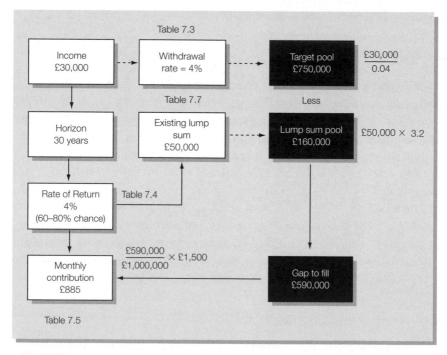

Figure 7.8 Determining financial goals is easy

(Table 7.4). Let's assume they feel comfortable with this. Using this rate of return over their investment horizon, we can see that £1 compounds up to £3.20 (Table 7.7). So, we can multiply the £50,000 lump sum they have by 3.2 to give £160,000, making the gap to be filled by their regular savings plan to be a mere £590,000.

Next we can calculate the level of monthly contributions needed to fill a hole of £590,000. From Table 7.5 the monthly contribution over thirty years to build £1 million using the 4 per cent rate of return is about £1,500. But they only need £590,000. So, the monthly contribution required is £1,500 multiplied by £590,000/£1,000,000 which is around £885 a month. Remember this is in today's terms and would need to be scaled up each year to take account of inflation.

The couple could have decided to be conservative and choose a 3 per cent withdrawal rate and 3 per cent real return during the accumulation phase, which would increase the monthly contributions they need to make to £1,600 to achieve their target income of £30,000 until they die, with greater certainty. These are the kind of trade-offs that you face and need to decide for yourself.

Calculations for the property purchase

In the same manner, but using a 6 per cent rate of return gives them a 'reasonable' chance of getting to where they want to go over the next twenty years or so, they would need to invest £350 per month (from Table 6.5: £150,000/£1,000,000 × £2,300). Don't get hung up with the fact that it is eighteen years and not twenty or that £345 has been rounded to £350. The actual return on the portfolio will not be exactly 6 per cent. If you are lucky or unlucky, it may be nowhere near 6 per cent! To be more certain of the outcome, they could save more, but they don't want to.

7.5 Useful calculations

In Figure 7.9, if you are interested, you will find the formulae to calculate basic estimates for your own investment plan. You probably need to use a spreadsheet, as the calculations are laborious using a calculator. Always bear in mind the limitations of such calculations. They do, however, provide you with a useful tool to look at the consequences of different courses of action, allowing you to make decisions aligned more closely with your goals.

$$\textbf{Final value} = \frac{\text{annual contributions} \times [(1 + \text{rate of return})^{\wedge \text{Number of years}} - 1]}{\text{Rate of return}}$$

$$\textbf{Annual contributions} = \frac{(\text{final value} \times \text{rate of return})}{[(1 + \text{rate of return})^{\wedge \text{Number of years}} - 1]}$$

$$\textbf{Pool size} = \frac{\text{required income}}{\text{withdrawal rate}}$$

Where ^ = to the power of

Figure 7.9 Formulae for your own calculations

7.6 Summary: investment goals

■ Have a clear idea of what you want to achieve from your investing and express it clearly.

■ Spend some time thinking about your goals using the simple five-step process.

■ Use the tables to calculate your target pool size and contribution levels given your investment horizon and expected portfolio return.

■ It is important to bear in mind that the actual return that your portfolio delivers is unlikely to be that chosen as your expected return. This is the great dilemma all investors face. Use Table 7.4 to get a feel for the chances that a specific rate of return can be achieved over the investment period you choose.

■ Failing to understand and use this type of data creates a large risk that you will be disappointed with the outcome of your investments.

■ More analysis on what type of portfolio mix has a good chance of delivering the returns you need and what some of the worst-case extremes that you may face is covered in Chapter 9.

■ You can change any or all of the following four things to increase your chances of success: scale down your goals; reduce the rate of expected return you use; increase the contributions you make; extend the time you invest for. The right combination for you, only you will know. But at least you now have the tools to work out what the implications are.

References

Maslow, A. (1970) 'A theory of motivation', in: *Motivation and personality*, 1st ed. Upper Saddle River, NJ: Pearson Education.

8

Smarter risk taking

Risk surrounds and envelops us. Without understanding it, we risk
everything and without capitalising on it, we gain nothing.

Glynis Breakwell (2007)

The quote above encapsulates exactly what we are trying to achieve in
this chapter that begins the process of building you a smarter portfolio. As
an investor you are surrounded and faced with risk with every decision that
you take. Place a deposit with a bank and you cannot be certain that they
will give you your money back – Northern Rock did after government inter-
vention and Icesave probably will, following the UK's employment of
anti-terrorist legislation to keep the funds in the UK! If you own equities
then 2008, amongst many other occasions, revealed that equity markets
fall, sometimes very painfully, as well as rise and that companies can and
do fail – Lehman Brothers, Woolworths, Waterford and Wedgwood to name
but a few.

The key to smarter risk taking lies in understanding what risks you face,
deciding whether or not they reward you adequately and ultimately if you
want them in your portfolio. Avoiding unwanted risks in your portfolio is
a big part of the game. As a sweeping generalisation, investors tend to own
too many risks that they would not want to hold if they understood what
they were and were actually aware that they were taking them.

To make the process a bit easier, we can break the risk down into market
risks and implementation risks, i.e. the risks of being in the markets and
how you decide to gain this exposure respectively. Figure 8.1 provides a
summary of these risks. Fortunately market risks are limited in number and
implementation risks can be largely avoided if you take the smarter
investing route.

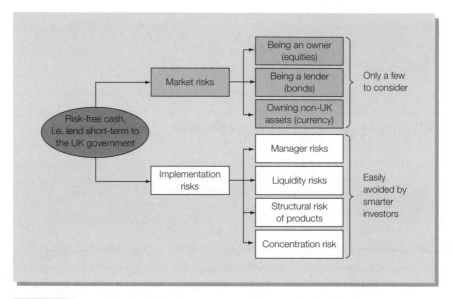

Figure 8.1 **Identifying the risks you face is the first step**

8.1 2008 – a violent introduction to risks

2008 was a great year for illustrating that many individual and professional investors simply had little idea of the risks that they held in their portfolios. Here are a few examples of the risks that were highlighted by the historic events that we witnessed in the markets:

■ The risk of being a company owner. On the high street, many illustrious names went into administration (e.g. Lehman Brothers, Woolworths, Wedgwood, Viyella) and the trading results of many have been severely dented. The UK market fell by over 30 per cent. Being an owner of a company through investing in equities does not guarantee positive returns in the short term although a long-run economic rationale does exist.

■ The (default) risk of being a lender. This is the risk of not getting your money back when you lend it to others, for example when you place a deposit with a bank. Many savers (known somewhat derogatively as 'rate tarts') chased the highest returns available, forgetting that they were lending money to companies and relying on them having sound business strategies. Icesave, Northern Rock, Singer & Friedlander all illustrated the risks of doing so. Risk and return go hand in hand. In addition investors who invested in corporate bond funds (i.e. they lent their money to companies) had a pretty rough ride with a common corporate bond index falling by more than 10 per cent. Bonds were supposed to protect them from equity market falls, yet many 'overlooked' the fact that a weaker economy also means more corporate distress – see below.

■ The currency risk of owning non-UK assets. It became considerably more expensive for a UK skier to enjoy a coffee on the slopes of the French Alps – in fact about 25 per cent more costly at around £5 a coffee! Pensioners living in Spain suffered a reduced income on their pensions paid in the UK and converted into euros. Conversely, investors who owned foreign assets (e.g. owning US equities) benefited as the value of these assets increased in sterling terms.

■ Liquidity risk, i.e. not being able to get your hands on your money when you want it. You may remember that between 2003 and 2006 commercial property funds were the latest hot asset class on the back of 20 per cent plus returns four years in a row. However, when the markets began to fall in 2007 and 2008, many investors in 'bricks and mortar' funds investing directly in commercial property suddenly had withdrawal restrictions placed on their money, in some cases up to six months or more.

■ Counterparty risk. Too many private investors had their portfolios stuffed full of 'guaranteed' products that promised to repay the principle invested irrespective of the returns in underlying markets, coupled with the opportunity for upside participation. Yet a guarantee of any sort in any walk of life is only as good as the person who signs it. Just ask the US$8 billion of investors who held Lehman Brothers structured notes and who will now be lucky to see 15 cents on the dollar.

■ Manager investment risk. The majority of active managers got beaten by the markets in the very environment in which they previously claimed they had the flexibility and skills to avoid excessive trouble. In fact some recent research indicates, for example, that 93 per cent of European eurobond managers lost out to the index over the one-year period to the end of October 2008, rising by the way to 98 per cent over five years. The equity managers fared little better with 76 per cent being beaten by the market in European Large Cap funds, rising to 84 per cent over five years. That's a pretty appalling (yet not unexpected) outcome given the *raison d'être* of the industry (iShares, 2008).

- Manager fraud. Bernard Madoff, the renowned manager of one of the most 'respected' hedge funds, allegedly made off with $50 billion of investors' cash, including that of some of the apparently most sophisticated investors. It was invested in what looks like the biggest Ponzi scheme scam ever.

- Concentration risk. Just ask the employees at Lehman Brothers what the concentration of risk means. Many lost their jobs (and the future capital they would derive from it) along with considerable parts of their wealth held in Lehman shares awarded to them as bonuses during their employment.

Well, with all those risks (and more) facing you, it may feel tempting to simply remain in cash – but that is not a realistic option. What we need to do is to explore what the risks are of stepping away from cash and how we can mitigate or avoid unwanted risk. Finally, we want to end up with risks in a portfolio that are understood, transparent, controlled and managed. This is not as hard as you think, when you break it down into bite-sized chunks.

8.2 The cost of capital

At this point it is worth introducing a financial concept called the cost of capital. Grasping this concept is a critical starting point for approaching the construction of robust and sensible investment portfolios. Like many concepts in investing and finance it is pretty simple to grasp. It is attempting to quantify what the cost of capital is that is the challenge. Let's take a high-level look at this important concept, which is in fact a two-sided coin, as you will see.

Two sides to the coin: risk and return

A company seeking to invest in its business can raise funds from three sources: from its own resources (retained earnings); from lenders (bank loans and buyers of their bonds); and from selling shares in its ownership. When a company raises capital to fund its operations it does so at a cost and the cost of capital rises with the perceived riskiness of the company. As witnessed in 2008, by a number of major banks going cap in hand to the taxpayers to raise capital to avoid insolvency, the cost of capital rises with risk. Some banks have had to give up independence and have been effectively nationalised due to ownership they have conceded. The interest they are paying on the preference shares that have been issued, for example around 14 per cent when base rates were around 1.5 per cent, reflects the severe risks the taxpayer is taking. That is the price these weak institutions have to pay for staying in business. On an individual basis, people with very poor credit records end up paying usurious interest to loan sharks as they can't get anyone else to lend to them. Financially sound individuals and companies should pay lower rates of interest.

The other side of the cost of capital coin is the expected return that an investor should receive from either owning a company's shares or lending money to it. The higher the cost of capital (i.e. the greater the risk), the higher the expected return an investor would anticipate. This is an important concept to grasp. It was a lesson quickly learned by bank depositors in 2008 – high deposit rates were needed to attract lenders to banks with weak balance sheets and poor strategies. The cost of capital is determined by the market, reflected in the price that it will pay for an asset. The higher the risk/cost of capital, the lower the price of the assets and thus the higher the expected return in compensation.

The cost of capital of equities is greater than that of bonds, not least because bond holders sit higher in the pecking order in the event of a company getting into trouble or going into administration. For example, in the 2008 bank bailout, those who took taxpayer capital must pay the preference share 'interest' first and it is anticipated that dividends to common shareholders will be significantly curtailed for some time. Take a look at Figure 8.2, which illustrates the returns that were achieved from investing in different asset classes historically.

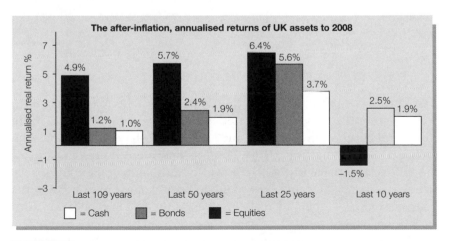

Figure 8.2 After-inflation returns of UK asset classes

Source: Barclays Equity Gilt Study, 2009.

8.3 Focusing on market risk

The term market risk, i.e. being an owner in companies by purchasing equities or becoming a lender by buying bonds, needs to be defined a bit more closely. What we are talking about here is the risk that remains once we have eliminated all the specific risk associated with an individual firm. The risks associated with a specific company (thus called 'specific' risk) can be eliminated quite quickly by adding more equities of different companies to it (see Figure 8.3). In fact, most company-specific risk is avoided by owning thirty or so stocks, but from a smarter investor's perspective, the more the merrier. The risk that you are left with is known as market (or systematic) risk.

In a seminal piece of work, which won Professor William Sharpe the Nobel Prize, he put forward the idea that only market risk – that is the risk after all specific company risk is diversified away – is rewarded. The more market risk you take, the higher the expected return. The model that he created is known as the Capital Asset Pricing Model, which sits at the heart of modern finance (despite its critics). This underlying message remains central to investment success.

From an equity perspective market risk is the remaining risk that you face if you own UK plc rather than just Lloyds Bank, for example. You can do this by owning equities of all the companies in the FTSE All-Share index through a fund of some sort – more on that later.

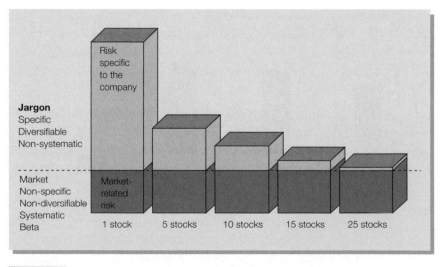

Figure 8.3 Company-specific risk is quickly eliminated

Later, this model was refined by Professors Eugene Fama and Kenneth French, two renowned academics in the US, who developed the idea based on empirical data that three risk factors define the characteristics of equity risk, rather than Sharpe's single market risk factor. They also noted that two risk factors define the broad characteristics of bonds. Their theory is commonly known as the 'Multi-factor Model' (Fama and French, 1993). We explore the implications of this for building portfolios below.

8.4 The risks and rewards of being a lender

One way to generate returns in your portfolio is by lending your money to the government by buying government bonds (gilts in the UK) or to corporations by buying their bonds. In essence, you lend them your money and they promise to pay you interest on the money and to give you your money back at a certain date in their future. Simplistically the interest paid should be sufficient to compensate you for the risk that they can't pay you back (because they go bust), inflation, and the fact that you are tying up your money. Most people placing a deposit would expect a higher interest rate from tying up their money for three years rather than three months. In the same way it is no surprise that companies or banks that have weak balance sheets and poor strategies will have to offer you higher returns (e.g. deposit rates) than stronger ones.

We will explore these two investment options in considerably more depth later, but the basic underlying risks are evident.

As you can establish from the cost of capital concept, as an investor the safest way to make a return from lending your money is to lend it to your government for the shortest time possible, i.e. overnight. You are not going to get a great return as you are not risking much, i.e. the government's cost of capital is low. This is often referred to as the 'risk-free rate' by investors (although there is much debate about what an individual or an institution's true risk-free rate actually is – but that is an unnecessary distraction at this point). You could get more return by taking more risk, which you can do in one of two main ways.

Lending to weaker companies

Lend your money to someone who has a higher risk of not paying you your interest and returning your capital. This risk is referred to as either credit risk or default risk. You will probably have heard of, or even used, the term 'AAA' rated, which implies financial solidity and a low risk of default – it has become part of our common language. This is a credit rating provided by a rating agency of which there are several. As you slide down the alphabet through the Bs and the Cs, the cost of capital rises as does the expected return reflected in the increased yield an investor receives for lending money to them. In other words, the risk of default rises for which investors need to be compensated. The question that needs to be answered is whether or not this 'default' risk is adequately compensated.

Lending your money for longer

If you leave money in your current account, where you have instant access to your funds, you don't generally expect to get paid much interest. However, if you placed a deposit for two years (leaving aside the credit risk issue above) you would expect to receive a higher rate of interest for tying up your money. That is because (a) your money can erode in spending power terms through the effects of inflation; (b) you have an opportunity cost of tying up your money which the borrower needs to compensate you for; (c) you have the risk of not knowing what return you will be able to reinvest the interest payments at. This is known as the time value of money. The flip side of the increased expected return from owning a bond that matures (i.e. pays back capital) further into the future is that its price, which moves to reflect the market's ever-changing expected level of return

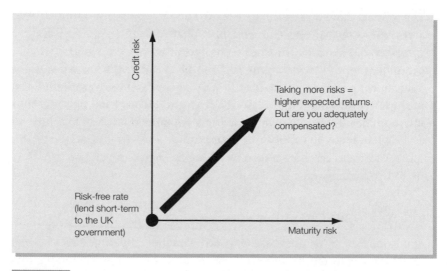

Figure 8.4 **You can take two key risks to increase returns**

by investors (called its yield), will be increasingly sensitive to movements in yields. This concept and more detail on how bonds work is covered later. This market risk is called interest rate risk or maturity risk. The question that needs to be answered is whether or not this 'maturity' risk is adequately compensated (see Figure 8.4).

Why many investors seem to land themselves in trouble is by not looking at the evidence on the risk/reward pay-off and assessing if compensation is adequate, combined with a lack of robust thinking as to why they own bonds in a portfolio in the first place. Both these issues will be addressed later.

8.5 The risks and rewards of being an owner

By buying equities you take on the risks associated with being an owner of a business. In the heady days when markets appear to go mad, it seems that people tend to forget that the stock market is not simply the electronic trading of pieces of paper, but the mechanism for valuing the future benefits of ownership in real companies run by real people with real products, reflected in the price of its shares. The level of your future wealth is inextricably linked to the fortunes of companies in which you are a part owner. Those fortunes depend on the ability of each company to employ their capital effectively, establish and execute a profitable business strategy, adapt to the uncertain forces that impact on the profitability of their industry and the sheer hard work of those who work there.

The rewards that you receive are the cash dividends that the company pays and rise in the share price attributable to the growth in earnings that the company can generate. In the shorter term these earnings can change, as can sentiment as to how much an investor should pay for these earnings. Share prices go up and down based on the market's collective interpretation of the latest information available. Bad earnings figures and negative sentiment can result in share price falls. In extremis companies can go bust and as a shareholder you can lose all your money.

Not all equities are the same

The Fama and French research, referred to above, breaks down the risk that an investor receives into three key components: the risk of being in the equity market as a whole, as opposed to simply holding 'safe' cash on which you earn the risk-free rate of return; the risk of owning smaller companies rather than larger companies; and the risk of owning less healthy companies. These characteristics relate to company size and the degree of financial distress the company is in. We will look at this concept in more detail in the next chapter.

The rewards are usually referred to as the market risk premium (above the risk-free rate), the size premium and the value (financial distress) premium relative to the market. Their research indicates that around 95 per cent of the return of an equity portfolio can be described by these three factors.

As an aside you can imagine that this could be a useful tool in testing active manager skill as many managers simply have styles with long-term biases towards these return-enhancing factors that they sell and charge for as skill. Comparing their risk-factor-biased portfolios against broad market benchmarks is not a fair comparison.

The market risk premium can be thought of as the risk premium for equities of developed markets and the risk premium for equities of emerging markets. Intuitively, it is relatively easy for many investors to accept that the risks of investing in, say, emerging economies in Eastern Europe, parts of Asia and South America are greater than those of investing in the developed nations like the US, UK, the Eurozone and Japan. The cost of capital is expected to be higher for a number of financial, political, social, ethical and legal reasons. The flip side of the coin is that the returns that an investor requires in compensation should be higher.

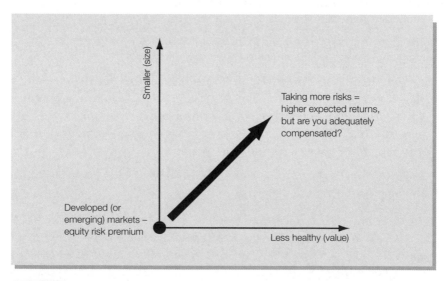

Figure 8.5 You can take two key risks to increase returns

Again, investors need to evaluate whether or not they believe that these incremental risks, relative to those of simply owning broad exposure to developed markets and picking up the equity market risk premium, are likely to deliver adequate compensation for doing so (see Figure 8.5).

Considerable debate rages around these incremental risk premia, but with a bit of thought and common sense you can decide whether they should be part of your portfolio – the old saying 'all things in moderation' applies particularly well to risk choices in portfolios.

8.6 Risk choices are limited

As you can see, when you strip investing bare, it is pretty uncomplicated. There are two main ways in which you can generate returns: by being an owner or by being a lender. Getting the right mix between these is the key step. These returns can be enhanced by taking on credit and maturity risk as a lender and emerging market, size and company health risks as an owner, but only if as an investor you feel that you are adequately compensated for doing so. As we have seen, manager risk rarely pays and is impossible to identify upfront. Other implementation risks can easily be avoided.

References

Breakwell G. and Barnett, J. (2007) *The Psychology of Risk: An Introduction*, Cambridge University Press, p. 1.

Fama, E. F. and French K. R. (1993) 'Common risk factors in the returns on stocks and bonds', *Journal of Financial Economics* 33, 3–56.

iShares (2008) Active Funds Performance Overview, Recent Trends.

9

Smarter portfolio construction

Building a sensible and robust portfolio is not as complicated or as difficult as people make out. For some investors, simply owning a broad exposure to global equities, for example using an index tracker fund and holding cash or National Savings Certificates that provide inflation protection, in the right proportions (Chapters 6 and 7 help you to define this), is sufficient. This is a sort of 90/10 portfolio, with 90 per cent of the value for only 10 per cent of the hassle. Such a strategy would put most fund managers out of business.

However, it probably makes sense to try to construct more robust and better diversified portfolios based on the evidence we have to hand, a bit of hard thinking and a good dose of common sense. What does not make sense is getting caught up in overcomplicated software models, taking on risks that are not adequately rewarded or the myriad of faddish sectors and markets pedalled by those who think that complexity justifies their fees. As you will see, the smarter investing approach is to keep things robust, transparent and simple, resulting in effective and survivable portfolios.

You only need to look back at the past thirty years or so to register just what might be thrown at you and your portfolio. We've had oil crises, war, terrorism, rampant inflation, low inflation, three major equity market crashes, irrational exuberance in the dot.com world and the housing market, the credit crunch and the recent spectre of deflation, to name just a few. It doesn't seem unreasonable to think that it makes sense to cover a few of these bases. You have the opportunity to build a portfolio for all seasons. As ever, in investing there are no right or wrong answers, just those that probably give you a better chance of surviving with your investment programme intact. It is worth bearing in mind the wise words of John Bogle:

'Asset allocation [your mix of building blocks] is not a panacea. It is a reasoned – if imperfect – approach to the inevitable uncertainty of the financial markets.'

And as William Bernstein succinctly agrees:

'Since the future cannot be predicted, it is impossible to specify in advance what the best asset allocation will be. Rather, our job is to find an allocation that will do reasonably well under a wide range of circumstances.'

9.1 The portfolio building process

The process from here is summarised in Figure 9.1. Having identified the investment and implementation risks that you face in the previous chapter, you now need to decide which risks you want to include and which to exclude. So, we need to come up with some criteria for why we should use a specific building block or not, look at the evidence that we have to hand that can guide us in making a decision, and then decide how much of each type of risk we should take.

9.2 Construction goals and approach

Over the period of your investment life, the one thing that you can be certain of is that the world, both in terms of politics and economics, will provide

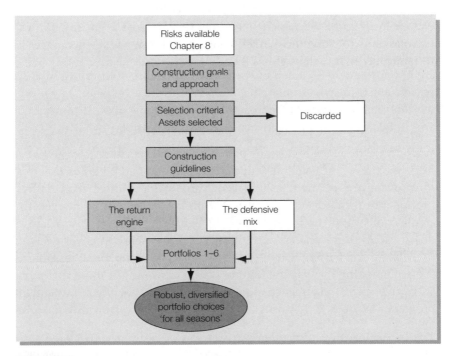

Figure 9.1 **The portfolio construction process**

some very considerable challenges and opportunities for the companies that you own or companies and governments that you lend to. The markets will do their best to value them through their pricing mechanism. As we saw in 2008, that can be a fast moving, volatile and painful process.

The goals of the construction process

It is impossible to tell what lies ahead, but history does provide us with some insight into the magnitudes and frequencies of both sides of the coin. If we accept that we face such uncertainty, the only protection that we have is to try to own a well-diversified mix of assets that have the potential within their structure, and the process through which they generate economic returns, to mitigate some of the risks that we, as investors, face. This is the 'portfolio for all seasons' we are aiming for.

The other key goal we are aiming for is a structure that is entirely transparent. A clear understanding and acceptance of what each asset class building block brings to the table, i.e. the key role it plays and the risks that it mitigates, will allow you to view your portfolio as a whole and not as its constituent parts. This is vitally important because at any point one asset class is likely to be doing better than another. Looked at in isolation the temptation is to chase the market. Looking at it as a whole encourages us to remember that each asset has its role and its time.

The construction approach

I have seen many approaches to constructing portfolios, from the seemingly sophisticated asset allocation models run by investment banks to the exceptionally simple two-building-block (bonds and equities) approach. Better practitioners will end up in approximately the right place, whatever process they adopt, and one cannot say that any answer is wrong if the split between growth and defensive assets takes into account the client's emotional tolerance for risk. You should be in the right ball park. The approach adopted here is based on solid investment theory and has a certain clear logic that makes great sense to most people.

To put in into context, it might help to review quickly the investment theory on which it is based.

The beneficial effect of combining asset classes whose return patterns are not exactly similar (i.e. they are imperfectly correlated) is to increase the return of a portfolio without increasing its bumpiness of returns, or alternatively to keep the same level of return and decrease the bumpiness of returns. This phenomena of diversification was first explored in depth and mathematically described by Harry Markowitz in the 1950s and is generally referred to as Modern Portfolio Theory (Markowitz, 1952). He won the Nobel Prize for it. Simply put, and without doing down Markowitz's achievement, you can smooth portfolio returns by owning blocks that are zigging, while other blocks you own are zagging, without giving up return. The more they zig and zag without relationship to each other the more the relationship between return and risk is improved. Modern Portfolio Theory still lies at the centre of much investment industry thinking today, despite its critics (Bernstein, 1996). Portfolios that display the best trade-off between risk and return are said in the lingo of the investment world to be 'efficient'. A rational investor might be expected to select the appropriate efficient portfolio to invest in.

As an interesting aside, it is perhaps ironic that Markowitz himself confessed that he did not use his Nobel Prize-winning equation when it came down to investing his own money! He simply states:

'I visualized my grief if the stock market went way up and I wasn't in it — or if it went way down and I was completely in it. So I split my contributions 50/50 between stocks and bonds.' (Zweig, 2007)

As another aside, means-variance optimisation (MVO) software, which is derived from the quadratic equation that Markowitz developed, is still widely used in the investment industry, but is rarely used with much common sense or insight. What it attempts to do is to identify portfolio structures at every point along the risk spectrum where the trade-off between return and risk is most favourable. The result is a graph that usually looks like a banana, referred to as the 'efficient frontier', but is of less practical use. Unconstrained optimisation tends to generate unintuitive portfolio structures, due to estimation error maximisation (Michaud, 1989). Outcomes are extremely sensitive to small changes in the return/risk relationship, and return in particular. Reflect on this comment if you are tempted by the sexiness and seemingly sophisticated nature of optimisation software, and advisers that use it:

'Despite the mysticism many perceive in these tools, understand that all these tools do is to solve a mathematical equation. They do not know what you are inputting into them and will calculate whatever you ask them to. These tools don't even know they are solving financial problems (or creating them).' (Loeper, 2003)

In accordance with Modern Portfolio Theory (MPT) a rational investor should seek to own an efficient portfolio. Another piece of seminal academic work provides us with an insight into how we can tackle the portfolio construction problem. James Tobin's Separation Theorem (Tobin, 1957) suggests that the most efficient portfolio available is the 'market portfolio', i.e. the market cap weighted global asset mix (i.e. all the bonds and equities in the world). No portfolio has a theoretically better set of risk/return characteristics. Thus, in a theoretical world, investors should own this market portfolio and add risk-free assets to it to create lower risk/lower reward portfolios, or leverage it if they wish to increase the risk of the portfolio beyond that of the market portfolio.

Our approach is a sort of common sense derivation, based around creating a reasonably efficient and effective pool of risky assets, taking the market risks we want to take and then diluting this risky pool by adding defensive, less risky assets to it to a level that is appropriate. I was talking this approach through with one of my clients, BoulterBowen WealthCare, one day and they coined it the 'whisky and water' approach – a great word picture, for which I thank them. Let's follow this simple analogy through.

Considerable care is taken in the creation of a blended malt whisky to create a distinctive flavour from a number of single malts that is robust and

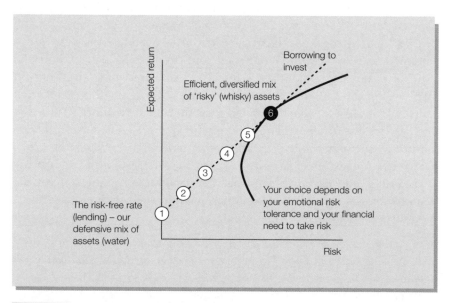

Figure 9.2 A simple yet effective approach

will remain consistent over time. That is our risky mix of growth/return oriented asset classes that meet our selection criteria. Whilst some will drink their Scotch neat, others, depending on their palate and desire to avoid ill effects, will dilute it with water to a flavour and strength that is right for them. That is the addition of our defensive assets that water down the strength of the pool of risky assets. The first step then is to create our blended portfolio of investment assets; the second is to identify what goes into the defensive, less risky mix; and the final step is to mix the two together to create suitable portfolio choices (see Figure 9.2).

9.3 Deciding on the asset class menu

There is an ever-widening choice of building blocks (asset classes) that you could invest in, from the more familiar cash, bonds, equities and property to the less familiar and more esoteric, such as commodities, hedge funds, gold, art, wine, cars, etc. The problem is that you have to decide, in a rational way, which to discard and which to use, and how much of each you should include. Pick up the money section of your Sunday paper and see how many 'opportunities' are on offer each week. Traditionally, these are categorised by the industry as equity, bond and alternative investments, which is helpful up to a point.

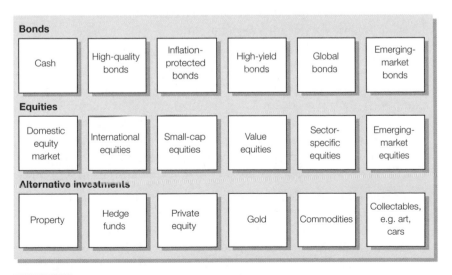

Figure 9.3 The choice can feel bewildering

What we will do in this section is to create a decision-making framework that will help you to decide which building blocks will sit well in your portfolio and which should lie on the scrap heap of marketing hype, market chasing and the opaque. In fact, with some common sense, a basic understanding of a few simple concepts, drawn together with some simple rules, you can put together sensible multiple-building-block portfolios without too much difficulty. The first thing to do is to lay down some criteria for inclusion in your portfolio. The second thing to do is to look at each asset class in turn, and make a judgement as to whether or not they should be included on your menu, given the tools we have at our disposal (historical data, economic and investment theory and a good dose of common sense).

Basic criteria for including building blocks

The criteria for inclusion fall into two main categories: those relating to the investment characteristics of the asset class and those that concern the ability of the asset class (i.e. the risks you want to take) to be replicated effectively. Let's look at the first category.

- *Criterion 1: The returns of the asset class should rely on market-based returns and/or investment theory, and not manager skill.* This comes back to the active versus passive debate that we hopefully settled in Chapter 4. You want to make sure that you understand and that you know where the returns are coming from (i.e. the economic rewards of being an owner and/or a lender). You do not want your returns to be based on the transient moment of luck of judgement of individuals – back capitalism every time, not individual skill!

- *Criterion 2: The return history should provide adequate insight into the characteristics that the building block exhibits.* Some investment opportunities come backed almost only with a good story and the air of hope (often sprayed around by the marketing department). Others come with short and flawed track records (such as hedge fund industry performance where very significant biases offer a misleading picture). We want to base our decisions on data that at least provides adequate insight into the ups and downs over preferably longer periods of time.

- *Criterion 3: The functional attributes that the asset class possesses should make a meaningful contribution at the portfolio level.* When an asset class is added to a portfolio mix, it needs to bring something positive to the table. It should deliver one of a number of contributions: provide an equity-like return, such as those derived from the UK equity market; it should offer the opportunity for higher equity returns than the broad market; or it should do a good job of reducing equity market risk. Remember that the risk of owning an asset class needs to be adequately compensated. Additionally, some asset classes do a better job at protecting wealth in different situations, such as unanticipated inflation, deflation or simply when the world is running scared (e.g. 2008).

The second category relates to the practical implementation of the portfolio strategy that you decide upon.

■ *Criterion 4: Products that cleanly replicate these characteristics should be available given the level of your assets and circumstances.* There is little point pursuing an asset class that you cannot access effectively either because the minimum economic investment is too high or access to the assets is based upon private transactions – private equity being a case in point for most individual investors.

■ *Criterion 5: Any products should have sufficient liquidity to allow you to rebalance your portfolio efficiently, when it drifts away from its long-term strategy, as it will.* A good and recent example is the use of bricks and mortar commercial property funds that directly purchased real estate on behalf of the fund. In 2008 redemptions were high in a falling market and emergency redemption clauses were invoked, tying in clients for several months in some cases. The ability of clients to adjust their own portfolios, just at the time they need to, is an important attribute.

■ *Criterion 6: Products have low all-in costs that eat up as little of the market returns on offer as is possible.* This is important because expensive products may take a significant proportion of the market return, to the benefit of all those involved in its management and distribution, while you take 100 per cent of the market risks. Costs really matter in this game, as you will see when we explore this point in more depth later.

Filtering out the good from the bad

In Table 9.1, you will see a summary of how different asset classes stack up against these criteria. In this table, we consider the more risky assets available – the whisky in the whisky and water analogy. The rationale for inclusion or exclusion is expanded upon in the individual asset class summaries provided in Chapter 11. These are my own judgements, based on the evidence that I have seen and the conclusions that I have drawn from

Table 9.1   Criteria for including risky asset classes

Criteria	1	2	3	4	5	6
Risky asset classes (the 'whisky')	Market driven returns	Adequate return history	Positive contribution to portfolio	Replication of risk factor	Adequte liquidity	Low-cost options
UK equity	✔	✔	✔	✔	✔	✔
Developed world ex-UK equity	✔	✔	✔	✔	✔	✔
Emerging market equity	✔	✔	✔	✔	✔	✔
Value (less healthy companies) equity	✔	✔	✔	✔	✔	✔
Smaller companies equity	✔	✔	✔	✔	✔	✔
Global real estate	✔	✕	✔	✔	✔	✔
Commodity features	✕(1)	✕	✔	✔	✔	✔
Hedge funds	✕	✕	✕	✕	✕	✕
Private equity	✔	✕	✕	✕	✕	✕

(1) *Investment theory rather than manager skill.*   = Excluded assets

it. Many investment professionals, advisers and individual investors, perhaps including you, may disagree. You need to have strong and defensible reasons for doing so and evidence to back up your case. The evidence used is explored in the individual asset class summaries.

Remember that you do not need to use all these asset classes in your portfolio. The important thing is that you understand why something is in there and not to include anything that you cannot get your head around. If you do, the chances are that at some point you will feel challenged as to why you own them and will be unable to make a rational decision to either discard or retain them. As you will see, I have prepared a range of portfolio structures for the 'whisky' and 'water' parts of the portfolio, depending on where you sit on the spectrum from a basic but effective, to a more refined but more complex portfolio.

The same process applies to more defensive assets, i.e. bonds and cash, which represent the 'water' in the 'whisky and water' analogy (see Table 9.2). It is worth noting that the contribution of different bond asset classes does depend on where and how they are used.

| Table 9.2 | Criteria for including defensive asset classes | | | | | |

Criteria	1	2	3	4	5	6
More defensive asset classes (the 'water')	Market-driven returns	Adequate return history	Positive contribution to portfolio	Replication of risk factor	Adequate liquidity	Low-cost options
UK gilts	✔	✔	✔(1)	✔	✔	✔
UK index-linked gilts	✔	✕	✔(2)	✔	✔	✔
Corporate bonds	✔	✕	✕	✔	✔	✔
UK cash	✔	✔	✔(3)	✔	✔	✔

▬ = Excluded assets

(1) Longer-dated gilts sit best in equity-dominated portfolios.
(2) Index-linked gilts have important inflation defences built in which are important for more cautious long-term investors.
(3) Where short-dated alternatives, particularly index-linked gilts, are not available.

Bonds and cash are often a confusing area for many investors. In short, bonds and cash play a defensive role and they need to provide relative calm either for cautious investors or as a balance against their risky assets. Sorting out how best to construct the defensive asset mix is explored further below.

Each asset class should contribute positively

Perhaps one of the biggest weaknesses in many investors' portfolios is that they have not, critically, understood how each asset class they include in their portfolio contributes towards bettering its structure and robustness.

As indicated above, each building block has a primary role to play in a portfolio: as a core part of the return engine (developed market equities); as a return enhancer over and above the core equity returns; or as a diversifier of equity market risk. Assets also respond differently to economic circumstances, such as inflation and deflation and at times of global crisis. Depending on your outlook, you can construct your portfolio with assets that cover the key risks that concern you. By and large, the key economic threat to investors' wealth, over the long-term, is inflation. Investors would do well to stack their portfolios with assets that provide long- and short-term protection from it.

Table 9.3 provides a summary of the contributions that each of the asset classes that meet the inclusion criteria exhibit.

Table 9.3   Asset-class contributions

Asset-class contribution	Key portfolio role			Environment		
	Core return	Return enhancer	Equity risk diversifier	Long-term inflation	Deflation	Global crisis
Growth-oriented assets						
UK equity	X			X		
Developed world ex-UK equity	X			X		
Emerging market equity		X		X		
Value (less healthy companies) equity		X		X		
Smaller companies equity		X		X		
Global real estate			X	X		
Commodity futures			X	X		
Defensive assets						
UK gilts			X		X	X
UK index-linked gilts			X	X		X
UK cash			X		X	X

As you can see from Table 9.3, being an owner of businesses and trusting in the long-term power of capitalism provides you with the return engine of your portfolio. You can try to squeeze some more juice out of the markets by taking on additional risks (i.e. owning firms with a higher cost of capital and thus a higher expected return). Asset classes that provide equity risk diversification do so at a cost – that of not owning equities – and are likely to deliver lower long-run returns. More volatile diversifiers sit best on the growth-oriented menu and less volatile assets sit best on the defensive menu.

9.4 Ground rules for the growth portfolio

The goal in creating the growth-oriented (whisky) mix is to create a diversified portfolio that will deliver strong, equity-like inflation returns over the long term. Hopefully, through diversification, this mix will deliver returns at least in line with UK equities over the long term, but at lower risk. In order to create an orderly construction of your portfolio, you need some basic ground rules.

Guideline 1: Carefully consider your home market bias

For many investors, when they think of growth assets and taking exposure to the equity markets they think about UK equities and the FTSE 100 (the 'Footsie') index. This is their natural reference point, despite the fact that it only covers the top 100 companies out of approximately 15,000 eligible global companies that you could be invested in. This is usually because it is familiar to investors, they recognise the key names – M&S, Shell, HSBC, etc. – and it makes investing in equities a bit more controlled. They feel less control over names like Cheung Kong Holdings or Macquarie Bank and therefore feel that they are more risky, as they know less about these markets, institutions and firms (French and Poterba, 1991). The other possibility is that investors feel an innate sense of confidence in their own economy, which is in fact over-optimistic. This is unlikely as the real growth of developed economies should be comparable over longer time periods and thus returns broadly the same. This liking for one's own market is known as home bias and is very common and pronounced across both institutional and individual investors.

Talk to an investment purist and they would say that the most effective starting point is fully backing capitalism across the globe and owning a share of more or less every listed company in the world, based on their market capitalisation. This, the purist would say, is an efficient portfolio that is highly diversified by company, sector and geography. You do not have to do anything to manage it because it is constructed on a market capitalisation basis and as different companies' share prices move and thus their capitalisations move (being the number of shares multiplied by the share price), so does your holding in each. No monitoring, no trading, no transactional costs eating away at your market returns. A pure investment in capitalism!

There is no right or wrong answer to this question and the balance that you adopt is ultimately a personal one. However, do not make it based on the fact that you think the UK will deliver better returns than other developed markets such as the US or Europe. That is either short-term market timing or misplaced longer-term optimism.

The reaction of many investors, when they look through a global equity fund to the country allocated, is a reluctance to trade a home bias in the UK for what appears to be a bias to the US, which has a greater slice of the pie because of the magnitude of the value of all of its companies. When it comes to structuring the growth-oriented mix, options at both ends of the spectrum (100 per cent home bias to a market cap weighted global

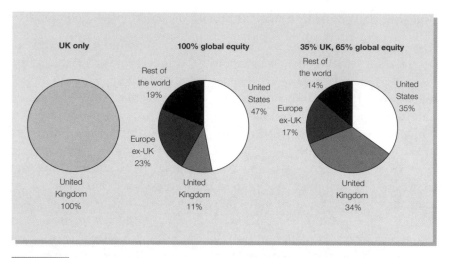

Figure 9.4 Breakdown of global equity markets by region

Source: Global Equity – MSCI World Equity Index.

portfolio) are provided, along with a compromise balance between the two (see Figure 9.4).

Guideline 2: Make material allocations to non-UK equities

As an investor, the central risk of UK equities performing poorly over short and longer periods of time should make it obvious that owning a more

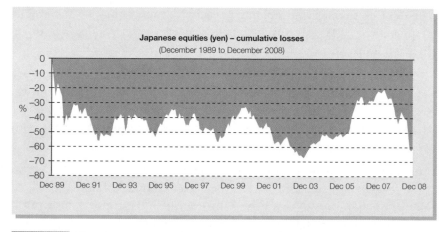

Figure 9.5 The Japanese equity market is a frightening reminder

Source: MSCI Japan Index.

diversified exposure to companies around the world makes good sense. In the shorter term the diversification benefit of investing internationally may be limited as correlations appear to increase at times of equity market trauma. However, the salutary lesson of the Japanese market that languished 60 per cent below its peak almost twenty years later is one reason why you need to diversify globally (see Figure 9.5).

A note on currency risk

As an extension to the home bias issue above, owning assets outside your home market, i.e. non-UK assets for a UK sterling-based investor, exposes you to currency risk. To keep things simple, let's consider an investment in the US equity market. You in fact own two assets: the underlying ownership in a number of US companies and the US dollar. Imagine that US equities rise by 10 per cent. For a US dollar-based investor, their return is that 10 per cent. For a UK investor, they will receive the 10 per cent plus the change in value of these assets depending on whether pound sterling has strengthened or weakened against the dollar. Imagine you originally bought £1,000 worth of US shares at US$2 to each £1. At the end of the year, the exchange rate is now US$1 per £1. Your shares are worth US$2,200 in dollar terms, but when you translate that back into pound sterling terms at the new rate they are worth £2,200!

Currency may be either beneficial or detrimental to your portfolio: beneficial when sterling weakens, as it did dramatically in 2008, and detrimental when sterling appreciates, as Figure 9.6 illustrates.

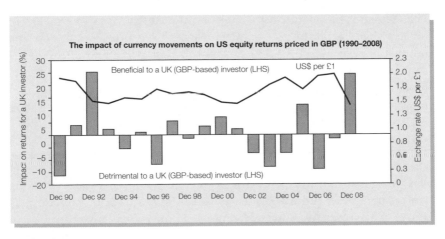

Figure 9.6   **Currency can act as a diversifier**

Source: MSCIBarra – US equity, Bank of England exchange rate.

There are several properties of currency worth considering. First, it is a rate of exchange and in itself has no economic return-generating mechanism like being an owner or a lender. Second, over the long run the exchange rate should be in line with the purchasing power parity between two countries. This principal is succinctly explained by the *Economist* and their well-known Big Mac Index:

'Burgernomics is based on the theory of purchasing-power parity, the notion that a dollar should buy the same amount in all countries. Thus in the long run, the exchange rate between two countries should move towards the rate that equalises the prices of an identical basket of goods and services in each country. Our "basket" is a McDonald's Big Mac, which is produced in about 120 countries. The Big Mac PPP is the exchange rate that would mean hamburgers cost the same in America as abroad.'

Third, currencies tend to be uncorrelated to equities in particular and thus provide some potential diversification benefit in an equity-oriented portfolio. They also tend to have low correlations between each other. Finally, currency movements have volatility more akin to equities than bonds.

How do you handle currency risk? The easy starting point is to avoid currency exposure in your defensive asset classes by owning GBP-denominated assets, e.g. National Savings Certificates or index-linked gilts. If you happen to own any global bond exposure, this should be fully hedged. You want to avoid the equity-like volatility being mixed in with your low-volatility assets.

When it comes to your equity exposure (and other risky assets) you could, like many institutional investors, take on the currency risk as a means of diversifying the portfolio. Countless papers have been written on the optimal level of hedging currency exposure, but at the end of the day it comes down to a practical issue. Virtually all global and country equity funds are unhedged, i.e. you will suffer the full impact of any currency movements, which could be in your favour or against you. The long-term investor can afford to take the view that these will even out over time. Perhaps they will, perhaps they will not.

On the other hand, avid active managers see currency as a separate asset class to be managed independently of the underlying asset classes. Picking market trends and turning points, as we know, is a difficult game to play and is best avoided by individual, and most professional, investors.

Guideline 3: Decide on your equity return enhancers

The return enhancing opportunities that exist relative to the broad developed equity market exposure (emerging market, value and small company premia) need to be decided upon. A bit more detail on these is provided in the asset class summaries in Chapter 11. The risk that you are taking is that you accept what appear to be higher risks, with hope and possibility of picking up the incremental premium. Periods will exist in the shorter and possibly longer-term where these tilts may not pay off against the broader market. That is one of the challenges.

Guideline 4: Decide on your equity market diversifiers

The bulk of the 2000s has been a salutary lesson in the fact that equity markets do not always go up or quickly bounce back, which was the delusion carried over from the raging bull market of the 1980s and 1990s. The UK market went nowhere from 2000 to 2008 (via an up and down ride). The spectre of Japan should sit in the back of any investor's mind. As Laurence Siegel of the Ford Foundation so encouragingly once stated (Siegel, 1997):

'Risk is not short-term volatility, for the long-term investor can afford to ignore that. Rather, because there is no predestined rate of return, only an expected one that may not be realised, the risk is that, in the long-run, stock returns will be terrible'.

Growth-oriented equity market diversifiers, such as property, may help to smooth shorter-term equity market falls, as well as providing some comfort over the long-term, if Siegel's warning comes true over your investing lifetime.

You need to decide if you want to include these asset classes or if you wish to ignore them, sticking with equities and simply reducing the risk you take by diluting your equity exposure with defensive assets. Read up about each in Chapter 11 and make your own mind up.

The degree to which each asset class helps to smooth the portfolio returns, i.e. how effective their diversification benefit is, depends on how highly correlated their returns are. Table 9.4 illustrates how effective these were at doing so over the period 1990–2008. Bear in mind that broadly a correlation of 1 to 0.7 provides marginal diversification benefit – most equity assets fall in that category; 0.6 to 0.4 provides better diversification; and around 0.3 to −0.3 returns are said to be uncorrelated, which is a much

Table 9.4 Asset class correlation matrix, 1990–2008

		Asset 1	Asset 2	Asset 3	Asset 4	Asset 5	Asset 6	Asset 7	Asset 8	Asset 9	Asset 10
UK equity	Asset 1	1.0									
UK value equity	Asset 2	1.0	1.0								
UK small cap equity	Asset 3	0.8	0.7	1.0							
World ex-UK equity	Asset 4	0.8	0.8	0.7	1.0						
World ex-UK value equity	Asset 5	0.8	0.8	0.7	1.0	1.0					
*World ex-UK small cap equity	Asset 6	0.7	0.6	0.7	0.8	0.8	1.0				
Emerging markets equity	Asset 7	0.7	0.6	0.7	0.8	0.8	0.7	1.0			
Global commercial real estate	Asset 8	0.5	0.5	0.5	0.6	0.7	0.7	0.6	1.0		
Commodities	Asset 9	0.2	0.2	0.3	0.3	0.4	0.4	0.4	0.4	1.0	
UK 1-month T-bills	Asset 10	0.1	0.1	0.1	0.1	0.1	0.1	0.1	0.1	0.0	1.0

1.0–0.7 = marginal benefit   0.6–0.4 = reasonable benefit   <0.4 = strong benefit

Source: refer to Appendix 1.
Note: US small cap used as a proxy.*

sought after quality by investors. In fact, if you could find four uncorrelated asset classes with equity-like returns, you could halve the risk of the portfolio without giving up any return. The problem lies in finding them! You can see that global commercial real estate and commodities provide useful potential diversification benefits.

Guideline 5: Make allocations that are meaningful but not overpowering

If you decide to make allocations to any return enhancing or equity market diversifiers, you should do so in a material way, but without overpowering the core broad equity market asset classes. So, you should probably make a 5 per cent minimum allocation to each of the growth-oriented mix and a maximum of 15 per cent to 20 per cent.

Guideline 6: Allocations should reflect your take on the arguments

The other important piece of guidance that you should take on board is that the allocations you make should reflect your confidence in the underlying evidence and arguments put forward. For example, if two asset classes have the same premia, but the evidence and argument support one case more than the other, you would not employ an equal weighting in your portfolio. You may decide on balance to exclude several asset classes, simply because you don't feel comfortable with them. My advice is don't own anything that you do not understand and feel comfortable with.

9.5 Building your growth-oriented portfolio return engine

When we put all this together we are now in a position to construct the growth-oriented (whisky) element of your portfolio.

The portfolios that I have come up with are set out in Tables 9.5a and 9.5b. Two sets of portfolios have been constructed, one with home bias and ranging from very basic UK-only to a more complex globally diversified model with partial home bias. The other uses a global market capitalisation weighted approach.

Table 9.5a Examples of growth-oriented portfolios

Home bias	Basic		Diversified	Style tilts
	UK	Global	Global	Global
UK equity market	100%	30%	25%	15%
UK value equities				5%
UK smaller company equities				5%
World ex-UK equities		60%	45%	25%
World ex-UK value equities				10%
World ex-UK smaller companies equities				10%
Emerging market equities		10%	10%	10%
Global commercial real estate			10%	10%
Commodities			10%	10%
Total allocation	**100%**	**100%**	**100%**	**100%**

It probably makes sense, as a minimum, to adopt the basic global structure in Table 9.5a to make sure that you have both the comfort of knowing that you are not wholly reliant on UK plc for your equity returns over your investing lifetime and that you have a small long-term allocation to faster-growing, higher-risk economies in the emerging nations. The global style tilts option is for those who feel comfortable with the evidence and arguments and are able (either directly or through a capable adviser) to manage this on an ongoing basis. In Part 4 possible implementation products are suggested for each of these allocations.

For those of you looking to take the purist route and simply own the efficient global market capitalisation weighted portfolio the options are set out below. The important thing to remember is that none of these are wrong, and complex does not necessarily mean better for you. Diversification does, however, make good sense, even if it does not work on every occasion. You should vary your own mix around these broad guidelines.

Table 9.5b Examples of growth-oriented portfolios

Global market cap	Basic		Diversified	Style tilts
	UK	Global	Global	Global
World (developed and emerging)	100%			
World equity (developed)		90%	70%	40%
World value equity				15%
World smaller companies equity				15%
Emerging market equities		10%	10%	10%
Global commercial real estate			10%	10%
Commodities			10%	10%
Total allocation	**100%**	**100%**	**100%**	**100%**

How effective is this portfolio construction?

There are three main levels to answering this question. The first is that the logic of the building blocks used makes sense: we have combined blocks that generate a strong core return with some higher risk blocks that should help to enhance returns and others that should provide some protection to equity market risk.

At the next level we can take a look back at how this portfolio would have performed over a given period of time. In Table 9.6 there is a comparison between UK equities and the global style tilts portfolio (as in Table 9.5a above) over the period from January 1990 to October 2008 (1990 is the common data start point for the assets included).

What is interesting to note is that while the risk has been the same, when measured by volatility, it appears that the downside impact of the worst-case periods has been reduced by the diversification into other asset classes. Returns have stood up well, delivering a cumulative 10 per cent or so extra over this time period than a simple investment in the UK market. Diversification is a tool worth using. Smarter investing requires that you simply stack the odds of success in your favour by making sensible decisions along the way.

Figure 9.7 provides a bit more detail in the comparison of the two choices – UK equities and our growth-oriented mix of assets – during two particularly tough periods for investors: 2000–2002 (the Tech Wreck) and 2007–2008 (the Credit Crunch). As you can see, diversification helped to reduce the cumulative losses incurred over this period. While this illustrates that diversification is an important decision, in periods like the early 1990s, when property fell substantially and global markets fared worse than the UK, it did not pay off; but that does not make it invalid. Investing is an imperfect science.

Finally, we can estimate, based on the assumptions that we make about each asset class going forward, (a) its return (i.e. the equity market return

Table 9.6 Portfolio performance comparision, 1990–2008

	Growth of £100	Return (real)	Risk %	Worst 1 year	Worst 5 years
UK equity (FTSE All-Share)	£202	3.8%	15%	−37%	−8.6%
Global style tilts portfolio	£220	3.9%	15%	−31%	−3.5%

Source: Simulated index data. Refer to Appendix 1 for details.

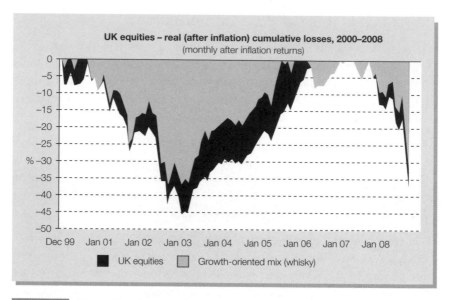

Figure 9.7 Diversification can help

Source: UK Equities; FTSE AU-Share; growth-oriented mix – refer to Appendix 1.

from developed markets plus any premia for emerging markets, less healthy (value) companies and smaller companies); (b) the risk of each; (c) the risk of the portfolio, given that the imperfect return correlation between building blocks should help to reduce the portfolio risk below the sum of its parts. The assumptions used are summarised in Chapter 11. The portfolio parameters have been calculated using Harry Markowitz's equation and represent a portfolio of assets that have been rebalanced back to their original allocation percentages at the start of each year. No costs have been deducted. The result is illustrated in Table 9.7.

Figure 9.8 shows that by taking a wide range of asset classes, some in themselves pretty risky, you can create a portfolio such as the global style tilts portfolio (the whisky) that has an expected efficiency higher than that of the UK/developed markets. Remember too that it provides protection from

Table 9.7 Portfolio comparison: estimated return and risk

	Expected return (real)	Expected risk (%)	Return per unit of risk
UK equity	5.0%	20%	0.25
Global style tilts portfolio	6.3%	19%	0.34

Source: Albion Strategic Consulting.

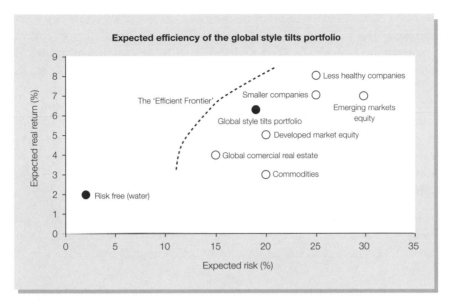

Figure 9.8 **The global style tilts portfolio is a reasonable structure**

the risk that the UK equity market simply fails to perform over our own investment lives.

Having created a sensible and robust growth-oriented portfolio, which should deliver equity-like returns over the longer term, we need to turn our attention towards the defensive assets mix. These assets will be used to water down the growth-oriented mix to a level that is consistent with your financial need to take risk and your emotional tolerance for it.

9.6 Building a robust defensive asset mix

This is an area that quite a few investors get confused about. One problem is that many investors feel that, having taken on bond exposure at the expense of equity exposure, they should try to get as much juice out of the portfolio as possible. Alternatively, they own fixed income in order to generate income to live off and again try to squeeze as much income as they can.

James Tobin and the 'whisky and water' approach would simply suggest that you take all the risk in the growth-oriented portfolio and simply add the risk-free water to it. Theoretically that sounds both rational and simple to do. But there is, perhaps, a little more to it than that. The first problem is what the risk-free asset actually is for an investor.

In order to try to make sense of creating our defensive asset mix, we need to take a step back and ask ourselves what the bond (fixed income) part of the portfolio is there for. The problem is that it means different things to different investors with different goals, different exposure to risky assets and different tolerance for risk. Simplistically, lending the government money on a short-term basis by buying Treasury bills is regarded as one reasonable proxy. But here's the rub: if you are a long-term investor, then your biggest worry is inflation and the erosion of your purchasing power, yet cash has proven itself to be a pretty poor store of purchasing power over time. So is cash really the risk-free asset for you? Perhaps we can best unravel this muddle by looking at the two extremes of investor.

Remember, though, that what we are talking about here is longer-term investors, say ten years plus, who will rely on their capital to support their financial goals, such as sustaining a comfortable retirement.

The cautious long-term investor

Imagine that you are an investor that finds the whole investment choice trade-off uncomfortable and that you are unable to take the risk of unfavourable outcomes in pursuit of favourable outcomes. Loss of capital scares you. Perhaps in light of this, you have set modest goals and lowered your retirement spending that your assets should be able to sustain.

As a long-term investor of this ilk, there are two things that you want to avoid and protect against. The first and most critical is inflation. Even at what seem relatively low levels of inflation, your spending power in retirement could be significantly eroded. If you are, for the sake of this example, sixty years old today the possibility is increasingly high that either you or your partner, if you have one, are going to live to a hundred. Inflation at what seems like a paltry 3 per cent per year will reduce £100 of spending power to just £30 pounds (see Table 2.1 at the start of the book). That is likely to be a risk that you simply cannot afford to take. The other risk is shorter term in nature, being that of suffering volatility and possibly losses on your portfolio on a month-by-month or year-by-year basis.

Many very cautious investors simply put their cash on deposit. Take a look at Figure 9.9 and ask yourself if that is a low-risk strategy, when the issue is one of purchasing power (leaving aside the credit risk issue of whether the bank the deposit is placed with is sound). The risk of a period of high and unanticipated inflation is a major risk to the long-term cautious investor.

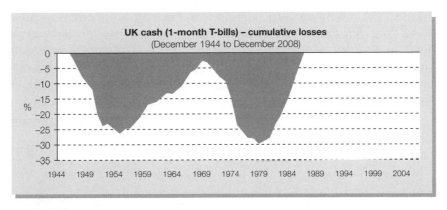

Cash is a poor store of purchasing power

Source: Barclays Equity Gilt Study, 2009.

The data series in Figure 9.9 does not take into account the tax, up to 40 per cent, that you pay on your bank deposits. Given that from 2000 to 2008 UK Treasury bills yielded only 1.9 per cent after inflation per year, you would not have been left with much change after tax. Remember too that chasing the highest rate of return on deposits is in effect chasing the banks with the poorest strategies and weakest balance sheets. There is no free lunch in investing. Cash is not a risk-free lunch.

To mitigate the risk of inflation effectively, investors should own assets that naturally protect against inflation. Equities, which do a good job over the long term, are excluded as they are simply too volatile for a very cautious investor (although a strong argument does exist for any long-term investor to hold even just 20 per cent in growth-oriented assets). More defensive options are debt instruments (i.e. where you are the lender) that have an inbuilt inflation protection mechanism in their structure. That points you towards index-linked securities issued by the UK government (other countries' index-linked securities do not provide protection against UK inflation risk). Your choice is between UK index-linked gilts (bonds) or index-linked National Savings Certificates, whose structure pays you an income and return of capital that is protected from inflation, based on the Retail Price Index. In practice they do a reasonably good job of protecting you against inflation. In contrast, conventional bonds perform very poorly at times of unanticipated rises in inflation: yields must rise to compensate investors for the new level of inflation and prices, as a consequence, fall.

Ideally, you would own shorter-dated index-linked gilts (e.g. five years) that have lower price sensitivity to changes in yields and therefore have a low level of volatility and thus short-term risk to capital. If these had been around since 1945 (index-linked gilts were first issued in 1984) Figure 9.9 would have shown no losses to purchasing power on short-dated index-linked gilts or National Savings Certificates.

In practice your implementation options are somewhat limited by availability of suitable products, although that is rapidly changing. This is discussed in more detail in Chapter 13.

The less-cautious long-term investor

At the other end of the risk spectrum, imagine that you are a pretty risk tolerant investor, comfortable with trading off unfavourable outcomes in pursuit of more aggressive favourable outcomes, and that you have a financial need to take this risk. As a consequence you own a pretty high allocation of equities/risky assets, let's say 80 per cent. Unlike the cautious investor, you are protected reasonably well from inflation by owning equities, real estate and commodities in your growth-oriented mix. You are not too worried by volatility, as reflected in your risky asset mix, unlike the cautious investor. What you really want to do is to own the best diversifier when the equity market crashes, but giving up as little equity exposure as you can.

UK gilts are a potentially strong diversifier of equity market risk. Despite their normally positive correlations to equities, at times of equity market trauma high-quality bonds (gilts) have the potential, although not the certainty, to act as havens of safety and liquidity, with commensurate positive consequences for yields (down) and prices (up) as investors flood into this asset class. As we explored previously, the further away the maturity of the bond (more precisely the 'duration' – a measure of this sensitivity – see Chapter 12), the more this positive effect is magnified.

'Only high quality, long-term bonds perform well in times of severe stress, allowing investors to view the opportunity costs of holding bonds as an insurance premium incurred to insulate portfolios from extreme positions.'
(David Swensen, CIO Yale Endowment)

This seems to make logical sense and the empirical evidence seems to support the case reasonably well. As ever, in investing you will be able to find occasions when this did not work. It is a question of balance. On balance it is not unreasonable to include some longer-dated gilts in risky portfolios.

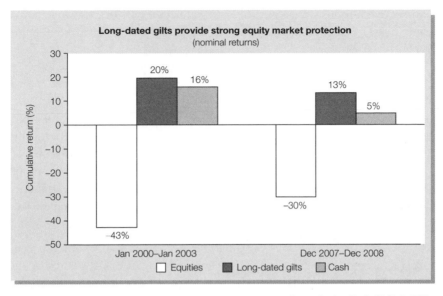

Source: Barclays Equity Gilt Study, 2009.

Figure 9.10 Balancing equity risk with quality, long-dated bonds

Take a look at the evidence in Figure 9.10, covering a couple of periods in the turbulent 2000s when equity markets crashed.

At the end of the day it comes down to a balance of evidence, logic and practicalities. For the investor seeking to avoid complexity they could hold

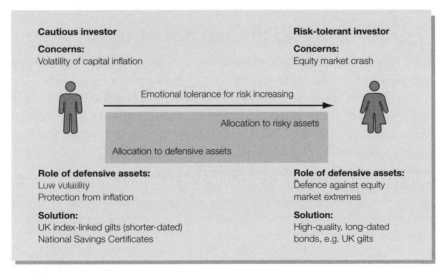

Figure 9.11 Summarising the role of defensive assets

shorter-dated index-linked gilts or National Savings Certificates to balance their risky assets. Failing that they could simply hold cash (see Figure 9.11).

Suggested structures for the defensive assets mix

So, in light of the above arguments and evidence, it becomes clearer what a well-structured defensive portfolio could look like (see Table 9.8). Ideally short-dated index-linked gilts would be used at the more cautious end of the spectrum and longer-dated gilts towards the more risk-tolerant end of the spectrum. The section below provides possible portfolio structures along the risk spectrum. Each investor needs to decide for themselves. The choice is a function of logic, complexity and product availability. Some compromises may need to be made.

Table 9.8   Well-structured defensive portfolios

Defensive assets mix		Smarter Portfolios				
	1	2	3	4	5	6
Basic						
UK cash	100%	80%	60%	40%	20%	0%
Risk-mitigation based						
UK index-linked gilts (short-dated)	100%	75%	50%	25%	0%	0%
UK gilts (long-dated)	0%	5%	10%	15%	20%	0%
Total allocation	**100%**	**80%**	**50%**	**40%**	**20%**	**0%**

9.7 Portfolios along the risk spectrum

Now that we have our growth-oriented and defensive asset mixes sorted out, we can combine these to offer different choices along the risk spectrum. These are set out in Table 9.9. They employ no extraordinary insight or the use of seemingly sophisticated software to create, just some common sense, a little bit of insight and some simple guidelines. As you can see, these are defined by incremental steps in growth-oriented assets of 20 per cent. Much below this and the portfolios are too similar to be able to distinguish any real difference between them and one risks levels of spurious accuracy in dividing up the risk spectrum much further. But do so if you wish to! Remember that there are no right or wrong answers, just some that are probably better than others.

Table 9.9   Portfolio choices along the risk spectrum

Home bias – global style tilts	Smarter Investing Portfolios					
	1	2	3	4	5	6
Growth assets mix						
UK equity market	0%	3%	6%	9%	12%	15%
UK value equities	0%	1%	2%	3%	4%	5%
UK smaller company equities	0%	1%	2%	3%	4%	5%
World ex-UK equities	0%	5%	10%	15%	20%	25%
World ex-UK value equities	0%	2%	4%	6%	0%	10%
World ex-UK smaller company equities	0%	2%	4%	6%	8%	10%
Emerging market equities	0%	2%	4%	6%	8%	10%
Global commercial real estate	0%	2%	4%	6%	8%	10%
Commodities	0%	2%	4%	6%	8%	10%
Defensive assets mix[(1)]						
UK Index-linked gilts (short-dated)[(2)]	100%	75%	50%	25%	0%	0%
UK gilts (long-dated)	0%	5%	10%	15%	20%	0%
Total allocation	**100%**	**100%**	**100%**	**100%**	**100%**	**100%**

Portfolio parameters[(3)]						
Expected real (geometric) return %	2.0	3.1	4.1	4.9	5.7	6.3
Expected risk %	3	4	8	11	15	19

(1) A basic alternative is to hold cash, but with the associated inflation and credit risks.
(2) In the absence of suitable products a combination of cash and longer-dated index-linked gilts could be used.
(3) Based on the asset class assumptions made – see Chapter 11.

Interpreting the risk and return numbers

Table 9.9 provides some rough guidance of the expected long-term annualised returns, which are based on the assumptions made for each building block and the allocations to each in the portfolio. These assumptions and how they were arrived at are set out in Chapter 11, which gives a greater insight into each asset class. What is important to remember is that (a) one can never be certain what the rate of return will be, and (b) that even if this estimate is correct over your investment lifetime, it will not be delivered steadily, year on year, especially with more risky portfolios.

The risk number provided is the expected annualised standard deviation of returns, which the industry calls risk. What it describes is actually quite useful. As a rule of thumb, if you add the risk percentage either side of the average return, this roughly defines the range within which two out of three annual returns is likely to fall. Use the expected return number as an approximation for the (arithmetic) average return – it is close enough for our purposes. So, for Smarter Portfolio 6, above, this would give a range of +25 per cent to −13 per cent (6.3% +/−19%). Nineteen out of twenty returns should fall within +44 per cent to −32 per cent. Remember that outliers are likely to occur in real life, perhaps more frequently than the statistics suggest. A portfolio like Portfolio 6 would have lost around 20 per cent or so of its value in 2008 – a painful, but not unexpected, outcome given the rough-and-ready range estimate above. Again, remember that in investing forewarned is forearmed.

In the next chapter we look at each of these portfolios in turn and link them to both your emotional tolerance for taking risk and your financial need to take it, which you explored in Chapters 6 and 7.

References

Bernstein, P. (1996) *Against the Gods*, New York: J. Wiley & Sons.

French, K. R. and Poterba, J. M. (1991) 'Japanese and US cross-border common stock investments', NBER Working Paper No. R1537.

Loeper, D. B. (2003) *The Alternative to Alternative Classes*, Wealthcare Capital Management.

Markowitz, H. (1952) 'Portfolio selection', *Journal of Finance*, VII(1).

Michaud, R. O. (1989) 'The Markowitz Optimization Enigma: Is Optimized Optimal?', *Financial Analysts Journal*, 45(1) (January/February): pp. 31–42.

Siegel, L. (1997) 'Are Stocks Risky? Two lessons', *Journal of Portfolio Management,* Spring 1997, pp. 29–34.

Tobin, J. (1957) 'Liquidity preference as behaviour towards risk', *The Revue of Economic Studies*, no. 67.

Zweig, J. (2007) *Your money and your brain*, London: Souvenir Press, p. 4.

10

Smarter portfolio choice

This chapter will hopefully help you to decide on the portfolio that is most appropriate for your circumstances. This is a function of your emotional ability to tolerate risk as well as your financial need and capacity to take it. You will be guided by your psychometric risk profile, if you undertake one, as well as the rate of return that you require to meet your goals and the certainty that it will be delivered by the portfolio you choose.

Take a look at the portfolio matrix in Table 10.1 below. It provides a useful comparison of the general properties of each of the six Smarter Portfolios. Remember that looking into the past is a useful exercise, but it cannot foretell the investment lifetime that you will experience. That said, one lesson can be learned; if you want higher returns you have to take higher market risks (i.e. own more growth-oriented, risky assets).

10. 1 Understanding and using the matrix

You can use the grid to try to match up your emotional risk profile score with the rate of return that you need to achieve your financial goals in the 'Upside opportunity' section. It then makes sense to look at the 'Downside insight' section that provides some pointers as to what you can expect from different portfolios. You can see, for example, that Smarter Portfolio 6 would have been down around 37 per cent in the crash of 2000–2002, whereas Smarter Portfolio 3 would have lost around 13 per cent. This can be used (as a very rudimentary alternative) in the absence of a psychometric risk profile score that helps to point you towards a sensible level of risky assets. Even if you have undertaken one, looking at the hard numbers on

Table 10.1 Portfolio matrix: comparing the six portfolios

Smarter Portfolio	6	5	4	3	2	1
Growth-oriented assets	100%	80%	60%	40%	20%	0%
Defensive assets	0%	20%	40%	60%	80%	100%
Emotional risk profile (FinaMetrica)						
Best fit score	100–89	88–69	68–54	53–39	38–17	16–0
Discomfort level	<76	<60	<45	<29	<2	n.a.
Minimum sensible horizon (years)	>15	>15	>15	>10	>5	>3
Upside opportunity						
Annualised real (after-inflation) return						
1900–2008 (1)	5%	4%	4%	3%	2%	1%
1990–2008 (2)	4.2%	4.2%	4.1%	3.9%	3.6%	3.2%
1990–2008 – growth of £100	£220	£219	£215	£207	£196	£183
Expected long-term return (3)	6.3%	5.7%	4.9%	4.1%	3.1%	2.0%
Years to double your money	11	13	15	18	23	36
Annualised real return with an 80% chance of being achieved (4)						
Over 10 years	1.5%	2.0%	2.0%	2.0%	2.0%	1.0%
Over 20 years	3.0%	3.0%	3.0%	2.5%	2.5%	1.5%
Over 30 years	3.5%	3.5%	3.0%	3.0%	2.5%	1.5%
Downside insight						
Risk (%)						
1990–2008	15%	12%	9%	6%	3%	2%
Expected (5)	19%	15%	11%	8%	4%	3%
Peak-to-trough falls						
1900–2008 (1973–1974) (6)	−73%	−61%	−49%	−34%	−18%	0%
1990–2008 (Aug 00–Jan 03)	−37%	−29%	−21%	−13%	−5%	−2%

Risk of loss (7)

Over 10 years

Over 20 years

Over 30 years

| | < 1-in-20 | | 1-in-10 to 1-in-20 | | 1-in-10 to 1-in-5 |

Risk of running out of money in retirement over 30 years (8)
Withdrawal per £100,000 of starting capital

£3,000 per annum

£4,000 per annum

£5,000 per annum

| | < 1-in-10 | | 1-in-5 to 1-in-10 | | > 1-in-5 |

losses can at least help you to manage your own expectations. During 2008, for example, the perception of risk rose dramatically as hard losses were suffered by investors, despite the likelihood that risk tolerance per se remains pretty constant through time.

The following notes are important in making sure you understand what key numbers/insights represent.

1   The returns for the period 1900–2008 represent the real (after-inflation) returns from the UK equity market in the same proportion as the allocation to risky 'growth-oriented' assets described in the Smarter Portfolio structure. As we explored above, the risk-free asset we will use in portfolios is short-dated index-linked gilts (or National Savings Certificates). These have only been around since 1984. They have little interest rate (maturity) risk and all returns and capital are broadly protected from inflation. As such, you would expect them to deliver positive real returns in all periods. This has been modelled using a 1 per cent real return prorated by the proportion of defensive assets in the Smarter Portfolio. A bit crude but not unreasonable. Using T-bills, on the other hand, would have magnified losses unreasonably due to the very high inflation in the 1970s and the erosion of purchasing power that resulted.

2   This uses market indices that are comparable to the market risk factors that we want exposure to. The indices used in the Smarter Portfolio models are listed in Appendix 1. Note that UK T-bills have been used to model short-dated index-linked gilts. Over the period 1990 to 2008 they have delivered low single-digit real returns. No costs of any kind have been deducted from the returns.

3   The expected return is the annualised average return that is derived from the asset allocation of the Smarter Portfolio (rebalanced annually) and the return, risk and correlation assumptions for each asset class in the mix. It was calculated using a piece of software called MVOPlus (www.effisols.com), developed by William Bernstein, a highly regarded investment thinker and practitioner. No costs of any kind have been deducted from the returns.

4   The annualised real return with an 80 per cent chance of being achieved is estimated using a Monte Carlo simulation process. This picks returns from the specific Smarter Portfolio return distribution, which is defined by its return (3, above) and risk (5, below). It selects a return for each forty years of an investment's life. It then creates 10,000 investment lives, providing a means for estimating the return with an 80 per cent likelihood of occurring.

5 The expected risk number is derived in the same way as the expected return in (3) above.

6 The 1900–2008 peak-to-trough represents the falls in the growth-oriented assets of the specific Smarter Portfolio. A zero per cent return is assumed from defensive assets which should return positive real returns in any year, given their structure. This assumption keeps things simple and provides a sense of magnitude of 'worst-case' markets; 1973–1974 places recent market turmoil in perspective.

7 The risk of loss is estimated using the risk and return distribution and a Monte Carlo simulation, as described in (4), above. Note that a 1-in-20 chance is a 5 per cent chance; a 1-in-10 chance is a 10 per cent chance and a 1-in-5 chance is a 20 per cent chance.

8 The chance of running out of money in retirement is based on the amount of income you draw each year (in today's money terms, i.e. taking account of inflation) per £100,000 of starting capital. This is one of the key numbers that you needed to decide upon in Chapter 6, as you developed your goals.

10.2 Smarter Portfolio insights

On the next six pages you will find a more detailed look at each of the Smarter Portfolios 1 to 6 (see Figures 10.1–10.6). Once you have narrowed down your likely suitable portfolio using the portfolio matrix, you can then use the relevant figure to look more closely at the characteristics of this portfolio. Compare and contrast different Smarter Portfolios to work out where you feel most comfortable.

Note that the previous notes correspond to those marked on each of the following figures.

Smarter Portfolio 6

Portfolio strategy

		Suggested time horizon	Emotional risk tolerance	
Risky	100%	Minimum	FinaMetrica – Best Fit score	100–89
Defensive	0%	15 years	FinaMetrica – Discomfort level	<76

Return insights

Annualised real returns

Historical	
1900–2008 – UK Equity (1)	4.8%
1990–2008 – Portfolio (2)	4.2%
1990–2008 – Growth of £100	£220
Expected real returns (3)	
Annualised	6.3%
Years to double your money	11

Portfolio real returns 1990–2008

Expected real returns (4)			
Likelihood	10 years	20 years	30 years
90%	–1.5%	1.0%	2.0%
80%	1.5%	3.0%	3.5%
70%	3.5%	4.0%	4.5%
60%	5.0%	5.5%	5.5%
50%	6.3%	6.3%	6.3%

Risk insights

Risk–Annualised standard deviation of returns

Risk % (5)	19%

Cash-like ▬▬▬▬▬▬▬▬▬▬▬▬▬▬● Equity-like

Annual real returns 1990–2008 (2)

Cumulative real losses 1999–2008 (2)

□ Portfolio 6   ■ UK equities □ Portfolio 6

Peak-to-trough (real returns)

1990–2008 (2)	Fall (%)	–37%	Fall (months)	29	Recovery	30
1900–2008 (6)	Fall (%)	–73%	Fall (years)	2	Recovery	9

Worst case loss of purchasing power 1900–2008 (6)

Effect on £100	1 year	5 years	10 years	20 years	30 years	40 years
1900–2008	£42	£35	£44	£65	£179	£241

Risk of loss (7)

Magnitude	1 Year	5 years	10 years	20 years	30 years	40 years
Loss (6)						
Loss >10%						
Loss >20%						

Risk of retirement ruin (8)

Years	Withdrawal rate – income taken per £100,000 of starting capital					
	£2,000	£3,000	£4,000	£5,000	£6,000	£7,000
Over 10 years						
Over 20 years						
Over 30 years						
Over 40 years						

Negligible	<1-in-10	>1-in-10	>1-in-5	>1-in-2

Figure 10.1 Detailed insight: Smarter Portfolio 6

Smarter Portfolio 5

Portfolio strategy

Risky	80%
Defensive	20%

Suggested time horizon

Minimum
15 years

Emotional risk tolerance

FinaMetrica – Best fit score	88–69
FinaMetrica – Discomfort level	<60

Return insights

Annualised real returns

Historical	
1900–2008 – UK Equity (1)	4.4%
1990–2008 – Portfolio (2)	4.2%
1990–2008 – Growth of £100	£219
Expected real returns (3)	
Annualised	5.7%
Years to double your money	13

Portfolio real returns 1990–2008

Expected real returns (4)			
Likelihood	10 years	20 years	30 years
90%	−0.4%	1.4%	2.2%
80%	1.7%	2.9%	3.4%
70%	3.3%	4.0%	4.3%
60%	4.6%	4.9%	5.0%
50%	5.8%	5.8%	5.7%

Risk insights

Risk – Annualised standard deviation of returns

Risk % (5)	15%

Cash-like ▬▬▬▬▬▬▬▬▬▬●▬▬ Equity-like

Annual real returns 1990–2008 (2)

Portfolio 5

Cumulative real losses 1999–2008 (2)

UK equities Portfolio 5

Peak-to-trough (real returns)

1990–2008 (2)	Fall (%)	−29%	Fall (months)	29	Recovery	30
1900–2008 (6)	Fall (%)	−61%	Fall (years)	2	Recovery	8

Worst case loss of purchasing power 1900–2008 (6)

Effect on £100	1 year	5 years	10 years	20 years	30 years	40 years
1900–2008	£54	£48	£53	£72	£173	£238

Risk of loss (7)

Magnitude	1 Year	5 years	10 years	20 years	30 years	40 years
Loss (6)						
Loss >10%						
Loss >20%						

Risk of retirement ruin (8)

Years	Withdrawal rate – income taken per £100,000 of starting capital					
	£2,000	£3,000	£4,000	£5,000	£6,000	£7,000
Over 10 years						
Over 20 years						
Over 30 years						
Over 40 years						

Negligible	<1-in-10	>1-in-10	>1-in-5	>1-in-2

Figure 10.2 Detailed insight: Smarter Portfolio 5

Smarter Portfolio 4

Portfolio strategy

Risky	60%
Defensive	40%

Suggested time horizon

Minimum
15 years

Emotional risk tolerance

FinaMetrica – Best fit score	68–54
FinaMetrica – Discomfort level	<45

Return insights

Annualised real returns

Historical	
1900–2008 – UK Equity (1)	3.8%
1990–2008 – Portfolio (2)	4.1%
1990–2008 – Growth of £100	£215
Expected real returns (3)	
Annualised	4.9%
Years to double your money	15

Portfolio real returns 1990–2008

Expected real returns (4)			
Likelihood	10 years	20 years	30 years
90%	0.5%	1.7%	2.3%
80%	2.0%	2.8%	3.2%
70%	3.1%	3.7%	3.8%
60%	4.0%	4.3%	4.4%
50%	4.9%	4.9%	4.9%

Risk insights

Risk – Annualised standard deviation of returns

Risk % (5)	11%

Cash-like ●━━━━━━━━━━━━ Equity-like

Annual real returns 1990–2008 (2)

Cumulative real losses 1999–2008 (2)

Peak-to-trough (real returns)

1990–2008 (2)	Fall (%)	−21%	Fall (months)	29	Recovery	28
1900–2008 (6)	Fall (%)	−49%	Fall (years)	2	Recovery	8

Worst case loss of purchasing power 1900–2008 (6)

Effect on £100	1 year	5 years	10 years	20 years	30 years	40 years
1900–2008	£65	£61	£63	£80	£158	£203

Risk of loss (7)

Magnitude	1 Year	5 years	10 years	20 years	30 years	40 years
Loss (6)						
Loss >10%						
Loss >20%						

Risk of retirement ruin (8)

Years	Withdrawal rate – income taken per £100,000 of starting capital					
	£2,000	£3,000	£4,000	£5,000	£6,000	£7,000
Over 10 years						
Over 20 years						
Over 30 years						
Over 40 years						

Negligible	<1-in-10	>1-in-10	>1-in-5	>1-in-2

Figure 10.3 Detailed insight: Smarter Portfolio 4

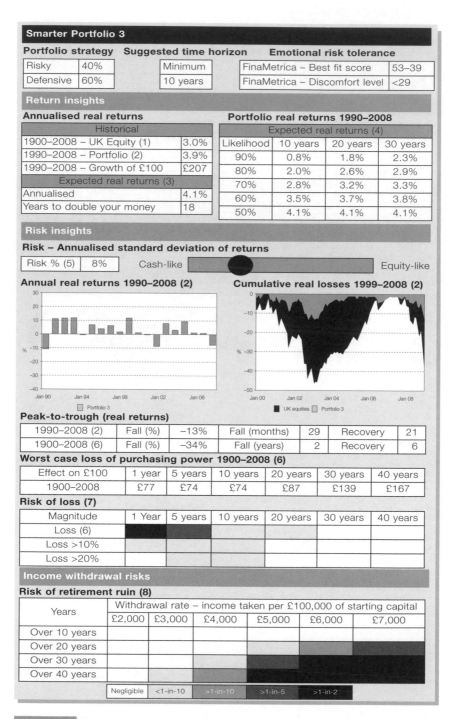

Smarter Portfolio 3

Portfolio strategy

Risky	40%
Defensive	60%

Suggested time horizon

Minimum
10 years

Emotional risk tolerance

FinaMetrica – Best fit score	53–39
FinaMetrica – Discomfort level	<29

Return insights

Annualised real returns

Historical	
1900–2008 – UK Equity (1)	3.0%
1990–2008 – Portfolio (2)	3.9%
1990–2008 – Growth of £100	£207
Expected real returns (3)	
Annualised	4.1%
Years to double your money	18

Portfolio real returns 1990–2008

Expected real returns (4)			
Likelihood	10 years	20 years	30 years
90%	0.8%	1.8%	2.3%
80%	2.0%	2.6%	2.9%
70%	2.8%	3.2%	3.3%
60%	3.5%	3.7%	3.8%
50%	4.1%	4.1%	4.1%

Risk insights

Risk – Annualised standard deviation of returns

Risk % (5)	8%

Cash-like ———— Equity-like

Annual real returns 1990–2008 (2)

☐ Portfolio 3

Cumulative real losses 1999–2008 (2)

■ UK equities ☐ Portfolio 3

Peak-to-trough (real returns)

1990–2008 (2)	Fall (%)	−13%	Fall (months)	29	Recovery	21
1900–2008 (6)	Fall (%)	−34%	Fall (years)	2	Recovery	6

Worst case loss of purchasing power 1900–2008 (6)

Effect on £100	1 year	5 years	10 years	20 years	30 years	40 years
1900–2008	£77	£74	£74	£87	£139	£167

Risk of loss (7)

Magnitude	1 Year	5 years	10 years	20 years	30 years	40 years
Loss (6)						
Loss >10%						
Loss >20%						

Income withdrawal risks

Risk of retirement ruin (8)

Years	Withdrawal rate – income taken per £100,000 of starting capital					
	£2,000	£3,000	£4,000	£5,000	£6,000	£7,000
Over 10 years						
Over 20 years						
Over 30 years						
Over 40 years						

Negligible	<1-in-10	>1-in-10	>1-in-5	>1-in-2

Figure 10.4 Detailed insight: Smarter Portfolio 3

Smarter Portfolio 2

Portfolio strategy   Suggested time horizon   Emotional risk tolerance

Risky	20%		Minimum		FinaMetrica – Best fit score	38–17
Defensive	80%		5 years		FinaMetrica – Discomfort level	<2

Return insights

Annualised real returns

Historical	
1900–2008 – UK Equity (1)	2.1%
1990–2008 – Portfolio (2)	3.6%
1990–2008 – Growth of £100	£196
Expected real returns (3)	
Annualised	3.1%
Years to double your money	23

Portfolio real returns 1990–2008

Expected real returns (4)			
Likelihood	10 years	20 years	30 years
90%	1.5%	1.9%	2.2%
80%	2.0%	2.4%	2.5%
70%	2.5%	2.6%	2.7%
60%	2.8%	2.9%	2.9%
50%	3.1%	3.1%	3.1%

Risk insights

Risk – Annualised standard deviation of returns

Risk % (5)	8%	Cash-like ▬▬▬▬▬▬▬▬▬▬▬▬ Equity-like

Annual real returns 1990–2008 (2)   Cumulative real losses 1999–2008 (2)

Peak-to-trough (real returns)

1990–2008 (2)	Fall (%)	−5%	Fall (months)	10	Recovery	10
1900–2008 (6)	Fall (%)	−18%	Fall (years)	2	Recovery	3

Worst case loss of purchasing power 1900–2008 (6)

Effect on £100	1 year	5 years	10 years	20 years	30 years	40 years
1900–2008	£88	£87	£86	£94	£120	£132

Risk of loss (7)

Magnitude	1 Year	5 years	10 years	20 years	30 years	40 years
Loss						
Loss >10%						
Loss >20%						

Risk of retirement ruin (8)

Years	Withdrawal rate – income taken per £100,000 of starting capital					
	£2,000	£3,000	£4,000	£5,000	£6,000	£7,000
Over 10 years						
Over 20 years						
Over 30 years						
Over 40 years						

Negligible	<1-in-10	>1-in-10	>1-in-5	>1-in-2

Figure 10.5 Detailed insight: Smarter Portfolio 2

Smarter Portfolio 1

Portfolio strategy

Risky	0%
Defensive	100%

Suggested time horizon

Minimum
3 years

Emotional risk tolerance

FinaMetrica – Best fit score	16–0
FinaMetrica – Discomfort level	n.a.

Return insights

Annualised real returns

Historical	
1900–2008 – UK Equity (1)	1.0%
1990–2008 – Portfolio (2)	3.2%
1990–2008 – Growth of £100	£183
Expected real returns (3)	
Annualised	2.0%
Years to double your money	36

Portfolio real returns 1990–2008

Expected real returns (4)			
Likelihood	10 years	20 years	30 years
90%	0.8%	1.1%	1.3%
80%	1.2%	1.4%	1.5%
70%	1.5%	1.7%	1.7%
60%	1.8%	1.8%	1.9%
50%	2.0%	2.0%	2.0%

Risk insights

Risk – Annualised standard deviation of returns

Risk % (5)	3%

Cash-like ⬤▬▬▬▬▬▬▬▬▬▬ Equity-like

Annual real returns 1990–2008 (2)

☐ Portfolio 1

Cumulative real losses 1999–2008 (2)

■ UK equities ☐ Portfolio 1

Peak-to-trough (real returns)

1990–2008 (2)	Fall (%)	0%	Fall (months)	0	Recovery	0
1900–2008 (6)	Fall (%)	0%	Fall (years)	0	Recovery	0

Worst case loss of purchasing power 1900–2008 (6)

Effect on £100	1 year	5 years	10 years	20 years	30 years	40 years
1900–2008	£100	£100	£100	£100	£100	£100

Risk of loss (7)

Magnitude	1 Year	5 years	10 years	20 years	30 years	40 years
Loss						
Loss >10%						
Loss >20%						

Risk of retirement ruin (8)

Years	Withdrawal rate – income taken per £100,000 of starting capital					
	£2,000	£3,000	£4,000	£5,000	£6,000	£7,000
Over 10 years						
Over 20 years						
Over 30 years						
Over 40 years						

Negligible	<1-in-10	>1-in-10	>1-in-5	>1-in-2

Figure 10.6 Detailed insight: Smarter Portfolio 1

11

An insight into key asset classes

This chapter puts some more meat on the bones of Chapter 8. The main focus is to provide a real understanding of the nature of equity investments. At the end of the day they are the core 'whisky' that drives portfolio returns and which are then diluted using shorter-dated index-linked gilts. The simplest, but reasonably effective, portfolio would be a combination of a UK (or global) index tracker fund (or Exchange Traded Fund – ETF – explained in the next section) combined with National Savings Certificates that are index-linked. How difficult was that!

Understanding the role of each asset class in your portfolio is important to feeling comfortable with it. If you don't get the story for the asset class, then simply exclude it from your portfolio. You don't want nagging doubts undermining your confidence in the robustness of your portfolio.

11.1 The thrills and spills of equities

Understanding the thrills and, just as importantly, the spills of being an owner of equities is central to understanding the challenges in both building and preserving wealth.

There are two emotional extremes that afflict equity investors: on the one hand, particularly in rising markets, it's easy to begin to believe that they are a route to quick wealth creation, and aren't that risky; after all, from 1980 to 1999, eighteen of the twenty years generated positive returns, and half of those generated after-inflation returns of more than 20 per cent a year. A sum of £1,000 invested over this period grew to £12,000 – now that was thrilling! In Figure 11.1 you will see

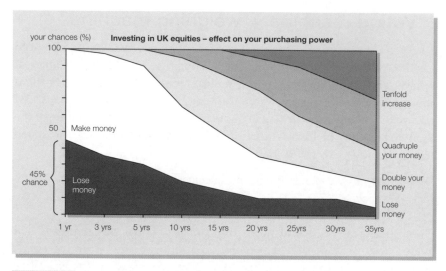

Figure 11.1 Chances of outcomes in equity investing

that the twenty-year bull market that multiplied your wealth more than tenfold was a rare event and that losses are as much a part of the game in the short term. Over time, gains begin to predominate as the hard cash generated by real companies begins to win through over sentiment.

On the other hand, the 40 per cent fall from 2000 to the end of 2002 was quite a spill, destroying large amounts of wealth for those drawn into the delusion that equities were a risk-free route to riches. That was quickly followed by 2008, when markets sank back to their 2003 low in dramatic fashion, losing over 35 per cent from the previous peak in late 2006. That's quite a sequence of spills, but far from the worst that has happened in the UK, let alone in other markets around the world.

Smarter investing requires you to get a handle on the thrills and spills of equities and how you can use them to drive your wealth accumulation and why it is so important to make sure that you hold sufficient insurance, by owning defensive assets to protect you if the worst happens, which it might.

11.2 Voting machine v. weighing machine

To get to the root of the issues that you face as an equity investor, you need to think about why equities can deliver long-term, mid-single-digit real returns, and why from time to time returns are simply so far away, both on the upside and the downside, from this long-run average. Let's perhaps start unravelling this issue with a 1934 quote from Benjamin Graham, one of the founding fathers of today's investment management industry. He stated (Graham and Dodd, 1996) that:

'In the short run the market is a voting machine; in the long run, it is a weighing machine.'

Spend a bit of time thinking about this statement, as it elegantly defines the fundamental difference between what investors are willing to pay for shares in a company at a point in time and what their true value is given the state of their company in the real world. When investors disconnect the relationship between real life and markets, problems arise.

The short-term voting machine

As a holder of equities, you become part-owner in real businesses, either in the UK or overseas, depending on what building block you are using. In the UK, there are about 2,600 public companies listed on the London Stock Exchange, AIM and Techmark exchanges, which you have the ability both to own and, through your rights as a shareholder, to have some say in how they are run. Globally there are more than 15,000 to become part-owner in. In return for investing capital, your reward comes in two distinct forms: the regular dividends that you get paid in cash; and the capital appreciation, or otherwise, reflected in changes in the share price. Together, these give you the total market return from your investment.

However, this total market return does not necessarily reflect the underlying value of companies and markets in the real world, but investors' emotional perceptions of what they are worth and these change with market sentiment. Some of the increases in share prices you experience may reflect a speculative change in perceptions, creating gains as it waxes and losses as it wanes. This is the market operating as a voting machine, as Graham puts it.

The amount investors are willing to pay for each £1 of future earnings depends on sentiment prevailing at the time and it is reflected in the ratio of the price of a share to its earnings, otherwise known as its price/earnings ratio. Higher ratios reflect the increased optimism that investors feel, reflected in the higher amount that investors will pay for future earnings. Changes in price that reflect changes in perception, and an increased willingness to pay up for earnings reflected in changes in P/E, are speculative returns.

Playing the game of capturing these shorter-term changes in sentiment is more akin to gambling than investing. A classic case is the technology boom and bust of the late 1990s and early 2000s, when investors paid high prices for non-existent or unlikely future earnings. John Bogle, a wise and rational investor, summed up investing as opposed to speculating most eloquently as follows (Bogle, 2002b):

'If there was a single dominant failing of the recent bubble, it was the market's overbearing focus on the momentary precision of the price of a stock rather than on the eternal vagueness of the intrinsic value of a corporation. Nonetheless, the price of a stock is perception, and acting on that perception is speculation. The value of a corporation is reality and acting on that reality is investment.'

Always beware of so-called experts who say 'it's different this time' and that a re-evaluation of earnings is required to explain why you should pay so much for earnings. This is probably a pretty good signal that a bubble is about to burst! Stock prices will fall when these above-normal earnings fail to materialise, which has always proved to be the outcome in investment bubbles.

The long-term weighing machine

In reality, the profits (earnings) of a company grow through increased sales and improved profit margins; improved sales come from good product development, focused marketing, well-chosen segments in which to compete, motivated sales teams, and taking care of existing clients. Better profit margins come from improved productivity through better skilled employees, better processes, strong corporate governance and technological efficiencies. Value is created in the real world by hard work, not wishful thinking. This true value is sometimes referred to as intrinsic value, a phrase coined by Benjamin Graham.

Returns from equities come from the dividends that companies pay (and in aggregate the market pays) and the capitalisation of their profits (earnings), resulting in a change in the price of stocks and in aggregate of the market. These dividends, plus your capital gains, equate to the total market return that you receive. However, only some of the price change is due to the underlying economics of each company, represented by their changing profitability and thus growth (or decline) in earnings per share; the rest comes from changes in investor sentiment.

Imagine that a company managed to increase its profits so that its earnings per share rose from £1.00 to £1.05, a growth rate in earnings of 5 per cent over a year. At the start of the year the P/E ratio was 15 and thus the price of the shares was £15 (i.e. £1.00 × 15). At the end of the year, if the P/E ratio remained constant at 15, the price of the shares would rise from £15 to £15.75 (£1.05 × 15), in other words a 5 per cent rise in price or capital gain, and the company also paid a dividend of 3 per cent, giving you a return from the endeavours of the company of 8 per cent. The dividends that you receive and the capitalisation of earnings growth, at a constant P/E, are sometimes referred to as investment returns and represent the return from the endeavours of the company. (You should note that a significant proportion of returns comes from the dividends you receive from your equity investments. This may be contrary to the belief that has grown up over the past couple of decades where changes in price seemed to contribute far more to returns than dividends.)

Imagine, though, that in this same year, investors began to feel bullish about the economy, the market in general and the firm in particular and were now willing to pay sixteen times earnings for the shares, instead of fifteen. This would result in a price rise from £15 to £16.80 (16 × £1.05) or a 12 per cent increase in price. Your total market return would be: 3 per cent dividend + 12 per cent price change = 15 per cent.

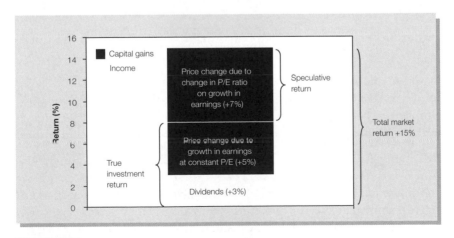

Figure 11.2 The elements of market returns

So, the difference between investment returns and market returns, in this case 7 per cent, is due to investors' changing perceptions affecting the level of the P/E ratio. This difference is sometimes referred to as the speculative return (see Figure 11.2).

The magnitude and longevity of these differences tell us that evaluating the intrinsic value of a company, or a market as a whole, is difficult and that emotions seem to cloud investment judgement, sometimes significantly. Strong growth in an economy tends to reinforce investor behaviours such as overconfidence, over-optimism and unwarranted self-belief, which, at extremes, leads to bubbles and subsequent busts. As Warren Buffett (1996) said:

> *'Nothing sedates rationality like large doses of effortless money.'*

In the long run, speculation zeros out

In the end, though, the link between investment returns and market returns must reflect what is really happening in the underlying economy and business world, a point well worth remembering. Put another way, long-run returns are attributable to investment returns and not short-term speculative excesses. In fact, in the USA, since 1872, real market returns and investment returns were comparable at around 6.5 per cent. Buffett again makes the point succinctly about investors in his company Berkshire Hathaway (Buffett, 1997):

> *'The longer a shareholder holds his shares, the more bearing Berkshire's business results will have on his financial experience – and the less it will matter what premium or discount to intrinsic value prevails when he buys or sells his stock.'*

Estimating the intrinsic value of an enterprise is not easy for most of us without the insight, experience and enthusiasm of the likes of Buffett.

11.3 An insight into equity market returns

As we explored, when constructing the Smarter Portfolios, equities are the engines of portfolio growth, delivering on average around 5 per cent after inflation per year in the UK. That means doubling your purchasing power once every fourteen years or so. That in itself should be quite a thrill, in return for having the stomach to hold them, although you may not, at first glance, think so. However, over thirty-five years, each £1 of spending power invested would buy over five times as much as you started with. That is the true power of time and compounding. At times, you may get an even bigger

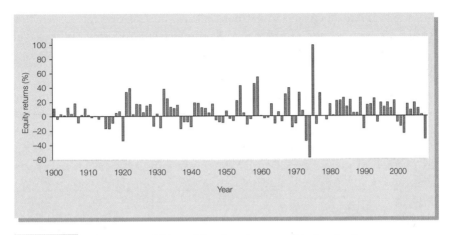

Figure 11.3 **Investing in UK equities is a bumpy ride (real returns 1900–2008)**   *Source: Barclays Equity Gilt Study, 2009.*

thrill, but don't bank on it. Be happy if you achieve the long-run average return you are hoping for. In fact, in investing, generating positive real returns of any sort over the period that you are investing is a bonus and reaching your target rate of return especially pleasing.

Taking a brief look at historical equity returns, here using the UK market, what is evident is that owning equities is a risky business, if you view risk as being the likelihood of suffering repeated highs and lows to reach your goals (see Figure 11.3).

If we now look at equity returns over different windows of time (Figure 11.3 shows single-year returns) we can see that time appears to have the effect of smoothing out the highs and lows. Looking at the same data series but working out the annualised (compound) return that equities delivered investors during this period, in real (after-inflation) terms we can quickly see why phrases like *'equities for the long term'* apply (see Figure 11.4).

Looking at Figure 11.4 reveals a few interesting insights. First, on average over this period UK equities have delivered real increases to investor purchasing power in the region of 5 per cent a year, providing a good hedge against long-term inflation. After all, companies can raise their prices and the value of their assets rise too. Second, several ten-year periods have existed where returns have been negative, including the ten years to the end of 2008. In the 2000s our perception of equity market risk has been heightened, particularly in comparison to the bullish 1980s and 1990s. Yet in the UK at least, all thirty-year periods have delivered positive increases

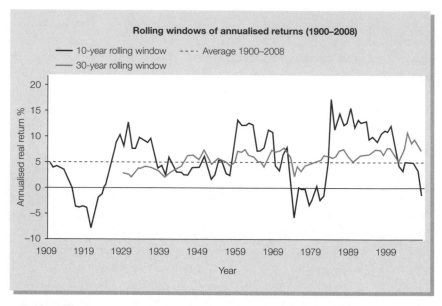

Figure 11.4 Equity investment is a longer-term strategy

Source: Barclays Equity Gilt Study, 2009.

to investors' purchasing power. Third, equity returns tend to revert towards the long-term return.

Reversion towards the mean

Early in my career I was given the insightful piece of wisdom that markets were like rubber bands stretched between two long-term points in time. At times, they are pulled away from their relatively relaxed norms to points at which they become stretched by the force of the hand of the speculative market. The further from the norm they go, the greater the force trying to return them to their unstressed position. At some point, which is hard to pick, they will spring back, sometimes overshooting dramatically for a time. Not a bad word picture to bear in mind.

Periods when markets have been overvalued (i.e. P/E ratios have been higher than average) have tended to be followed by periods of lower-than-average returns as markets return to mean levels of value, and vice versa. The fallibility of this approach is that the magnitude and longevity of periods of outperformance can be extremely extended, and the market turning points and speed of mean reversion cannot be judged with any accuracy. If it were easy, investment professionals would prove it in outperformance – something we simply do not see en masse, as we explored earlier in the book.

There are many documented instances of rational investors holding out against the opportunity to make speculative returns because it was felt that the market had moved away from fundamental economic reality, including Warren Buffett and his 'not getting' the tech-stock thing. At the time, even the Sage of Omaha came in for some serious, but ultimately unwarranted, stick from his critics.

Equity returns on a global basis

Around the world, people have generally fared well in real terms by being investors in equities over the long run (see Figure 11.5). The 'weighing machine' that Benjamin Graham refers to is in effect weighing all of the effort, hard work, innovation, creativity, productivity and determination of managers and employees day in, day out, which have contributed to the growth of capitalist economies over the past century.

As you can see in Figure 11.5, returns above inflation have ranged from around 3 per cent to 7 per cent. Returns for Japan, Germany and France over the 109-year period were more muted than for the others due to very

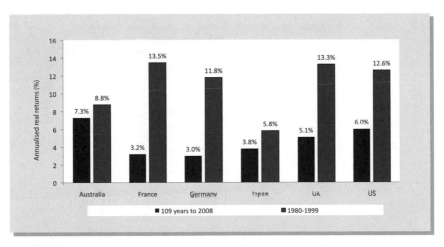

Figure 11.5 **Long-term annualised real returns from global equity markets (1900–2008)**

Source: Copyright © 2009 Elroy Dimson, Paul Marsh and Mike Staunton, Triumph of the Optimists: 101 Years of Global Investment Returns, *Princeton University Press, 2002 and Credit Suisse Global Investment Returns Yearbook 2009.*

high inflation at times earlier in the century. During the bull market from 1980 to 1999, returns were well above the long-run average. These rates of return, where in the UK your purchasing power would have doubled every five to six years, were clearly unsustainable. While we would all like to see this repeated, it is unlikely.

Equity markets crash both frequently and with magnitude

However much you should be trying to focus on long-term goals, the latent fear of periods of serious market trauma should lurk in the back of your mind; markets can and do crash. The surprising thing is not that they do, but just how frequent, traumatic and prolonged they can be both in the UK and around the world. You need to understand the potential frequency, magnitude and longevity of these crashes if you are to give the markets the due respect that they deserve. Owning a diverse portfolio is the only real protection.

Let's take a look at the UK market and see what crashes investors have experienced since 1900. Figure 11.6 shows UK equity market falls since 1900; it reveals the cumulative falls from top to bottom of the market and how long it would have taken for your wealth to return to a level where it could buy as much as when the market was at its previous peak. The data

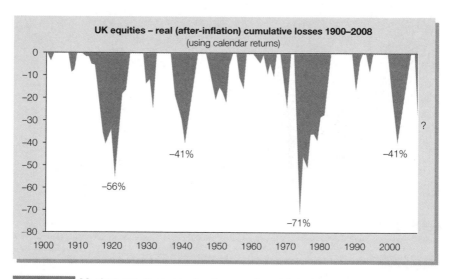

Figure 11.6 Market crashes can be frequent and harsh

Source: Barclays Equity Gilt Study, 2009

is for year-end to year-end, which may to some extent mask the true high to low of the market, but it is good enough for our purposes. Markets have the potential to destroy significant wealth.

Equities have more extreme surprises than statistics suggest. If returns truly fell in a binomially, or a bell-shaped, distribution, as assumed by the industry, then you would expect that the poor returns of 1974 would be expected, statistically, once in 1,400 years and the great returns of 1975 to happen every 33,000 years. Statistics don't fully capture the nature of true markets.

Perhaps the best-known case of investors being caught out by market extremes was the fall of Long Term Capital Management, a hedge fund that blew itself up despite the presence of two Nobel Prize-winning economists and leading market traders. Their models said that what happened couldn't happen; it did, they lost 90 per cent of their capital in a month and effectively went bust. Expect the unexpected might be a good motto to adopt.

Figure 11.6 provides a pretty scary graph and an indication that most investors are likely to need some defensive assets in their portfolio, somewhere (e.g. it may come from owning defensive assets in an investment sense, as described earlier, or from a final salary scheme, state pension, etc.). As you can see, equity market crashes are relatively frequent occurrences.

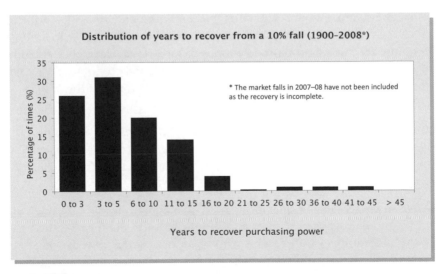

Figure 11.7 It may take longer than you imagine to get back to where you started

Source: Copyright © 2009 Elroy Dimson, Paul Marsh and Mike Staunton, Triumph of the Optimists: 101 Years of Global Investment Returns, *Princeton University Press, 2002 and Credit Suisse Global Investment Returns Yearbook 2009.*

On a global basis market falls have been even more pronounced at times with Japan, Germany and France losing 97 per cent, 91 per cent and 85 per cent around the time of the Second World War. Remember too that some markets closed entirely, such as that in Russia at the time of the Revolution. Being an owner of production is not without its risks!

While it may appear from these numbers that equity markets tend to bounce back reasonably quickly, don't be deceived. Figure 11.7 gives a sample of equity market falls around the globe. Look out.

Let's take a look at equity returns going forward.

11.4 Developed equity market returns

As we established earlier in the book, you should earn a reward for the additional risks that you incur from investing in equities as opposed to owning risk-free cash or bonds. You could lose your money, you have no certainty that dividends will be paid, or any certainty that your shares will appreciate. In the pecking order of claims on a company's assets on liquidation equities are at the bottom of the pile, below secured bankers, bond holders and other creditors; this more risky position (i.e. the higher cost of capital) demands greater reward for investors.

This reward or premium is known as the equity risk premium. Measuring it in the past is simple enough; however, like many arguments in investing, not only are there short-term exceptions to long-run averages, but also different time frames tell different stories. Academics and economists argue ad infinitum about the level of the equity risk premium but as the *Economist* succinctly put it in 2003:

'Yes, over long periods equities have done better than bonds. But there is no equity "premium" – in the sense of a fairly predictable excess over bond returns on which investors can rely . . . Searching for a consistent, God-given premium is a fool's errand.'

All I can say, as a practitioner rather than an academic, is that over the long run a premium appears to exist and should do so in the future, otherwise we would simply invest in bonds with lower risk. As the objective of good, simple, long-term investing is giving yourself the greatest chance of success, and equities have a greater chance of delivering long-term real returns than either bonds or cash, if you are a long-term investor you should have a natural bias towards equities.

As investors, we should be reasonably confident that companies operating in free capitalist economies should be able to continue to pay dividends and to increase their profits and collectively generate real growth in a nation's economy over the long term. They have done so in the past over reasonable periods of time. In the long run, we can therefore be reasonably confident that eventually investment returns and market returns will be similar – they have to be.

In the long run, you would expect the return from equities to be related to the growth in dividends as higher corporate profits (i.e. earnings) are generally assumed to lead to higher dividends. At the end of the day, equity returns have to reflect economic reality. That provides us with a simple model for coming up with future long-term rates of return from equities. In terms of potential levels of return over the next decade, assuming a dividend yield of 3 per cent in the UK and a not unreasonable assumption of earnings growth of 5 per cent in nominal terms and inflation at 3 per cent, and assuming a constant P/E ratio, we get the following estimate of real expected equity return:

3% dividends + 5% earnings growth − 3% inflation = 5% real return

If you believe that the P/E ratio will contract from this point forwards (it would not have been a bad assumption to make by the dispassionate investor in 2000 for example), returns will be lower and vice versa.

The cost of capital of developed markets is similar

It is important to remember that the cost of capital and the expected returns of developed market equities should be roughly the same, long term, across developed markets. On this basis, the use of non-UK developed market allocations is driven entirely by the desire to diversify UK equity risk and not driven by a return opportunity. The issue of home bias was explored previously.

Insights into the future

The problem you are up against as an investor, as you have seen on many occasions throughout this book, is that you have little idea what your own investment path will look like within all the range of possible outcomes that could exist. History gives a feel for what they possibly might look like, but there are no certainties. We can reflect on

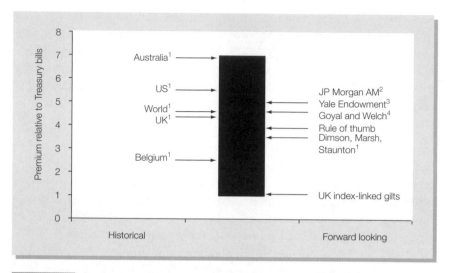

Figure 11.8 Estimating the equity risk premium is not an exact science

Data sources:
1 Dimson, E., Marsh, P. and Staunton, M., 'The Worldwide Equity Premium: A Smaller Puzzle' (7 April 2006). EFA 2006
  Zurich Meetings Paper. Data 1900–2005.
2 JP Morgan Asset Management long-term capital market return assumptions, 30 November 2007.
3 Swenson, D. F. (2000) Pioneering Portfolio Management, New York: The Free Press.
4 Goyal, A. and Welch, I., 'A Comprehensive Look at the Empirical Performance of Equity Premium Prediction' (11
  January 2006). Yale ICF Working Paper No. 04-1.

what has been; use simple rules of thumb like that above; see what
other well-respected practitioners think; and look at what some of the
academic research suggests. Figure 11.8 captures these different
elements, focusing on developed markets. A floor of around 2 per cent
in real (after-inflation) terms exists as one would simply own index-
linked gilts issued by the UK government with little risk instead. On the
left-hand side you can see what the risk premium was across different
markets and how it has been quite wide and averaging a little over 5
per cent above the risk-free rate. On the right-hand side we can see
what others believe the future may hold. A long-term equity risk
premium of around 4 per cent above risk-free assets, giving a real return
of 5 per cent (assuming risk-free assets deliver around 1 per cent real
returns) is not unreasonable.

11.5 Emerging market equities

Investing in emerging markets, i.e. economies that are developing from an
agricultural to an industrial and service-oriented structure, offers two benefits: first, these markets may be out of sync with the UK market, providing

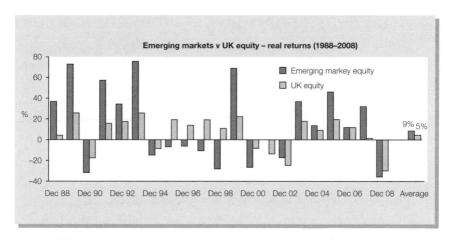

Figure 11.9 Emerging market equities deliver higher expected returns with higher risks
Source: MSCIBarra

a diversification benefit; and second, investors expect higher long-term returns relative to developed equity markets partly due to projected higher growth rates in these economies, but also in compensation for the additional risks they take on, i.e. the cost of capital is higher. These risks include: political instability; currency risk; a lack of open and free markets; higher costs to invest; insufficient legal protection for owners; limited liquidity; and poor corporate governance. Over the period 1988–2008 emerging markets delivered around 9 per cent a year after inflation versus around 5 per cent delivered by UK equities (see Figure 11.9).

Market fads of chasing, for example, BRIC economies (Brazil, Russia, India and China) are common when advisers talk of emerging markets, but should be avoided. It makes more sense to remain broadly diversified across all emerging markets. Due to the volatile nature of emerging market investments and the increasing globalisation of equity market trauma, an allocation to emerging markets should be moderate and based on the expectation, but not guarantee, of enhanced returns and diversification benefit. Figure 11.9 illustrates just how volatile investment in emerging markets can be on a standalone basis. Remember that as part of a portfolio they do contribute positive attributes.

11.6 Value (less financially healthy) companies

As we explored in Chapter 8, these are often described as companies that are cheap or undervalued. Perhaps a more apt term for value stocks is distressed stocks. Value stocks are often categorised as weak or underperforming companies, whose stock prices have been written down by the market as a consequence, possibly to below their true or intrinsic value. Financial measures that are frequently applied to value stocks are:

- High book-to-market (BtM) (i.e. the underlying value of a company's net assets).

- Low price relative to earnings (low P/E ratio) or, in other words, the amount that an investor is willing to pay for each pound of future earnings that the company generates.

- High dividend yield, which reflects the payout of cash today as opposed to reinvestment in the business.

On the other hand, growth stocks are companies whose earnings are growing rapidly and appear to have the ability to grow further. Even if growth rates are already high, that will not put off some investors, provided that they believe the market consensus is wrong. In a growth investor's view, earnings growth drives stock price performance and performance is largely independent of the stock value today.

At face value, value wins

Much of the academic work relating to the value premium is from the USA, although the presence of a global value premium is increasingly being researched. In short, the data suggest that a premium exists for investing in value stocks compared with growth stocks and that this is statistically significant. Figure 11.10 illustrates that this is so in both developed and emerging markets.

But there are no guarantees! Considerable periods of time can exist, and have existed, over which value stocks have underperformed growth stocks, sometimes to quite an extent, such as in the late 1990s tech boom. From the start of 1997 to the end of 1999 the UK larger cap value shares were beaten by UK large cap growth shares by almost 12 per cent per year. This creates a dilemma: do you try to obtain the value premium by holding more value stocks in your portfolio? If so, are you prepared to sit out what could be lengthy and painful periods of underperformance and hope to be rewarded? It's not recommended that you try to time when to be in value

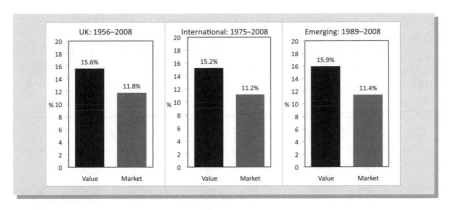

Figure 11.10 **The value premium appears to exist in global equity markets (annualised returns)**

Source: Dimensional UK Value Index, Dimensional International ex UK Value Index, Fama/French Emerging Markets Value Index. UK market – FTSE All Share 1962-present, 1956 to 1962 Elroy Dimson, Paul Marsh and Mike Staunton, Triumph of the Optimists, Princeton University Press, 2002, MSCI World ex-UK Index (net div.), MSCI Emerging Markets Index (gross div.). Refer to Appendix 1 for full details.

stocks and when to be in growth stocks. As ever with market-timing decisions, the longevity with which value and growth styles can seem seriously out of kilter, combined with rapidity and magnitude of turn-arounds, makes this a really tough game to play.

So, to make an additional allocation to value stocks requires you to feel confident that this premium is actually a reward for taking more risk, not just a data anomaly.

Why have value stocks outperformed growth stocks?

That is a good and relevant question. Rex Sinquefield is an investment academic and chairman of Dimensional Fund Advisors, a firm that specialises in providing passive products with the ability to tilt portfolios using capitalisation and style classifications. He states (Tanous, 1997b):

'On average, they're going to have future earnings problems. That's a source of risk. The market doesn't like that. So, small stocks and value stocks seem to be associated with higher rates of return. But it's really a cost of capital question. The value companies are struggling, and because they have this kind of risk they have to pay more for equity capital. The high cost of capital for the firm means a high rate of return for the investor.'

Eugene Fama reinforces this view (Tanous, 1997a):

'To me, stock prices are just the prices that produce the expected returns that

people require to hold them. If they are growth companies, people are willing to hold them at a lower expected return ... Value stocks may continue to take their knocks. Their prices reflect the fact that they are in poor times. As a result, because people don't want to hold them – in our view because they are riskier – they have higher expected returns.'

A sense of balance is provided by John Bogle (2002a) who, with his years of experience and insight, fails to see the existence of the value premium. His thoughts are based largely around his belief in a return-to-mean for markets over time and that costs and additional risks make the victory pyrrhic:

'Place me squarely in the camp of the contrarians who don't accept the inherent superiority of value strategies over growth strategies.'

At the end of the day, I don't think either you or I are any the wiser. The only thing worth remembering is that the market, for whatever reason, requires that perceived risks are rewarded. If you wish for the higher returns that value stocks, or for that matter small cap stocks (see below), potentially provide, you will be taking on more risk, and this risk in the widest sense will not just be measured by volatility of returns. Place your bets in moderation. If the value premium turns out not to exist then you should end up, over the long term, with a market-like return. So, to some extent, the risk of making an allocation is reduced.

11.7 Smaller companies

As we explored earlier, a premium (the small cap (or size) premium as it is known) is paid to investors for the additional risks that they take relative to larger company stocks. Put another way, their cost of capital is higher. Small cap stocks, like value stocks, appear to have characteristic that cannot be diversified away. Thus, according to the manual of investing, the equities of smaller companies (small cap stocks) will outperform those of larger companies, over time. Some investors try to capture this premium by adding additional exposure in their portfolios, over and above the smaller companies already in the index, to smaller companies. This strategy may work, but it is not guaranteed to succeed. You need to make your own mind up.

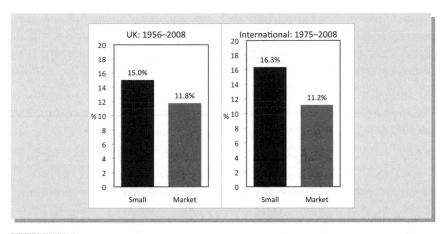

Figure 11.11 **The smaller company premium appears to exist in global equity markets (annualised returns)**
Source: Dimensional UK Small Cap Index, Dimensional International ex UK Small Cap Index. UK market – FTSE All Share
1962-present, 1956 to 1962 Elroy Dimson, Paul Marsh and Mike Staunton, Triumph of the Optimists, Princeton
University Press, 2002, MSCI World ex-UK Index (net div.), MSCI Emerging Markets Index (gross div.). Refer to Appendix
1 for full details.

What does the data tell us?

Looking deeper into the data and arguments behind the small cap premium will allow you to decide for yourself whether you want to include an additional exposure to them. Take a look at Figure 11.11.

However, you would be wise to remember that such averages mask periods, sometimes as long as twenty years, over which you would not have received this premium. The swings between periods of outperformance and underperformance of small cap stocks relative to the market may tempt you into trying to time your entry and exit into small cap stocks to capture the periods of outperformance and avoid periods of underperformance. Pick up the money section of any Sunday paper to see how much pressure there is on you to time markets. Don't be tempted because even the most astute professionals find this hard to do. Being a contrarian is not a route to an emotionally easy life!

Why does the small-cap premium exist?

Now we get to the crux of the debate. I wish I could answer this question, but I can't. In fact, when you review the discussions and ideas of academics and practitioners in the industry, you see that their views are varied and inconclusive. This should be a warning to you that owning small cap stocks is not a sure thing. However, there does appear to be some form of risk that cannot be diversified away, for which you are apparently being rewarded. My reading of research on this subject would seem to suggest that a premium may exist, but that it is not certain, and it is less convincing than the value premium.

An interview with Eugene Fama (one of the leading academic researchers of value and size effects) by Peter Tanous (1997a) about the small cap effect included the following exchange:

Fama: 'The risk in my terms can't be explained by the market. It means that because they move together, there is something about these small stocks that creates an undiversifiable risk. The undiversifiable risk is what you get paid for.'

Tanous: 'What causes that risk?'

Fama: 'You know, that's an embarrassing question because I don't know.'

Even Eugene Fama concludes the following:

'The size premium is, however, weaker and less reliable than the value premium.' (Davis et al., 1999, pub 2009)

Dimson, Marsh and Staunton (2002), leading academics at the London Business School, stated:

'It appears inappropriate to use the term "size effect" to imply that we should automatically expect there to be a small cap premium.'

And finally, John Bogle (Bogle, 2002a) again provides us with a balancing viewpoint:

'We see that the long period is punctuated by a whole series of reversion to the mean. Virtually the entire small-cap advantage [in the USA] took place in the first 18 years ... On balance these to-and-fro reversions have cancelled each other out, and since 1945 the returns of large-cap stocks and small-cap stocks have been virtually identical ... So ask yourself whether the evidence to justify the claim that small-cap superiority isn't too fragile a foundation on which to base a long-term strategy.'

There is no clear-cut answer. You have to go with what you feel comfortable. My advice would be to make any bets away from the total market with moderation. Remember that in a broad market index such as the FTSE All-Share, you already own about 6 per cent in small cap stocks. In the end, if no small cap premium actually exists, you should end up with a market-like return over the longer term, thus mitigating the allocation risk for long-term investors.

11.8 In summary – equity asset classes

You should now be able to come to some conclusions about equities. These are summarised below:

■ Equities are the return engines of portfolios, beating both bonds and cash. In the UK they have beaten inflation by around 5 per cent a year since 1900.

■ Returns in the long run reflect economic reality.

■ You can estimate the future real returns for equities by adding the current dividend yield to the projected growth in earnings.

■ In any year, you have about a two in three chance that returns will be positive.

■ Over twenty years, there is a very good chance that you will have positive growth in purchasing power, although global market evidence and Monte Carlo simulation urges caution. Let's say a one in ten or so chance exists that you will lose purchasing power over this time frame, which is not overly pessimistic.

■ Equity returns are volatile and their risk (i.e. their measure of volatility around the mean return – explored earlier) is somewhere in the region of 20 per cent for developed markets.

■ Real life shows that extreme returns tend to be larger and more frequent than estimated using bell-shaped (normal) distribution statistics. Your conclusion on market trauma should be: it happens; it happens frequently; in all markets; and can be very painful and sometimes long-lived when it does. *Caveat emptor*!

■ Markets have a tendency to revert to the mean level of long-run returns. However, the timing and pace of this reversion appears to be impossible to predict. Periods of above-average returns are often, but not always, followed by less-exciting returns and vice versa.

■ Incremental allocations to value, smaller company and emerging markets equities are expected to deliver returns over and above the broad market due to the higher cost of capital of the companies involved. Any allocation should be based on the balance of evidence and in moderation.

The two non-equity asset classes that met the selection criteria that allowed inclusion on our asset class menu were commercial property (real estate) and commodity futures. Let's take a closer look.

11.9 Commercial property – a diversifier

The UK's obsession with residential property has hopefully been put into perspective in 2008. Two important points come to mind. First, a house that you live in is not an ATM machine, spewing out cash every time you remortgage and build a new extension on to it. Second, and more importantly, owning residential property (buy-to-let) is not a substitute for a well-diversified investment portfolio to achieve and sustain your financial goals. A good run in the late 1990s and up to 2006 or so clouded many people's judgement and stilted their dinner party conversational skills. It could form part of a sensible mix of assets, but should not be your only asset. Apart from anything else, owning property directly is not without its hassles, of 'the roof is leaking' variety, from tenants.

The asset class we are talking about is commercial property, i.e. industrial estates, shops and shopping centres and office blocks. This provides diversification away from the residential property market. The other distinction is that ownership is indirect, rather than direct, through owning real estate investment trusts (REITs), which are shares where the underlying assets are properties and the vast majority of rental income is passed on to the shareholders.

Where do returns come from?

Historical data series show that unleveraged property returns, as economic theory would suggest, fall between equities and bonds. In terms of economic rationale, property represents a series of cashflows like a bond, made up of the regular payment of rent and the residual value of the building. The more certain the occupancy and length of rental lease, and the quality of the tenant, the lower the volatility of the capital value of the building. As such, buildings with high-quality tenants on long-term leases tend to act more like bonds and are less volatile as the income dominates returns. On the other hand, properties with short-term tenancies, the ultimate being hotels, tend to have more equity-like volatility in their capital value (see Figure 11.12). In the short-term, sentiment and supply and demand will affect the capital values.

The returns exhibited by REITs tend to be more volatile than those of 'bricks and mortar' funds that became so popular in the UK in the 2000s. The latter funds purchase properties directly with investors' money, making both valuation and liquidity an issue. The illusion that they were less

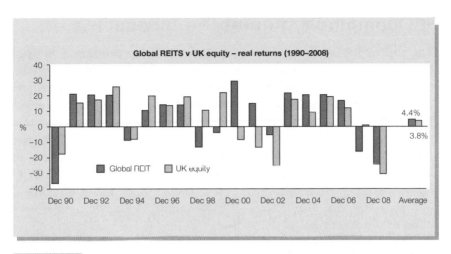

Figure 11.12 **Commercial property is a useful addition to the mix**

Source: S&P Global REIT index.

volatile, perhaps akin to bond funds, has vaporised in the asset mark-downs
and the imposition of exit restrictions on investors in the funds that
occurred in 2008. The corporate structure of real estate holdings, i.e.
whether the property is held directly by a fund or owned by a publicly
listed company, should have little effect on return and volatility in the long
term on an unleveraged apples-to-apples basis. Long term, publicly listed
REITs should deliver comparable returns to bricks and mortar funds.
Holding a global REIT passive fund makes sense from a diversification perspective.

The reality is best summed up by David Swensen (Swensen, 2000)

*'The absurd notion that simply changing the form of corporate ownership alters
fundamental investment attributes corresponds nicely to the idea of alchemy.
The higher volatility of REIT shares reflects an appropriate upward adjustment
of artificially dampened risk observed in appraisal-based return series.'*

Property tends to have a low correlation to equities, providing a diversification benefit, as property performance is usually linked to rental value
growth, in turn linked to economic growth, unlike the earnings of non-
property companies that are less correlated to economic growth (UBS,
2006). This is borne out in a correlation of 0.5 that is exhibited between UK
equities and global property. This diversification is achieved without the
substantial return give-up of holding bonds or cash.

11.10 Commodity futures – a bit esoteric

The commodity boom during the mid 2000s raised investor awareness of commodities. As ever, many chased returns as commodity prices rose on the back of Western consumer demand and production delivered by countries such as China and India. In many respects the true argument that surrounds this less well known and understood investment is one of risk reduction, not return, as we will explore. To begin to understand the introduction we need to take a step back and think what is going on when we say we are going to invest in commodities. What do we really mean?

The first point to note is that direct commodity prices are unlikely to deliver long-term real returns as they make up the inflation basket. Second, it is likely that any short-term imbalances in supply and demand are likely to even out over time. It is perhaps imprudent then to believe that commodity prices themselves will be the source of long-term real returns, as many in the industry do. In addition, direct investment in commodities is impractical for individual investors, as the consequences of taking delivery of a million barrels of crude oil are undesirable.

For that reason many commodity funds were launched that invested in the shares of companies involved in the extraction and processing of commodities. This is a leveraged play on the underlying commodity price, with the danger that the share price and the commodity price become disconnected. Perhaps the firm's strategy is poor, or its employee relations pitiful, or the management team weak. Success becomes an active management risk and should be excluded, for the many reasons we covered at the start of the book.

That leaves us with commodity futures funds, which have the potential to be a useful addition to the asset class menu, as they appear to provide the opportunity of real returns and are uncorrelated with bonds and equities. This is despite the fact that each individual commodity future in itself is a more or less zero sum bet.

What is a futures contract?

A futures contract involves two people; traditionally, on one side is a hedger, like a farmer looking to lock in the price of his crop, such as wheat, at some point in the future, and on the other side of this contract is a speculator who is looking to take on the price risk, making money if the price of wheat rises and a loss if the price of wheat falls. The futures contract reflects a recognised quantity of the commodity and the expiry date. Futures are rarely held to maturity as you then have the obligation of taking delivery of the commodity. Gains or losses are settled.

Where do commodity futures returns come from?

Given, as we said above, commodity prices will be comparable to inflation in the long term and that supply and demand imbalances will even out over time, at first glance you would be forgiven for wondering what all the fuss is about. Commodity futures fund returns do not come from under-lying cash generation that comes with being an owner of a company or a lender to it, but from the properties of the futures markets and the owner-ship of a basket of futures contracts. If you are intrigued, then read on (if not, then exclude them from your growth-oriented assets, substituting them for equities).

Recent research concludes that investment into a diversified basket of com-modity futures has historically produced strong real returns (Gorton et al., 2004) and may well do so again in the future, given some of the underlying characteristics of a diversified basket of uncorrelated futures contracts. The return of the well-known RJ CRB Commodities Index, which is made up of very approximately one-third energy, one-third metals, and one-third agri-cultural commodities, is illustrated in Figure 11.13.

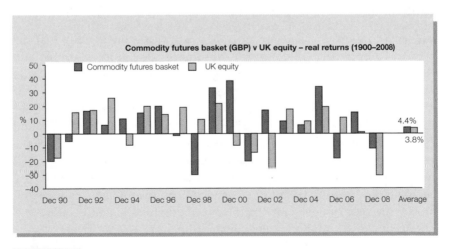

Figure 11.13 **Commodity futures have historically delivered strong uncorrelated returns**   *Source: www.crbtrader.com.*

Returns come from two main sources: the return on collateral provided against which futures contracts are purchased and from the 'commodity strategy' premium (Ibbotson Associates, 2006), which is made up of an insurance-like premium and what is known as a rebalancing bonus. Understanding what each element is and its likelihood of being captured going forward presents a more robust approach over the naïve extrapolation of historical data, or the simplistic expectation of an upward movement of commodity prices.

The insurance premium represents compensation for accepting the risk of unexpected deflationary commodity price movements from those wishing to hedge this position; it is paid through the futures contract being lower than the expected spot price – a situation described by Keynes as 'normal backwardation', a rather bizarre term to those on the outside of the futures markets. However, with the weight of money flowing into commodity futures, this could be expected to decrease, perhaps entirely, entering into a state of 'cantango' where the futures price is actually above the expected spot price; although recent research suggests that 'backwardation' may be the consequence of low inventory levels (Gorton et al., 2007).

The rebalancing bonus represents the return benefit that is accrued by owning a basket of uncorrelated/low-correlated individual futures (agricultural products, oil, metals, etc.) with high standard deviation that is rebalanced regularly. Even if the net excess return on each individual futures contract is zero (implying no insurance premium), a reasonable excess return can potentially be generated by regular rebalancing of the basket (a buy-low-sell-high strategy).

The contribution of each element is debated, with some arguing that the return is primarily due to the insurance premium (Gorton and Rouwenhorst, 2004) and others arguing for the rebalancing bonus (Erb and Harvey, 2006). It is likely that all these factors, in some proportion, contribute to the historical excess return evidenced. The rebalancing bonus alone and the uncorrelated nature of the basket's returns to equities and bonds make this a potentially attractive diversification asset class in the context of a portfolio. The conclusions that can be drawn from the research are as follows: commodities do not offer investors a consistent risk premium; commodity volatility is comparable to that of large company US stocks; the risks of large outlying losses is not excessive; and commodities are uncorrelated with bonds and equities (Kat and Oomen, 2006).

The decision to include them in your portfolio

Even in the absence of any real return, the uncorrelated nature of commodities should drive down risk, freeing up the risk budget to be spent elsewhere, i.e. adding higher-risk assets in search of returns. Recent research appears to indicate that correlations between commodity futures and traditional financial assets have remained unchanged over the past fifteen years despite the upsurge in interest and investment in commodities (Buyuksahin et al., 2007). Any allocation that you make should be based on a conservative return estimate and the positive risk-reducing benefits of adding an uncorrelated asset class to the portfolio.

11.11 Defensive assets

The defensive assets in your portfolio don't really need much more explanation than they have already received, but let's just summarise what we know. In our 'whisky and water' approach to building portfolios, the assets we have covered above are the 'whisky' and the simplest form of 'water' is cash.

Cash

As we discovered (see Figure 9.9) cash can be a pretty poor store of purchasing power at times of unanticipated and rapid rises in inflation. In its common form of implementation – placing a deposit with a bank – 2008 delivered a tough message to many that it is not a riskless asset. While the latter problem can easily be mitigated with some sensible implementation choices (covered in Chapter 13), the erosion of purchasing power requires a better solution.

Index-linked gilts and National Savings Certificates

The potential damage that inflation can reap on an investor's portfolio needs to be taken seriously. Defensive assets need to perform the role they are charged with robustly and efficiently. As we previously explored, defensive assets play two key roles – defending against equity market trauma and protecting the value of the assets assigned to them, in terms of volatility and purchasing power.

As such, shorter-dated index-linked gilts and index-linked National Savings Certificates are therefore strong contenders for risk-free assets for

most individual investors. Due to their structure, both of these govern-
ment-backed investments provide low risk to real capital. Let's look briefly
at each in turn.

Index-linked gilts: these are IOUs issued by the UK government. The principal amount you lend the government is adjusted for the rate of inflation
and the interest payable to you twice a year is based on the inflated level of
the principal. It is important to note that there is an eight-month lag in the
inflation linking to the Retail Price Index on current index-linked gilts. This
does give rise to the risk on very short-dated gilts that the inflation protection is weak in the event of a rapid inflation spike.

An argument could be made for owning index-linked gilts that have a
maturity of around five years or so as you then get a relatively low volatility
with strong inflation-protection characteristics. As mentioned earlier, a
bond's sensitivity to changes in yields is defined by its duration, where
duration is a weighted average of the maturity of all the income streams
from a bond or portfolio of bonds, measured in years. It helps to provide a
measure of movement of the price of a bond to a movement of 1 per cent
in yields. If the duration of a bond is three years, a 1 per cent rise in yield
will result in a 3 per cent fall in price and vice versa. This is often referred
to as the bond 'see-saw'. As such, a bond with a five-year maturity will have
a duration of around three years or so (its exact duration depends on a
number of factors that are irrelevant to this discussion).

If you own them directly and until they mature, you have the certainty that
they will deliver inflation-protected capital and interest payments along
the way. You can purchase index-linked gilts via most online brokerages if
you are a DIY investor.

Your other option is to own a fund or Exchange Traded Fund that invests
in them. As you will see, passive products exist for both. The issue you face
is that the index-linked gilts are marked-to-market, i.e. you will see the
interim volatility in their prices as the market responds to changes in the
real yields it demands for lending money. Most products tend to replicate
the entire market for index-linked gilts, with an average maturity of about
fifteen years and duration of thirteen years or so. That makes them quite
volatile. If that worries you, you could hold some cash to reduce the
volatility of your defensive assets. Over time you will receive inflation protection as you still own a basket of index-linked gilts.

Index-linked National Savings Certificates: these operate in much the same
way and are backed by the UK government. The main differences are that

they calculate the inflation protection on a monthly lag only and the most you can put into any one issue is £15,000, so you have to build your position slowly. To some extent the route you take may depend on how much money you have. They tend to offer real rates of return of around 1 per cent over inflation and you pay no tax as an individual on the interest (although the lower rate compensates in part for this). To find out more about them take a look at the clear website www.nsandi.com. The longest maturity of any issue is five years.

Longer-dated (conventional) gilts

As we covered in Chapter 9, conventional gilts and those with longer maturities provide concentrated equity market trauma protection, in theory (see Figure 11.14). The longer duration provides more diversification 'bang' for your 'buck' of equity allocation foregone. As ever in investing, there are no certainties. It seems a reasonable strategy to take based on the theory and the evidence. Conventional gilts perform poorly at times of unanticipated inflation as yields rise and prices fall. Combined with their volatility, long-dated gilts sit poorly at the more conservative end of the investor spectrum.

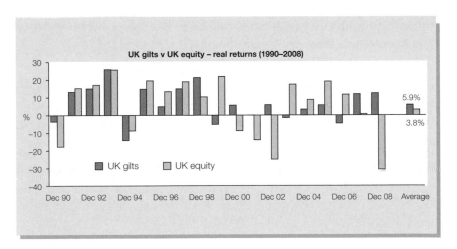

Figure 11.14 **Longer-dated gilts usually provide benefit during equity trauma**

Source: Barclays Equity Gilt Study, 2009.

11.12 Key asset classes excluded

A number of investment types have been considered but excluded from the menu, in particular hedge funds, and private equity, which are currently receiving wide attention and investor focus.

'Investors require unusual self-confidence to ignore the widely hyped non-core investments and to embrace the quietly effective core investments.' (David Swensen, 2007)

Hedge funds and funds of hedge funds

Hedge funds superficially appear to provide appealing characteristics to investors, either as low-correlation, strong-return, low-risk funds of funds, or as high-return-generating single funds. Care must be taken when using industry return numbers, given the biases that exist that considerably over-state returns and understate correlations and volatility. Industry claims that on an aggregated industry level hedge funds generate skill-based alpha should be looked at with a high degree of scepticism. Increasingly, questions are being raised as to what hedge funds are actually offering; recent research suggests that this may in fact be systematic exposure to alternative sources of market-based returns (beta) rather than manager skill (alpha).

When I wrote the first edition of this book, I was somewhat sceptical about hedge funds and resolved that the only way an allocation should be made was through a fund of funds structure and limited to 5 per cent of the portfolio. Perhaps, following 2008 when the hedge fund universe was down by 18 per cent and funds of funds were down over 20 per cent, my final 'Guideline 6' for considering hedge funds was well timed:

'Finally, be prepared for disappointment. Hedge fund investing is not alchemy and most managers have not yet seen a financial market crisis such as the Russian bond crisis that brought down Long Term Capital in 1998. At the very least accept that absolute return hedge funds are an unproven option.'

The difficulties of understanding the underlying strategies, selecting truly skilful managers (or even competent funds of funds), due diligence, and very high costs (2 per cent annual management fees and 20 per cent performance, plus 1 per cent and 10 per cent for funds of funds) in what is still a zero sum game make their inclusion unjustifiable. They are excluded.

Private equity

Private equity appears to provide exciting opportunities for public market-plus returns. In reality, capturing these higher returns comes at the price of illiquidity and higher risk. A Yale study of 542 buyout deals illustrated a gross return of 48 per cent compared to that of the market's 17 per cent, and a net 36 per cent after costs. Yet when the effects of leverage were taken into account between these transactions and the public market, creating an apples-to-apples comparison, this resulted in the latter outstripping the buyout deals significantly. These risks are compounded by the fact that only the top decile of managers is likely to deliver returns that compensate for these additional risks.

This implies the need for superior manager selection skills, access to manager funds, and high investor asset levels for direct access and appropriate levels of diversification. High costs decrease the upside opportunity further. For the individual investor, the benefits of private equity are outweighed by the practical problems of entry and diversification. They are excluded.

11.13 Summary of asset class assumptions

Inevitably, when it comes to planning your financial future, you need to make some assumptions about the asset classes (i.e. risk factors) that you will use to build your portfolio. For what they are worth, those used in the

Table 11.1 Asset class assumptions made

Building block	Expected real return	Premium	Risk
Growth-oriented, risky assets			
Developed equity markets	5% p.a.		20%
Emerging equity markets		+2% p.a.	30%
Value (less healthy) equities		+2% p.a.	25%
Smaller company equities		+2% p.a.	25%
Global real estate	4% p.a.		15%
Commodity futures	2% p.a.		20%
Domestic (UK) equity		**5%**	**20%**
Defensive assets			
Shorter-dated UK index-linked gilts	2%		3%
Longer-dated gilts	2.5%		10%

Note: The correlation matrix used can be found in Table 9.4.

portfolio construction process in this book are set out in Table 11.1. They represent the base numbers from which the 'expected' return and risk numbers for each Smarter Portfolio are derived. You need to decide for yourself.

References

Bogle, J. C. (2002a) The telltale chart. Bogle Financial Markets Research Center. Available from: http://www.vanguard.com.

Bogle, J. C. (2002b) The investment dilemma of the philanthropic investor. Bogle Financial Markets Research Center. Available from: http://www.vanguard.com.

Buffett, W. (1997) 1996 Annual Report: Chairman's Letter. Berkshire Hathaway Inc. Available from: http://www.berkshirehathaway.com/1996ar/1996.html.

Buffett, W. (2001) 2000 Annual Report: Chairman's Letter. Berkshire Hathaway Inc.

Buyuksahin, B., Haigh, M. and Robe, M. (2007) 'Commodities and Equities: "A Market of One"?' (31 December). Available at SSRN.

Davis, J. L., Fama, E. F. and French, K. R. (2009) 'Characteristics, Covariances, and Average Returns: 1929–1997' (February 1999). Center for Research in Security Prices (CRSP) Working Paper No. 471.

Dimson, E., Marsh, P. R. and Staunton, M. (2002) *Triumph of the optimists: 101 years of global investment data*, Princeton, NJ: Princeton University Press, p. 145.

Economist (2003) 'Taking stock', June 6.

Erb, C. B. and Harvey, C. R. (2006) 'The Tactical and Strategic Value of Commodity Futures', Social Science Research Network Working Paper, 12 January.

Gorton, G. B. and Rouwenhorst, K. G. (2004) 'Fact and Fantasies About Commodities Futures'. NBER Working Paper Series, Working Paper 10595, National Bureau of Economic Research.

Gorton, G. B., Hayashi, F. and Rouwenhorst, K. G. (2007) 'The Fundamentals of Commodity Futures Returns', Yale ICF Working Paper 07-08.

Graham, B. and Dodd, D. (1996) *Security analysis: The classic 1934 edition*. New York: McGraw-Hill.

Ibbotson Associates (2006) *Strategic Asset Allocation and Commodities*. Commissioned by PIMCO.

Kat, H. M. and Oomen, R. C.A. (2006) 'What every investor should know about commodities'. Part II Multivariate Return Analysis, AIRC Working Paper Series.

Swensen, D. F. (2000) Pioneering portfolio management. New York: The Free Press, p. 220.

Tanous, P. J. (1997a) 'An interview with Eugene Fama – Investment gurus'. Available from: http://library.dfaus.com/reprints/interview_fama_tanous.

Tanous, P. J. (1997b) 'An interview with Rex Sinquefield – Investment gurus'. Available from: http://library.dfaus.com/reprints/interview_sinquefield_tanous.

UBS (2006) 'Pension Fund Indicators 2006'.

4

Smarter implementation

Hopefully at this point you have a good idea of what mix of building blocks to use in your portfolio. Now, you need to turn this plan into reality. Unfortunately, many investors fail to follow through, blinded and confused by the plethora of choice. Here is some guidance on pulling the trigger.

Chapter 12: Hire an adviser or do it yourself?

This is an important step. You need to decide whether you want to take on the full responsibility for implementing your portfolio strategy and the ongoing management of your portfolio, or whether you want to appoint an adviser to do this for you and act as your guide over time. This chapter is designed to help you to decide which course of action is right for you. It also provides some good tips on finding the right sort of adviser.

Chapter 13: Smarter product choices

Here you will find guidance on selecting the best passive (index) products in the marketplace. Simple selection criteria are provided, along with a few ideas of some of the asset class implementation products that you could take a look at, as a start. This is a very rapidly expanding universe and you need continually to be alert to new products being launched. Even if you employ an adviser, you need to be able to scrutinise the choices that they are making on your behalf.

Chapter 14: Costs – what a drag

If you sat down and worked out how much of your money was being siphoned off by the investment industry, you would be amazed. Costs matter, as John Bogle would say. Gaining a real understanding of what your all-in costs are, and the effect they may have on the success of your investment programme, is time well spent for a lose-the-fewest-points investor.

Chapter 15: Standing firm on index funds

One of the challenges as you try and put an investment plan into action is that as soon as you speak to anyone in the industry, the chances are that they will try to persuade you that they can beat the markets. Their argument often ends up as an attempt to malign index funds and persuade you that by buying them you are consigning your investment programme to mediocrity. Identifying and refuting the common put-downs will help you to have the confidence to stand your ground.

12

Hire an adviser or do it yourself?

The choice to run your own Smarter Portfolio or to hand over its implementation and ongoing management to an adviser is a big decision that you need to think carefully about. The choice depends on a number of issues, which we will explore below.

The key point that I want to make is that good advice and ongoing guidance over your lifelong investment journey from a leading adviser is worth its weight in gold. Poor advice and implementation could, on the other hand, have a seriously detrimental effect on your wealth, which in turn will impact on the aspirations that you have for your future lifestyle.

We will look at both options in turn, which will hopefully help you make the decision that is right for you. We will then look at how you go about selecting a leading adviser or a good platform for running your DIY portfolio on. Neither route is better than the other in any absolute sense, but one will be the better option for you.

12.1 Hiring an adviser

There is no straightforward method for deciding whether hiring an adviser is right for you. But you will probably have a gut feel as to whether you feel comfortable with establishing your own financial and investment plan and implementing and managing it over time. If you do then you may want to manage it yourself. If not, you will need to look for a strong adviser.

As a starting point it may depend how much money you have and what it represents. The ideas in this book apply to anyone investing; from someone putting £50 into their portfolio every month to build a nest-egg to someone looking to invest £10 million. If the money you are investing represents a small nest-egg that is never likely to be the core of your future financial well-being, you may think that it should be reasonably simple to invest yourself. It may be that this money is part of a money purchase pension plan run by your company and that you need to direct the monthly contributions you make in a sensible manner into the investment funds available on the plan menu. Again a DIY approach may make sense.

However, as wealth increases and as it becomes a central part of your future financial security and desired lifestyle, so the decisions that you make become more critical and complex. Worries such as running out of money, knowing that you are still on track despite recent markets, handling the paperwork and dealing with all the other issues that wealth brings are common. The lack of time in people's lives to think about and handle these issues compounds the stresses that can accompany wealth.

Table 12.1 may help you decide between the two. Ring the answers that apply to you and see where you come out. Totally unscientific but it should get you thinking!

Table 12.1   **Hire an adviser or adopt a DIY approach?**

	Adviser	DIY
Your investments:		
Simple investment affairs?	No	Yes
Critical to your financial security and lifestyle?	Yes	No
Investment of pension plan contributions only?	No	Yes
Annual ISA allowance only?	No	Yes
You have wider wealth issues?	Yes	No
Your skills, interest and time:		
Uncertain what to do, despite reading the book?	Yes	No
Disinterested in investment matters?	Yes	No
Time poor?	Yes	No
Dislike paperwork?	Yes	No
Want ongoing guidance and handholding?	Yes	No
Want someone else to take care of it all?	Yes	No
You feel you can handle these administrative tasks:		
Selecting best-in-class products?	No	Yes
Raising cash regularly, if needed?	No	Yes
Rebalancing your portfolio when it gets out of line?	No	Yes
Managing the tax consequences of rebalancing?	No	Yes
Aggregating your wealth position for review?	No	Yes
Monitoring your progress towards your goals?	No	Yes
Happy to pay around 1% of your assets a year to an adviser?	Yes	No

Source: Albion Strategic Consulting.

Only you can decide, but I am sure that you will have a pretty good feel for where you come out.

12.2 What attributes will a leading adviser have?

You can obviously see from the Table 12.1 that an adviser plays a number of key roles. Perhaps the most valuable thing that an excellent adviser can deliver is helping you to relax about your wealth, confident in the knowledge that your lifetime plan is robust, that your assets are invested in an appropriate and effective way and that you will be kept informed of the progress you are making towards your goals. That to many will be money well spent. The added bonus is that you can throw all the administration their way too! There are three key things that help to define a leading adviser.

They will be working for you, not against you

While that sounds pretty obvious the problem is that most of the advice industry, from renowned private banks and wealth managers to the IFA on the high street, remains conflicted by its business model. Misselling scandals have become common news as rapacious product-oriented solutions have been sold to clients, where decisions have been made on the basis of what is good for the adviser and not what is good for the investor.

Very serious conflicts of interest can arise from the remuneration structure of an adviser. Many advisers today are still, unbelievably, paid through commissions from products they sell. Investors feel that the advice is therefore free, as they don't need to write a cheque. But the truth is very different. Over time the commission and trails (ongoing income to the adviser) will significantly erode your performance and ultimately your wealth, relative to better solutions. Product suppliers, particularly insurance companies, still push the commission payable to an adviser as the lead benefit when selling their products to them, not how beneficial it will be to their clients. Enough! Don't go anywhere near a commission-based adviser. They are too conflicted and are unable to offer you the most effective investment solution (passive/index funds).

Some advisers call themselves fee based as they charge a fee, but which is then offset by the commissions that the products they sell generate. Again, they cannot offer you passive funds because they don't pay commission. They cannot then provide you with the best advice, given the evidence.

Finally, there are an increasing, if still small, number of fee-based advisers who may or may not charge you upfront for creating and putting into action a robust wealth plan (a percentage of your assets or a specified amount) and then an ongoing fee for monitoring and managing this plan and keeping you both informed and unstressed. This ongoing fee will probably be around 1 per cent of your assets that they manage and should slide downward depending on the value of your assets. Any commissions or trails that they receive on legacy products in your portfolio should be paid in their entirety to your account. They should also be passing on the direct factory gate costs of any products that are used in your portfolio such as ISA and pension wrappers. They should be taking no cut of any trading revenue.

If they can tick all of these boxes then they are pretty much unconflicted and are working for you, not against you. They will be keen to set out and confirm all of their fees in a transparent and clear manner and should be working hard to drive down factory gate costs of all the products that they use as part of their wealth management solution.

They will have broad wealth management insight and robust solutions

As wealth becomes more complex (often but not always due to size) a number of important areas need to be tackled by the adviser. The process

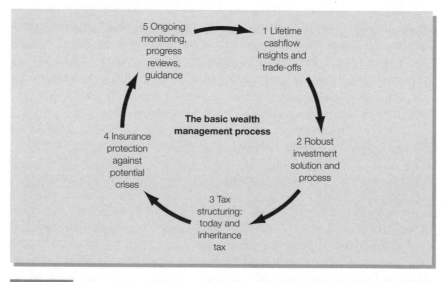

Figure 12.1 A decent adviser should have a disciplined and clear process

that they take you through to create a plan should be robust, systematic, documented and evidently undertaken with every client. An ad hoc approach reflects a lack of clear thinking and discipline, attributes best avoided in an adviser. Figure 12.1 provides the very basic outline of the wealth management process.

The development of a sensible financial plan requires a thorough insight into the collective assets of an individual and most likely their family, along with their projected income and expenditure over the coming years. The process is known as lifetime cashflow modelling and acts as a useful tool for discussion, running different lifestyle scenarios and trade-offs and testing the likelihood of successful outcomes, given the investment portfolio that you decide upon. These tools do not deliver definitive answers; how can they, when most of us cannot predict what will happen in either the markets or our own lives a year ahead, let alone thirty years ahead? But the process of thinking this through is important and valuable.

A leading manager should be using some form of lifetime cashflow modelling tool to facilitate a deep and thoughtful discussion about your wealth and aspirations. They should be able to give you an insight into the likely success or failure of the plan and resolve the inevitable trade-offs that exist, between what you hope for and reality.

They will have an effective investment process

Again, a decent adviser will have developed and will be able to explain clearly what their investment philosophy and process is. The way in which they arrive at your asset allocation should at least match the ideas set out in this book, and you should challenge them to explain to you why their approach differs, if it does.

If they are truly evidence based, then they should have reached the conclusion that passive implementation, to capture the bulk of the market rewards on offer, is in your best interests. If they don't then that surely raises questions about what they are doing and that potential conflicts of interest exist. These may be as simple as enjoying being entertained by active managers trying to sell their wares (a form of legalised bribery known as marketing budgets). Many of the larger wealth management companies and private banks offer in-house actively managed products, which makes everyone big bonuses at the end of the year, despite the fact they are fee based. More likely it is because they have never reviewed the evidence and are overconfident in their ability to pick winning managers. Start by talking first to leading advisers offering a passive investment solution. There are a few around and this band is growing slowly but surely.

12.3 Checklist for finding a leading wealth advisory firm

One of the major issues that investors looking for advice face is trying to find a firm of advisers that they can trust and who are likely to provide them with robust advice. Having read this book it should be more evident what you are looking for. Table 12.2 provides some pointers on how to locate one and some of the questions that you should ask.

The Institute of Financial Planning is a well-regarded organisation that is seeking to drive the professionalism of the financial planning business. Within their membership, if you look closely and use the criteria above, you will find many of the leading advisers. Their website is well worth a visit as it provides much background information on hiring a manager and a database for narrowing down those you might want to talk to: see www.financialplanning.org.uk.

Caveat

The due diligence that you perform on your adviser is your responsibility. Remember too that hiring an adviser is a process that demands some of your time and decision-making. You cannot abrogate all responsibility to them for your financial well-being. You need to understand and own the strategy that is put in place. They are there to hold your hand over time, monitor and update you on your progress. You need to be engaged in the process as it is your future lifestyle that is at stake.

12.4 The do-it-yourself option

The DIY option will suit you, either because your investment affairs are pretty simple or you have the time and inclination to undertake the tasks that could otherwise be subcontracted to an investment adviser. Going it alone requires you to set up a workable system for buying, selling and safe-keeping the investments that you buy. It will also need to keep a record of the details of each transaction that you undertake to allow you to fill in your tax return appropriately and accurately. The most effective route today for the DIY investor is to open an online brokerage account.

Table 12.2 Adviser checklist

Their credentials	
They must be registered with the Financial Services Authority. Check www.fsa.gov.uk	✔
They are fee based, charging a percentage of your investable assets p.a. (no commission offset)	✔
They take no other income from you of any kind, or from anyone else	✔
They offer a passive investment solution	✔
They offer some form of lifetime cashflow modelling as part of the planning process	✔
Likely to be a Member of the Institute of Financial Planning	✔
Individuals in the firm are probably Certified Financial Planner accredited*	✔

Some useful questions	
Do you have any conflicts of interest you need to declare to me?	✔
Are you a truly fee-based adviser?	✔
Can you show me every charge/cost I will incur if I become a client?	✔
How many other clients with similar assets to mine do you handle?	✔
Please describe your approach to creating my wealth plan?	✔
Please describe what you believe in from an investment perspective?	✔
What are my chances of achieving a successful outcome?	✔
Can I read your investment process document?	✔
How will you show me that I remain on course?	✔
Could I see a example of one of your progress reviews?	✔
Do you ever directly handle my money?	✔
Do you provide an advisory service or can you make decisions on my behalf?	✔
Could I talk to some of your existing clients?	✔

Soft attributes	
You feel comfortable that they know their stuff	✔
They enjoy discussing issues you raise	✔
They provide clear ideas and talk to you in terms that you understand	✔
You feel that they are working for and with you	✔
You feel that you could become professional friends	✔

* Other professional qualifications include: Diploma in Financial Planning (DipPFS), Associateship of the PFS (APFS) or Chartered Financial Planner status.

Choosing your investment platform

Some decades ago, owning individual securities directly through a brokerage account was the main method of investing and getting a stockbroker to look after your money was the norm, despite the hefty commissions and some pretty dodgy dealing practices that would not pass muster in today's more regulated markets.

An online brokerage account becomes the conduit through which to own, safe-keep, record-keep and rebalance your long-term Smarter Portfolio. It allows you to buy funds, ETFs and index-linked gilts at low transaction costs, usually around £10 per trade. These firms include the likes of Selftrade (www.selftrade.co.uk), TD Waterhouse (www.tdwaterhouse.co.uk), Barclays Stockbrokers (www.stockbrokers.barclays.co.uk) and the Motley Fool (www.fool.co.uk). Most banks have online brokerage options as well. There is no shortage of choice. You need to decide which firm is best for you. A few things to check out would be: who owns them, where the assets are custodied, what their charges are and if they charge for inactivity – one of your investment goals!

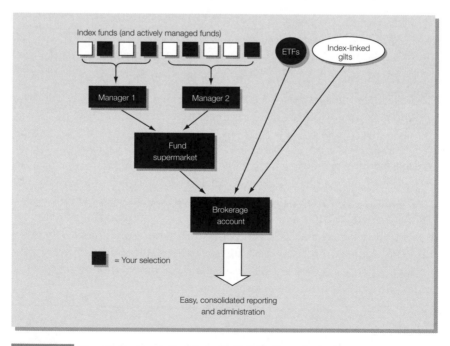

Figure 12.2 Investment needs drive administration choices

Figure 12.2 illustrates how you can use a brokerage account to consolidate your investments. Some brokerage firms have charges for inactivity (something you will be aiming for), so look out.

Getting started

The generic process for getting started follows along the lines of the list below. Some of these issues are addressed more fully in the sections below.

- Make sure the brokerage firm provides access to the funds you wish to own.
- Open an account.
- Transfer cash or securities. Make sure that the platform you choose allows 'in specie' transfers (securities) or else you may have to cash in your existing investments on which you will suffer costs and possibly taxes. Some platforms may charge, but this is usually on the way out, not on the way in.
- Decide your entry strategy, i.e. the time you will take to invest your money, which is different to picking the time you think it is best to enter the market – that is market timing.
- Make the trades – there won't be that many as you will not own many funds or ETFs.
- Invest any income that your portfolio throws off, which it probably will.
- Rebalance the assets back to their original mix when they get out of kilter, as they will from time to time. Use cash balances first.
- That's about it – not too much excitement or glamour!

A small point to remember is that if you are investing regularly in a number of ETFs, brokerage transaction costs will add up. Work out how much it will cost you as a percentage of your monthly investment – a penny saved is a penny earned. A £10 commission per trade on a £1,000 monthly investment split between four ETFs is 4 per cent of your capital needlessly given up. This route is probably best for investing larger sums or where the annual expense ratio of an ETF is substantially below that of comparable index funds and offsets the commissions.

Making a lump-sum investment

If you are a investing a lump sum, perhaps from an inheritance, a bonus or the sale proceeds of your business, you face a dilemma: what happens if equity markets crash after you put your money into them or returns are particularly weak over a long period of time?

It's a real problem, as any investor putting money into equities at the end of 1999 or mid 2007 quickly found out. Imagine that you have £1 million to invest and you decide to put it all into equities; you would be pretty upset if you invested it and within a year or two it was worth only £500,000. Let's do some simple maths: remember that 50 per cent down requires your portfolio to rise by 100 per cent, not 50 per cent, to get back to where it was; also, if your portfolio delivered 5 per cent in real terms a year from that point forwards (our estimate of average real returns from developed market equities), it would take you almost fifteen years to get back to its initial level of purchasing power. This is a very real risk that could damage the outcome of your investing programme. How can you avoid getting hit in this way?

The first thing you can do is own a diverse portfolio where your eggs are spread between a number of baskets including property, commodities and defensive assets. As such, you will have some protection, provided all these investments don't fall at once.

Second, you could try to gauge whether you think that equities look attractive relative to their long-term levels. That sounds a bit like market timing, but there may be some merit in taking what is a somewhat contrarian stance. To do this you need to have some measure of valuation that you can use and compare current valuation levels to the historic average. You can do this in a crude way by using what is known as the price to earnings ratio (or P/E ratio), which describes what the market is prepared to pay for each £1 of corporate earnings. The higher the P/E ratio, the more optimistic people are about future earnings growth. The long-term average P/E ratio in the UK is in the region of 12–14 times earnings, yet at times it has risen (and fallen) well beyond this. In 2000 the P/E for the market was in the high twenties. In the USA at that time it was around forty times, compared with a long-run average of fifteen. When prices (and P/E ratios) end up well above or below their historic levels, you might expect that they will revert towards more normal levels to bring them back in line, given that long-term earnings are likely to be reasonably stable. To quote Robert Shiller (Campbell and Shiller, 2001), who predicted the crash in 2000:

'Metaphorically, when one is mountaineering, one can enjoy the exhilarating view from up high on a mountain, and may look forward to the possibility of discovering a way up to a much higher level. But one will reflect that, realistically, at a random date years from now, one will probably be back at ground level.'

The problem for you is that while this may be true, you simply don't know when that random date is.

The solution then, if you are concerned about a fall in the equity market and you could live with any gains foregone, is to average your way into the market. You could decide on the number of years that you will do this over and then pick a Smarter Portfolio with a lower growth-oriented asset mix and move up one portfolio a year until you reach your required long-term strategy allocation.

The downside is that you could lose out if the markets forge ahead. It is a risk management issue and one that only you can resolve. In short, own a diverse portfolio and average your way in. Fortunately, it is not so much of a problem if you are building a portfolio using monthly contributions, as you will be averaging in across the whole of your accumulation stage.

Setting up your administration system

Once you are up and running you need to think about how you are going to go about administering your portfolio, with the least fuss and bother. Few of us like paperwork; in fact, for some people the feeling of anxiety about investing is as much to do with handling the administration as it is to do with living with a portfolio. Fortunately today, there are efficient and simple ways to administer a portfolio, particularly if you are a rational, long-term, buy-and-hold investor using index tracker funds and/or exchange-traded funds.

When setting up a portfolio you will have some initial administration to do as well as some regular maintenance work, which can be kept to a minimum. When you buy a fund or ETF, you will need to keep a record of your ownership of it, including: its exact description and any fund code that identifies it; the number of units/shares you own in each fund (active or index) or ETF; any buying and selling of these investments, including how many units/shares were traded and the date and the price at which the transaction took place; and any dividends from equities or coupon payments from bonds that you received. That should all be taken care of by your online brokerage account, if you use one. If not, you will receive contract notes from the fund companies that you need to organise and file appropriately.

In the case of income, you should check if the fund can automatically reinvest it for you to save time and effort. Remember, if you receive cash, you need to put this to work as soon as possible. This class of shares is often called accumulation shares. In the UK you may be liable for tax on any income, if you are a taxable investor, even if it is immediately reinvested.

You will need this information to fill out your tax return, declaring the income received and capital gains that you have realised during the fiscal year if this pot of money is taxable. Fortunately, most of these items are all produced either by brokers or the fund companies themselves. The degree to which you can minimise administration will be a function of the number of investments that you have decided upon for your Smarter Portfolio, the products you have chosen and the platform that you use. Remember, though, that your investment needs should drive your decision-making and not your desire to reduce the administrative hassle.

How you administer your investments will depend upon your own individual circumstances and the vehicles that you use. Time spent thinking about what administrative issues are going to arise from your portfolio and how you are going to handle them will save a lot of time and angst down the road. Here are some pointers that you should bear in mind.

- Choosing the right investments is your primary decision, which may dictate the administrative process. Remember that the same products may be sold through a variety of channels and one may be more administratively effective and/or cost-effective than another. Try to keep things as simple and as cheap as possible.

- When you receive information from your broker or fund company deal with it immediately. It won't take long. Otherwise, the temptation is to throw it on to the 'I'll do it later' pile and the hurdle of dealing with it becomes greater with each envelope that arrives.

- If you are a keen technology user, keep as much information online as possible.

- Careful record-keeping is essential and if your filing system is working, finding the information to do your tax return will be far easier for you or anyone you employ to do it.

- Don't avoid the admin. Set up an efficient system to control it.

Portfolio maintenance

Portfolio maintenance is made up of three tasks: tracking, monitoring and rebalancing. It should not take you more than a few hours once a year to keep things in order. Figure 12.3 summarises what you will have to deal with. At the end of the day, it is your money and you need to know how much you have, how anyone managing your money is performing and whether your plan is on track to meet your goals.

Making sure that you are on track to achieving your goals is important. Working out roughly where your accumulated wealth needs to be in the future, say every couple of years, is a good discipline. If you are retired and drawing an income, your goal may be to make sure that your purchasing power pool remains intact.

You can use the tables (or formulae) in Chapter 7 to calculate rough figures in real terms for target points along the way. Remember that the amount

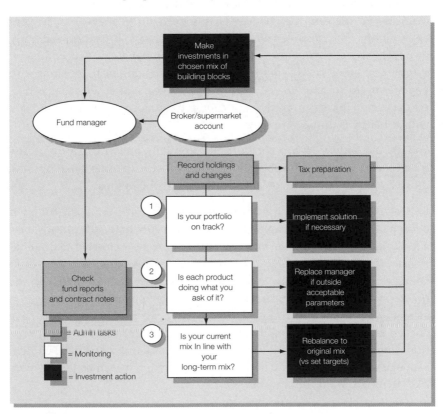

Figure 12.3 **Continual tracking, monitoring and rebalancing**

you see in your actual portfolio will be in tomorrow's money, reflecting the nominal returns you have made. To get back to real terms, you need to keep a note of inflation each year and use this to turn it back into today's money. Inflation data can be easily obtained from the Bank of England website. To make the conversion:

■ Create an index for inflation. Start with 100 and multiply this by 1 plus the rate of inflation, e.g. 5 per cent inflation will be 1 + 0.05. The inflation index in year 1 becomes 105. Say in year 2 inflation is 7 per cent, you multiply 105 by 1.07 to give 112.4.

■ To calculate your portfolio's purchasing power, divide whatever your portfolio is worth, say £125,000, by the inflation index divided by 100 = 125,000/1.124 = £111,210.

If you find that the portfolio value is falling behind your goals, at least you will know and you can contribute more, take a chance and increase the aggressiveness of the building-block mix (an inadvisable strategy in most cases as you increase the chances of missing your goal), or rein in your expectations. It is possible you get lucky and returns surpass expectations, in which case you can either reallocate assets elsewhere or expect a better standard of living later. Don't be tempted into making rash decisions with your portfolio structure based on one or two years; after all, what is one, two or even five years in thirty? Contribute too much or spend less and you will be happy if things get better.

You should only look at your portfolio annually at most; any more frequently and you will probably shock yourself with the inevitable ups and downs. Time does a good job at smoothing out the bumps.

Each year, take a look at how your investments have done against their chosen index. Say, for example, you own a FTSE All-Share index fund – take a look and see what the total expense ratio is now, how closely the fund has tracked the index, how large it is and if there have been any changes in strategy or personnel. In the event that performance is out of line with the market, you may have to take remedial action by replacing the manager or at least keep them under close scrutiny. This is a rare event if you have chosen an index fund carefully. Remember that 'out of line with expectations' means both above and below the benchmark index you have chosen. A manager whose results are better than expected may well be taking more risks than you want him to – beware.

Rebalancing your mix of building blocks

Rebalancing is the process of returning your portfolio back to its original mix, as over time building blocks will generate different levels of return, and the assets in the mix will become skewed in favour of the better-performing asset.

If you believe that markets revert to their long-run average – not a bad assumption to believe in and you would be in good company – then by rebalancing your portfolio, i.e. selling some of the building blocks that have outperformed and buying those that have underperformed, you may be positioning the portfolio appropriately to avoid/capture any mean reversion. It provides a discipline of buying low and selling high. However, there are no certainties that this will pay off over the timeframe you are investing over. As such, you should primarily view rebalancing as trying to maintain the risk/reward profile of your portfolio over the time you are invested for and which you chose in the first place. You just have to ignore the fact that, over some time periods and with the benefit of hindsight, it may turn out that it could have been better not to rebalance at all.

Perhaps the most succinct statement on rebalancing comes from David Swensen (Swensen, 2000), who invests for Yale University in the USA:

'Over long periods of time, portfolios allowed to drift tend to contain ever-increasing allocations to risky assets, as higher returns cause riskier positions to crowd out other holdings. The fundamental purpose of rebalancing lies in controlling risk, not enhancing return. Rebalancing trades keeps portfolios at long-term policy targets by reversing deviations resulting from asset class performance differentials. Disciplined rebalancing activity requires a strong stomach and serious staying power.'

He makes the point that in a severe bear market such as 1973–1974 the rebalancing investor was forced to buy more equities as markets continued to fall. Equally, rising equity prices needs a strong stomach as selling equities as part of a rebalance appears, at the time, to be a loser's strategy.

When should you rebalance? That's a question that has no definitive answer. Recent research (Lee, 2008) comes to the following conclusion:

'Aside from avoiding excessive trading, there are no optimal rebalancing rules . . . The good news for investors is that without an optimal way to rebalance, the burden of producing returns through optimal rebalancing is lifted. Return generation is again the responsibility of the market . . . The optimal rebalancing

strategy will differ for each investor, depending on their unique sensitivities to deviations from target allocation, transaction frequency, and tax costs.'

Some investors rebalance every year, which may be reasonable in steady markets. However, it probably makes sense to set a target for rebalancing, for example when the risky assets/defensive assets mix has moved by 10 per cent or more. Too low a target and you will be forever tinkering with the portfolio and incurring transaction and tax costs; in any case, small deviations are probably statistically insignificant, given all the assumptions that you have made to get to that allocation in the first place. Too high a target and you will expose your portfolio to too much risk, which could be costly. An example of a sensible rebalancing strategy for, say, a 40 per cent defensive and 60 per cent risky growth-oriented mix would be to allow the portfolio to run to 70 per cent in risky assets and 30 per cent in defensive assets and vice versa. Then rebalance.

The tax consequences and trading costs of rebalancing a portfolio need to be taken into consideration. If you sell equities that have gone up in price, you may incur significant capital gains, which may outweigh the added risk of holding a higher proportion of equities than intended. Remember that if you are making regular contributions to an investment plan, you can allocate new contributions into the building block that is underweight. By doing so you can avoid having to crystallise any capital gains in the outperforming asset classes you own. Even if you are not contributing regularly, your portfolio will be throwing off cash in the form of dividends from your shares and coupons from your bonds, which you could use.

12.5 Don't forget about tax

Managing your tax situation well is a very important component of successful investing. As an investor, it makes sense to use any legal tax breaks that you are given by the Chancellor. In most countries there are tax incentives designed to encourage you to invest more for your future and to rely less on the state. Remember that legally paying the taxman at a future date instead of today, or even altogether, can have a significant beneficial effect on your total portfolio returns over the long run. Tax breaks come in a number of forms.

Retirement (pension) savings

In the UK retirement saving is tax efficient, as you are given a tax break for saving into your pension plan. A 40 per cent rate tax payer investing £60 of their pay will get the benefit of £100 in their plan as their contribution is exempt from tax. Apart from these contributions receiving favourable tax treatment, capital gains and some forms of income are largely exempt from tax, although this changes depending on the Chancellor's whim. Pension funds are tax-exempt in many jurisdictions.

Personal tax shelters

In some jurisdictions, individual investors are provided with tax-deferred or tax-free investment structures. In the UK, for example, you can invest, with taxed income, up to £7,200 per year in an ISA for 2008–2009 and £10,200 for 2009–2010, which effectively shields you from most income or capital gains tax in the future. You should seriously consider taking advantage of this tax break. The Chancellor is rarely so generous.

Personal allowances

Again, some jurisdictions have allowances that allow you some capital gains tax free. The base cost of your investments, i.e. the price you bought them at, may also be increased over the years, thereby reducing any taxable gains that you must pay tax on later. This is the case in the UK. Remember that these can be used if you find you have to rebalance your portfolio at some time. With a buy-and-hold index fund/ETF strategy, you should have little need to crystallize capital gains, particularly when you are accumulating wealth. The Inland Revenue website (www.hmrc.gov.uk) provides the latest allowances. It does make sense to use up your capital gains allowances as it means the level of unrealised capital gains in your portfolio will be lower over time with less tax to pay if and when you liquidate your portfolio.

Harvesting and offsetting losses

Many jurisdictions allow you to offset capital losses that you make against capital gains. The magnitude and time scale over which losses can be carried forward varies from country to country. Some jurisdictions have rules to stop you from simultaneously selling and repurchasing stocks, known as bed-and-breakfasting.

Planning upfront how you are going to maximise the tax-efficiency of your investment plan is worthwhile and if you are going to spend money on advice, this is a good place to do so. In general, there are three key points to be made here if you are a taxable investor:

■ First, maximise the tax breaks that are legally afforded to you by your government. It will make a significant difference to your wealth in the long run.

■ Second, if you are unsure about what breaks are available to you for each pool of money you are investing and exactly how you can take advantage of these breaks, seek advice from your accountant. Alternatively, phone the Inland Revenue, if you are a UK taxpayer, as they are remarkably helpful and efficient.

■ Finally, your building block mix needs to be driven by your investment needs, not by tax planning. Being tax efficient within the context of your long-term building block mix makes sense.

That's it really for the DIY investor! It really is not too difficult to turn your theoretical portfolio into reality.

References

Campbell, J. Y. and Shiller, R. J. (2001) 'Valuation ratios and the long-run market outlook: an update'. Cowles Foundation Discussion Paper No. 1295, 1–19.

Lee, M. I. (2008) *Rebalancing and returns*, DFA.

Swensen, D. F. (2000) *Pioneering Portfolio Management*, New York: The Free Press.

13

Smarter product choices

It is no good getting to this point in the book, thinking 'what do I do now?' then shutting the book and entering a state of investment inertia. You need to work out how you are going to implement your portfolio strategy and the products that you are going to use to capture the market risks that you want to and pull the trigger.

Even if you have decided that you are going to use an adviser to help you, this chapter is important because it will provide you with a framework to analyse the product selection choices that they make and to question them about their choices. It is your money and you need to be comfortable that you are invested in the best products available.

At this point you will have selected your Smarter Portfolio and chosen the level of home bias, asset class diversification and return tilts that you feel most comfortable with. Now you need to decide how you can best replicate the risk factors that you want exposure to in your portfolio. That process requires the establishment of some selection criteria, which we will review below.

Fortunately the products available to passive investors are improving in both depth and quality. The bad news is that this means more products to sift through, although that is not too onerous. One of the consequences of the efficacy of passive investing and the development and ease of purchase and sale of exchange-traded funds (ETFs) is that they have become a market-timing tool for active managers. As such, product development has turned into a reductionist slice and dice of markets and sectors, creating a lot of noise. Solid, broad asset class products have been slow to be developed, but are increasing. That is good news. Stick to the criteria we set, and the selection process is relatively painless.

As a final point before we get started, while passive (index) investing is relatively new to the UK, it has been used very broadly in the institutional marketplace for many years. In the UK index strategies now represent around 20 per cent of all institutional assets (IFSL, 2008) and they are used widely by individual investors in the US and Australia. You are not going out on a limb using passive products. In fact it is worth noting that the global passive assets under management had reached US$5,000,000,000,000 (i.e. US$5 trillion) at the end of 2006 (Pensions & Investments, 2007). That is a lot of noughts and a lot of money; to put this in perspective, global pension fund assets stand at around US $18 trillion. You are not alone!

13.1 The serendipity of index-fund investing

The previous two chapters will hopefully have reinforced your conviction that passively managed index funds or ETFs are the way to go, and that costs really do matter. Just because a fund or ETF is passively managed does not mean that it necessarily holds the investing moral high ground. There are some shockingly structured and costly index products out there and you need to be wary of which you choose. Fortunately the selection criteria and process is pretty simple to pick the good from the bad. As Warren Buffett is reported to have said (Bogle, 2002):

'When the dumb investor realizes how dumb he is and invests in an index fund, he becomes smarter than the smartest investor.'

Play the game with the highest probability of success and invest in passively managed index products wherever possible. Choose the lose-the-fewest-points approach. The Dilbert cartoon by Scott Adams shown here sums up the situation perfectly. For those of you in the UK, a mutual fund is the equivalent of a unit trust or OEIC.

Going down the market-replicating route, you will achieve a number of really critical practical, as well as investment, benefits. These are consistent with your philosophy of losing the fewest points:

■ You are likely to beat the majority of actively managed funds over the long run, even if over short periods some active managers outperform the market.

■ If you choose a good fund you will probably never have to change managers during your investing lifetime, saving yourself a lot of angst, tax and transaction charges.

■ You don't have to worry about whether your fund manager is destroying your investment strategy with bad decisions or drifting away from the risks you wish to take.

■ You immediately and dramatically reduce the number of providers and products that you need to consider. This makes your selection process simpler and improves the chances of selecting the best product.

Here is how you can go about that process.

13.2 Choosing your market index

For each asset class exposure in your Smarter Portfolio, you have to decide what benchmark you are going to set and try to replicate it, such as the broad UK equity market. It needs to fully reflect the characteristics that you want in your portfolio and provide the basis for reviewing how well each product is doing in capturing these characteristics. In most cases this benchmark will be a published market index, such as the FTSE All-Share index, which covers a specified group of securities tracked in accordance with some clear and consistent rules. There are many indices to choose from and picking the right one is important. Below are some pointers for doing so.

Your broad market exposures

For your broad market exposures that form the core of your equity allocation, the return benchmark should be the return of the whole domestic market, which provides a diversified and representative benchmark as it includes most public companies, be they large or small and weighted according to their market size. A few very small firms may be excluded.

In the UK the FTSE All-Share is the index of choice for the rational investor. The 'Footsie 100', on the other hand, which is commonly quoted in the media, represents only the biggest hundred companies out of about 2,800 companies listed on the main and the AIM stock markets (the latter tends to be small companies) and only around 80 per cent of the market in terms of capitalisation. Figure 13.1 illustrates how important it is to choose the

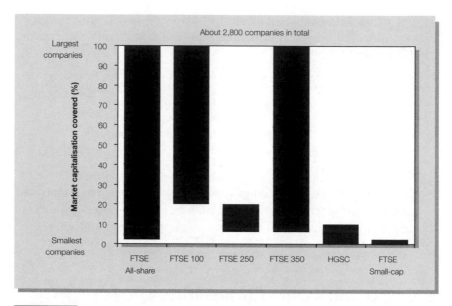

Figure 13.1 UK equity index comparisons

most appropriate benchmark index for your fund or ETF. The general rule of thumb is 'the broader, the better'.

From a global perspective, a world index from either MSCI or FTSE most likely represents the core broad market exposure you need. You need to note that the FTSE All-World series includes some emerging market exposure whereas the FTSE World series does not.

Building-block benchmark choices

The benchmarks that you could use for the various asset classes are set out in Table 13.1. In some cases you can see that for a couple of building blocks, more than one suggestion has been made.

You should always seek to use total return indices where the income, in the form of dividends from equities and coupons from bonds, is reinvested in the market, as opposed to price indices where it is not, as a significant proportion of your long-term returns come from reinvesting income. This applies particularly to your accumulation phase, where you should be reinvesting all the income.

When you select a fund, such as an index (tracker) fund, it is imperative to make sure that you are selecting a product that tracks the index you want

Table 13.1 **Asset class benchmarks**

Growth-oriented, risky asseties	Market index
Broad market exposure	
UK equity market	FTSE All-Share Index (not the FTSE 100)
World ex-UK equities (developed)	FTSE World ex-UK Index
	MSCI World ex-UK Index
World (developed and emerging)	FTSE All-World Index
World equity (developed)	MSCI World Index
	FTSE World Index
Emerging market equities	MSCI Emerging Markets Index
	FTSE All World All Emerging Index

Non-equity asset classes	
Global commercial real estate	S&P Global REIT Index
	FTSE EPRA/NAREIT Global Dividend Plus Index
Commodities	Reuters Jeffries CRB Index
	Dow Jones AIG Commodity Index
	Rogers International Commodity Index
	S&P Goldman Sachs Commodity Index

Risk factor tilts	
UK value equities	FTSE 350 Value Index
	MSCI UK Value Index
	FTSE UK Dividend Plus Index
UK smaller company equities	FTSE Small Cap Index
	Hoare Govett Smaller Companies Index
	FTSE 250 Index
World ex-UK value equities (developed)	MSCI World ex-UK Index Value
World ex-UK smaller companies equities (developed)	FTSE Global Small Cap ex UK Index
	MSCI World ex-UK Index Small Cap
World value equity	FTSE World Index Value Index
	MSCI World Index Value
World smaller companies equity	FTSE Global Equity Index Series Small Cap Index
	MSCI World Index Small Cap

Defensive assets		
UK cash		UK 1-Year T-Bill
		UK 3-month LIBOR
UK Index-linked gilts	(short-dated)	FTSE British Government Index Linked Gilt 0–5 years
	(long-dated)	FTSE British Government Index Linked Gilt (All stocks)
	(long-dated)	Barclays UK Government Inflation-Linked Bond Index
UK Gilts	(long-dated)	FTSE British Government Index (All stocks)
	(short-dated)	FTSE British Government (0–5 year) index

it to track. Just because a fund is called a UK Index Tracker, it does not mean it is tracking the FTSE All-Share index, in fact many replicate the FTSE 100, thereby missing out the medium-sized and smaller companies. The same applies to exchange-traded funds; make sure you know what they are replicating.

13.3 Product structures

When you come to selecting a product, you are presented with two main structures in the UK. That of investing via a unit trust or Open Ended Investment Company (OEIC) which are fund structures that you co-invest in with other investors, and exchange-traded funds that act like shares and are listed on the stock exchange. It is important to understand the differences between the two. Investment trusts are also covered although they are very limited in number when it comes to index replication.

Unit trusts and OEICs

In the UK, funds are known as unit trusts or Open Ended Investment Companies (OEICs), and in the USA they are referred to as mutual funds. In a fund, your money is pooled with other investors' money, but it remains yours and not part of the managing company's balance sheet, unlike when you make a deposit with a bank, or if you take out a with-profits policy with an insurance company. The assets are held by a custodian and an independent board of trustees are meant to look after the interests of investors in the fund. They appoint the custodian and fund managers. For your protection, the manager simply has a management contract to execute trades on the custodial account. Funds are a simple way to gain diversification across the whole market, which would be difficult for you to achieve cost-effectively on your own. You own units or shares in the fund, which are priced daily.

While investing via funds has been a very effective way for individuals and institutions to gain access to broad company ownership or lending opportunities, one structural drawback is that you are exposed to the whims, to some extent, of the other investors in the fund. Large investments into or out of the fund will result in large transaction costs which are charged against the fund's performance. Even if you are a long-term buy-and-hold investor you will pay your share of their costs. Depending on what fund you own, this may range from the negligible to the significant. Some more forward thinking fund management firms have introduced dilution levies on entry and exit that force each investor to wear their own costs, which no-one can really argue with.

A well-structured fund with a wide number of investors and large in size still provides a very worthy structure for the individual investor. In the UK passively managed index funds are often referred to as 'trackers'.

Exchange-traded funds (ETFs)

These should be considered alongside index funds as the vehicle of choice for a rational investor. Exchange-traded funds are similar to index funds but are shares listed on a stock exchange, which usually reflect the basket of securities that constitute a chosen index. It should be noted that some ETFs are derivative backed and this exposes the investor to both basis risk (i.e. the risk that the derivate contract does not deliver the index return) and, to a limited degree, counterparty risk, i.e. the risk of default of the other side of the derivative contract. However, the UCITS III (adopted on an EU-wide basis that set certain guidelines on products and the sale of funds across borders) help to ensure that this exposure is limited to around 10 per cent of the ETFs net asset value. The funds and ETFs that you buy should be UCITS III approved. The assets of an ETF are ring-fenced and in the event of the collapse of the product provider, investors have recourse to the ring-fenced assets.

Many of the world's major institutional investors use ETFs to help position their portfolios. At the end of 2008 there were around 1,600 ETFs globally and US$711 billion of assets invested in them. Europe's share of the number is 632 with U$142 billion invested (BGI, 2008).

ETFs tend to have low total expense ratios. One point to note is that many of them pay dividends, which you will need to reinvest yourself.

Investment trusts

Investment trusts share many of the properties of funds but are companies listed on the stock exchange and are, in some ways, like ETFs. Investment trusts are usually actively managed, but some replicate specific indexes like an index fund. They can be bought through brokers. A quirk of investment trusts is that they trade at either a premium or a discount to their net asset value or NAV (effectively the liquidation value of selling all the stocks). These arise through supply and demand mismatches and also the perception of the management of the investment trust and perhaps the leverage (borrowing) they are able to use. Somewhat surprisingly, index-replicating trusts also seem to trade at discounts and premiums to the NAV. Costs can be lower than for OEICs and unit trusts. Some investors look to take advantage of the changes in discounts, but that is a secondary and difficult game. They may be worth a look, but your best bet lies in the index funds and ETF universe.

13.4 Selecting the best passively managed index funds and ETFs

One of the great advantages of taking the index route, apart from giving yourself the best chance of achieving your goals, is that selecting a product is straightforward. Over the past couple of years, the choice and quality of index funds and ETFs have improved markedly, as Table 13.2 illustrates. Still, there are probably fewer than 100 UK-based index tracker funds and ETFs to choose from, across all building blocks, some of which you can discard quickly as they track inappropriate indices or building blocks. It's easier to choose from 100 index funds/ETFs than from 3,000 active funds, and the process of choosing the best is far simpler.

Tracking error is your critical selection criteria

The ultimate goal of using an index tracker fund, or ETF, is to gather as much of the market return as you can. The degree to which returns differ from the chosen index is known as tracking error (i.e. the standard deviation of returns relative to the index). This can be caused by a number of factors, which we will look at below. Tracking error of 2 per cent is the outer limit of what is acceptable and the lower the better. Remember that even small differences can mount up over time due to the effects of compounding.

An established fund will be able to prove what its tracking error has been, demonstrate the consistency of its replication process and make you feel comfortable that it will be able to reproduce its strong results in the future. Some funds publish tracking error. If for some reason they don't, just compare the returns on a year-by-year and cumulative basis against the index, e.g. the FTSE All-Share index, or ask their customer service team for the data. If the differences are large, on the upside as well as the downside, the fund is not well managed, or is replicating a different index from the one you think it is. There is no reason to choose a new index fund, which is unproven in its ability successfully to track the index. Here are some of the ways in which tracking error occurs.

Table 13.2 Guidelines for selecting index funds

Criteria	What to look out for
Index being tracked	■ Check it is tracking your chosen index ■ Remember – *total return* not *price* index
Tracking error	■ As low as possible, preferably less than 1% ■ Check cumulative returns versus index over five years ■ Avoid if significantly below (or above) index
Total expense ratio (TER)	■ Look for a very low TER. Less than 0.3% is good
Initial fee	■ Don't pay one
Fund size and age	■ Larger funds tend to be easier to manage ■ Avoids effects of a big investor pulling out ■ Five years' minimum record
Fund turnover	■ Less than 5% for broad equity markets
Replication process	■ Check what process is used ■ Ask why it makes sense for this fund
Manager experience	■ Always look for a team that has done its job well ■ Stability is a plus, as experience counts
Redemption fee	■ Fine if it is short term (one year)

Replication methods affect tracking error

The way in which the investment manager chooses to copy the index is important. There are three common methods that are used.

■ **Full replication**: As its name suggests, each company in the index is purchased by the fund. This would give you zero tracking error in a world where transaction costs are zero, but it's not the world we live in. Inevitably, transaction costs will create some tracking error. In addition, smaller funds may suffer from having to buy odd lots of stock that cannot be split as the amount being purchased is too small. Corporate actions and dividend payments also create activity that may generate tracking error.

■ **Sampling (or partial replication)**: In this case, the manager takes the view that the cost of creating and maintaining a portfolio with all the securities in the index is greater than the tracking error risk of holding only some of the securities. The manager will use some form of optimisation model to put together a sample of securities that mimics the index as closely as possible.

- **Derivatives**: This method is less common and places most of the funds in cash and purchases derivative instruments that mimic the market. Sometimes funds use both sampling and derivatives.

You should always check to see what type of process is used and ask why it makes sense for this kind of index. Take a look and see what other providers are doing.

Fees and costs contribute to tracking error

Fees always go a long way towards explaining tracking error, as not all index funds are made equal. Some charge very low fees of a few basis points (100ths of 1 per cent) and others as high as 1 per cent for domestic retail products. Better still, find out what the total expense ratio (TER) of the fund is. Never pay an initial fee for an index fund. Some index funds are taking the 'mickey' with high upfront fees and high TERs. Vote with your wallet and avoid them. Chapter 14 covers costs in detail.

Size may contribute to tracking error

This is important due to lot sizes, explained above. It may affect the decision as to how the fund is replicated, which may not be the most effective method to use. Being in a small fund may expose you to additional tracking error if a large investor suddenly withdraws. Size may also imply limited manager experience.

Turnover may contribute to tracking error

In some jurisdictions, such as the USA, turnover is very important to the taxable investor and should be avoided as much as possible. Some funds may perform as well as other funds and have similar tracking error but after-tax returns may be lower as a result of portfolio turnover. In the UK, a unit trust or an OEIC does not pay capital gains tax, so turnover is less important, at least from a tax perspective. It does matter though from a transaction cost perspective.

Manager experience will affect tracking error

Index investing is not just a 'plug it into the computer and sit back' process. Skilled index managers are aware of each of the elements of their process where tracking error can occur and they manage them very tightly. There is no substitute for experience and success. We will look briefly at one of the most respected index investor in the industry later.

There are enough high-quality index funds and ETFs for you not to have to stray outside these parameters for your core building blocks, but 'tilt' asset classes are still an issue. Currently, index bond funds and ETFs are a bit limited in the UK. Over time, index fund fees are expected to fall and more managers will enter the market. It is likely that your choice of asset classes/risk factors will also increase. Getting it right upfront is very important as you don't want to have to switch later on, particularly if you are a taxable investor. It is worth remembering that although there are limited funds to choose from, you only need one excellent fund for each asset class to build your portfolio with.

13.5 Passive providers

There are several dominant providers of passive products in the UK, whom you may wish to contact to get hold of some literature and prospectuses to review. There is also a wide range of smaller providers, whom you may want to seek out too. This is not a definitive list or in any way a recommendation – it just helps to steer you to some of the longer-established firms with the widest choice of building blocks. Some are omitted, not by implication but for the sake of simplicity. The onus is on you to work out which is most suitable for you.

Passive index fund providers

In the UK, according to the Investment Management Association's website (see below) there are around 50 index funds available to UK investors. The main index fund providers in the UK include: Legal & General (www.legalandgeneral.co.uk), AVIVA, which was formerly called Norwich Union (www.aviva.co.uk), Fidelity (www.fidelity.co.uk), and HSBC (www.hsbc.com). There are quite a few others too. The quickest way to get a list is to use the Investment Management Association's website using the direction provided below. In the USA, Vanguard is a leading provider of index funds and at the start of 2009 announced its arrival in the UK retail market. It is offering its funds only via advisers. This is a big step forward in the UK, providing some serious competition to the current crop of providers. Hopefully they will make their funds available to direct (DIY) investors too.

One group, Dimensional Fund Advisors (DFA), is perhaps best described as a passive risk factor fund provider. It focuses specifically on creating efficient portfolios that deliver pure risk factor exposures (i.e. value and small cap exposures) across global developed and emerging markets, rather than trying to replicate specific and common market indices. It manages them carefully to try to avoid some of the attritional costs that are associated with traditional index fund replication. They are only available to individual investors through selected advisers around the globe, including a growing number in the UK. If you use an adviser you should perhaps ask the question.

Exchange-traded fund providers

When selecting an exchange-traded fund (ETF), a similar focus exists: check the total expense ratio and see how closely the ETF tracks its chosen index. See how much money is invested in the ETF you are looking at – bigger is generally better. Start with the bigger providers such as 'iShares' (www.ishares.co.uk), Lyxor Asset Management (www.lyxoretf.com), db x-trackers (www.dbx-trackers.com) and EasyETF (www.easyetf.com). It may be worth noting that iShares ETFs are predominantly backed by an underlying basket of securities, db x-trackers and Lyxor are almost exclusively swap (derivative) based and EasyETF offer a mixture (IndexUniverse, 2008). My preference would be to own a basket of actual securities – it seems cleaner and more transparent. However, you may need to make some compromises on this as you may not be able to find appropriate products. Certainly try to fill your core allocations using ETFs backed by a basket of securities.

Keep a look out for new products. Be prepared to reinvest dividends.

Where to find information on indices

As part of your research into different asset classes and as part of your monitoring once you have established a portfolio, it is useful to get your hands on historic index data. This includes the following websites: www.mscibarra.com for UK and global equity markets (in US$ and local currencies), www.dowjones.com for its commodities index (in US$), www.crbtrader.com for its commodity index (in US$). The hardest index time series to find are the FTSE Indices and they generally have to be paid for. However, the www.ftse.com website does provide some useful information on how their indices are constructed.

In terms of monitoring your portfolio, index returns for each building block should be provided online by the provider. If not, ask the product provider for them. You have a right to know. Most ETF providers supply quite detailed information on the tracking error of their products.

Where to find useful information on funds

The easiest place to access information is online. If you are familiar and comfortable with the internet, you can access a wealth of information that can help reduce the number of possible funds needed to replicate your asset class mix. In the UK, progress has been slow, relative to that in the USA, in providing good information to investors. Things are improving, but no single website is perfect. Below are brief descriptions of some of the leading providers of information on funds in the UK, and in some cases globally. These are free sites at the basic level. Some charge fees for additional research. As a tip, where you cannot simply select index funds on those sites, search by TER to narrow down the field. Good index funds tend to have the lowest TERs.

Investment Management Association (IMA): www.investmentfunds.org.uk

This is the trade body for the UK's investment management industry. It provides good background information. The site has an investor menu and an option called 'Find a Fund'. This allows you to search funds available to UK investors in a number of ways including by total expense ratio and index tracker. Search and find the bulk of index funds available. Sort by total expense ratio (TER). You can see that TERs range from around 0.3 per cent to over 2 per cent! It's a good start but you will need to use other sites to gain a better insight into the detail of each fund.

Trustnet: www.trustnet.com

Trustnet's site covers all of the UK's unit trusts, OEICs and ETFs. You can click on the exchange-traded fund option to get a list of GBP-priced ETFs (sort on the currency column). You will need to look more closely at each fund by clicking through the link on the fund name. Some firms provide information, whereas others don't. For those funds that provide information you can compare the fund's performance versus the index and get a feel for its tracking error, size and fees. Expense ratios can be obtained by cross-referencing to the IMA site. Do some investigation yourself.

Table 13.3 Some suggestions for your product search

Market Index	Possible products	Structure	TER*
Broad equity market exposure			
FTSE All-Share Index	Legal and General UK Index Trust	Fund	0.52%
	Fidelity MoneyBuilder UK Index Fund	Fund	0.27%
	db x-trackers FTSE All-Share	ETF	0.40%
FTSE World ex-UK Index	Aviva Investor International Index Tracking Fund	Fund	0.95%
	db x-trackers FTSE All-World ex-UK	ETF	0.40%
MSCI World ex-UK Index	None at present	–	–
FTSE All-World Index-ex UK	db x-trackers FTSE All-World ex-UK	ETF	0.40%
FTSE All-World Index	None at present	–	–
MSCI World Index	iShares MSCI World	ETF	0.50%
	db x-trackers MSCI World TRN Index	ETF	0.45%
FTSE World Index	iShares FTSE Developed World ex-UK	ETF	0.50%
MSCI Emerging Markets Free Index	iShares MSCI Emerging Markets	ETF	0.75%
	db x-trackers MSCI Emerging Markets TRN Index	ETF	0.65%
FTSE All-World All-Emerging Index	None at present	–	–
Non-equity asset classes			
S&P Global REIT Index	None at present	–	–
FTSE EPRA/NAREIT Global Index	EasyETF FTSE EPRA/NAREIT Global Index	ETF	0.50%
FTSE EPRA/NAREIT Global Dividend Plus Index	iShares FTSE EPRA/NAREIT GlobalProperty Yield Fund	ETF	0.59%
Reuters Jeffries CRB Index	Lyxor ETF CRB GBP	ETF	0.35%
Dow Jones AIG Commodity Index	ETFS All Commodities DJ-AIGCI (USD)	ETF	0.49%
Style tilts (value and small)**			
FTSE 350 Value Index	None at present	–	–
MSCI UK Value Index	None at present	–	–
FTSE UK Dividend Plus Index	iShares UK FTSE UK Dividend Plus	ETF	0.40%
FTSE Small Cap Index	None at present	–	–
Hoare Govett Smaller Companies Index	None at present	–	–
FTSE 250 Index (more a mid–small cap index)	iShares FTSE 250	ETF	0.40%

Market Index	Possible products	Structure	TER*
Global value	There are limited options here**	–	–
	Regional high dividend ETFs act as the only proxy	–	–
Global small	There are limited options here**	ETFs	Look up
	Regional small cap ETFs from iShares	ETFs	Look up
Defensive assets			
Cash			
UK 1-year Treasury Bill	None at present – watch this space	–	–
UK cash (e.g. LIBOR or SONIA)	Fidelity Cash Fund	Fund	0.40%
	db x-trackers Sterling Money Market ETF	ETF	0.15%
Index-linked			
Index-linked National Savings Certificates	www.nsandi.com provides details	Certificate	No charge
Directly held (choose maturity – buy-and-hold)	Via a brokerage account	–	Trade cost
FTSE British Government Index-Linked Gilt (0–5 years)	None available at present – watch this space	–	–
FTSE British Government Index-Linked Gilt (All stocks)	Legal and General All Stocks Index-Linked Gilts	Fund	0.22%
Barclays UK Government Inflation-Linked Bond Index	iShares £ Index-Linked Gilts	ETF	0.25%
Conventional gilts – longer-dated			
FTSE British Government Index (All stocks)	iShares FTSE UK All Stocks Gilt	ETF	0.20%
Shorter-dated			
FTSE British Government Index (0–5)	iShares FTSE Gilts (0–5) years	ETF	0.20%

*December 2008
**Dimensional Fund Advisors Ltd offer style funds via select advisors

FT Funds: http://funds.ft.com/funds

The *Financial Times* has established a fund-rating service, which uses a similar database of funds to some of the other sites and provides a search mechanism based on its own classifications of fund risk. This is a useful site and can again be used with the other sites.

Morningstar: www.morningstar.co.uk

This is a global group that provides information on the universe of funds available to UK investors and provides a rating system for funds based on stars. This is a widely used service in the USA. Some investors use the rating system as some sort of endorsement of future market-beating performance for higher-rated funds, which it is not.

On the website, go to the 'Fund' tab on the home page and choose the 'Fund Screener' menu option and then use the drop-down menus to look at the fund options. Again you have to sift out the index funds for yourself. If you click on the fund name you get a brief summary. You may want to use the IMA's site first. There is also an ETF tab too.

Morningstar rate funds in each category from one-star (poorest) to five-star (strongest), based on risk-adjusted performance. Reading the fund rating reports provides some useful insights

Caveat

This brief review of a few independent fund information websites represents my own personal opinions. Use and evaluate them yourself. At the end of the day, you need to be comfortable with the information that you have to hand before you commit your money. You should take advice if you feel you need it. Using these sites, you should be able to come up with a shortlist of funds. You can request literature from the fund companies by phone or online and get answers to any questions that you may have. Ask them whatever you want. They want your money and should be pleased to help.

13.6 A possible shortlist – *caveat emptor*!

Table 13.3 provides a few product names to start your search with. Broadly, you can find pretty reasonable passive products that provide you with exposure to the risks that you are seeking to take on in the more core elements of your portfolio (UK, global and emerging equity, global real estate and commodity futures). Tilts to value and small cap stocks are a little less well covered, if you are trying to invest on a DIY basis. If you are using an adviser, then you may want to see if they use the Dimensional Fund Advisors' (DFA) range or other instutionally accessible products. Remember that you may have to balance the wish to gain exposure to a specific type of risk, with less than perfect product solutions. If you don't think the product is robust enough then perhaps you should consider reallocating that part of the portfolio and waiting until new products arrive on the market.

13.7 Using active funds (if you must)

I know that some of you will still be tempted! The hope of beating the markets over the certainty of underperforming the market by costs of an index fund is a strong, if irrational, emotion. Perhaps the most valid reason is if you cannot find an ETF or index fund to replicate the asset class you really want in your portfolio. This is particularly true in the return-enhancing tilt allocations, where index products for UK investors remain scarce at this point.

Sifting out the fact from the fiction is not an easy task in the actively managed fund world as marketing departments have plenty of scope to paint a rosy picture as to why their firm is the one that will win. The fact that they all claim to beat the market is a bit of a clue as to what you are up against! Past performance has been the driver for advertising campaigns and the sale of funds around the world. Yet you know that past performance tells you little about future outperformance. It is true that a few truly talented managers are out there – the problem is sorting the wheat from the chaff. Picking truly talented managers is as difficult as picking stocks. There are two key steps: the first is to find the right sort of manager, and the second is to find the right sort of fund.

Locating the right type of manager

Picking the right manager is a difficult task, given that performance is of little help. As a result, you need to make a qualitative assessment of a manager whom you will never get to meet and on whom you will get precious little information other than a glossy marketing biography. There are, however, some underlying characteristics that you should be looking for. They don't define a good manager but good managers are likely to be found in this subset. In short, the few managers who you want managing your money tend to have a passion for investing, bordering on obsession, have integrity and put your best interests at the forefront of whatever they do. Here are some things to look out for:

- **Independence**: Independent private firms tend to have longer-term motivations based on quality and reputation rather than gathering assets to deliver profits to a parent company's bottom line, above all else.

- **Aligned interests**: It is always good to see a fund manager who has a direct and significant stake in the funds he or she manages. Look at websites closely – those that do are likely to tell you. In addition, firms that are focused on investment quality tend to restrict the size of their funds, closing them to new money rather than just see them balloon into unmanageable beasts with diluted excess return potential.

- **Longevity**: Too many managers jump ship for money. You should be looking for someone with the conviction that what his or her firm is doing is the best way to be doing it, and it is worth staying with. Remember that if you are a taxable investor, cashing out and reinvesting to follow a manager could be very costly. Remember, you need them to stick around for twenty to thirty years. Unfortunately for you, only seventeen fund managers in the UK have been managing their fund for more than fifteen years! True.

- **Process**: Some fund management firms have disciplined, quantitative processes that seek to take the emotion out of investing, which helps them to be a little more contrarian in their approach. Disciplined processes that can be demonstrated to work, with strong proof statements, are worth considering and provide an alternative to concentration of future performance in the hands of a single manager who may retire or move funds.

Locating the right type of fund

- **Index choice**: Make sure you only look at funds that are trying to beat your chosen benchmark index.

- **Screening**: Narrow the universe of funds further by screening out persistently poor performers, particularly those with high costs.

- **Costs**: Always check fee levels and total expense ratios. Pick funds at the lower end of the expense spectrum. There is no evidence that higher fees lead to better performance, except in the cars that the managers drive. Avoid initial fees, and funds with high turnover. Costs mean greater hurdles to success.

■ **Information ratio**: In plain English this tells you how much return a manager creates through their skill, rather than that from the market, for the additional risk (tracking error) that their decisions incur, relative to the market. The higher this ratio, the better. Information ratios, after fees, of 0.5 and above, over a reasonable time frame, are considered good; yet even with a ratio of 0.5, you need at least fifteen years to know whether this is generated by skill or luck!

■ **Up and down markets**: It is worth taking a look at how the manager has performed in both up and down markets. Hopefully, a good manager will be able to demonstrate their skill in most conditions. Many managers in the late 1990s did well in the bull market by overexposing their clients' money to technology stocks, but looked woeful when this gamble came home to roost. It is always worth asking what the worst period has been, why that was and how they responded.

■ **Cash balances**: Look for funds where cash balances are and have been low. Cash, over the long run, will always be a drag on performance.

■ **Limit the number of funds you own**: While many investors are seduced by the prospect of beating the market over the long run, many inherently understand that the risk of a manager underperforming exists, and own several similar funds. Unfortunately your investments will resemble the broad market pretty closely, and you now own an index-like fund but with active fees.

One particular problem you face is that if you find a manager you like and they move, you will have to sell up, crystallise capital gains, perhaps need to pay tax to the Chancellor that could still be in your portfolio, and probably pay additional fees to get into the manager's new fund. These costs could seriously erode much of the good work they are doing. All in all, this advice may not seem very helpful, but there is no easy way to select good active funds that will outperform over the long run. If you find one, let me know. If you can't, you know what to do.

In conclusion

When selecting products to implement your Smarter Portfolio:

- Choose a reasonable market index for each risk factor you are seeking to replicate.
- Start with the main providers of funds and ETFs.
- Screen possible solutions against the criteria provided.
- Consider the risk exposure replication method carefully.
- If no or very weak products (for tilts) exist, consider getting reallocating exposure.
- Monitor on an ongoing basis.
- Keep an eye out for new products – they will be emerging rapidly.

References

Barclays Global Investors (BGI) (2008) *ETF Industry Preview Year End 2008*.

Bogle, J. C. (2002) The investment dilemma of the philanthropic investor. Bogle Financial Markets Research Center. Available from: http://www.vanguard.com.

IndexUniverse.com (2008) 'More on Counterparty Risk (Swap-based ETFs)', October, www.indexuniverse.com.

IFSL (2008) 'Fund Management 2008', www.ifsl.org.uk.

Pensions & Investments (2007) 'Index Managers: Wow, $% trillion', 19 March.

14

Costs – what a drag

A book that places a lose-the-fewest-points philosophy at its core would be incomplete without taking a good look at the effect of costs on an investment programme.

14.1 Why do we throw our money away?

The adage 'a penny saved is a penny earned' has never been more apt than when investing. Yet investors tend to be poor at understanding the true effect of costs on their wealth; surprising, given that in other walks of life they would be indignant about similar usurious levels of costs. Costs make a significant difference to your lifestyle in the future. After setting your long-term investment policy, controlling them is the most important factor in investment success, although controlling your emotions is right up there too.

To get your attention, on what sounds like a boring subject, take a look at the bullet points below. To quote research by the FSA (James, 2000):

'One must invest about £1.50 in an actively managed unit trust ... in order to obtain the market rate of return on £1; and that ...

Obtaining the market rate of return on £1 requires an investment of about £1.10 to £1.25 in an index tracker.'

Now that is a worrying statistic for every investor. The industry croupier is stealing from your pocket. Costs are also higher in the UK than the USA where these levels are closer to $1.30 for active funds and $1.10 for index funds. Yet as investors we seem unconcerned with costs for some strange reason; only 14 per cent of respondents to a survey in the UK (Autif, 1998) said that reasonable charges were the main reason that they chose a fund. Most buy on past performance, which you now know to be a lottery. There seem to be number of reasons for this:

- We don't have to pay cash to settle the bills – it all comes out of performance, and thus feels painless.

- We are used to paying for professional services such as accountants and lawyers, where we get something for our money, so why not investment managers?

- We have an innate feeling that in a competitive market higher costs will result in higher quality. That's simply not the case.

- We underestimate the long-term effects that small differences in annual costs make to the result of investing. Exponential effects over time are hard to calculate in our heads.

- We fail to identify just who has their hands in our pockets.

Let's run through an example of the costs that you will incur as an investor. These are much more than just the annual management fees that a fund manager will charge. To understand the effect of costs we will look at two hypothetical actively managed funds – High Cost Fund and Low Cost Fund – towards the end of this chapter.

14.2 More than just management fees

Funds incur a wide range of seen and unseen costs. Let's start at the beginning:

Cost 1: Management fees

This represents the direct remuneration that the fund manager gets from you in return for managing the fund and which is calculated as an annual percentage of assets managed. As a brief aside, some funds that focus on paying income may take management fees from your capital so that they can pay a higher level of income – watch out, as your capital will be quickly eroded by this practice and inflation, our second cost.

Cost 2: Inflation

This is the one unavoidable cost. You can only spend *real returns*. All annual fees eat away heavily, in percentage terms, at your real returns. For example, 2 per cent costs from a 10 per cent return before inflation means that 20 per cent of your returns are eaten up by costs. But 2 per cent costs after inflation of 3 per cent leaves you with only half of your nominal return. Always think of the effect of costs on real returns.

Cost 3: Initial fees

Initial fees, sometimes known as upfront fees, sales fees, or loads, are taken from you at the outset, purportedly to cover the cost of advice. If you have a true fee-based adviser they should pass all of this back to you. High upfront fees are the norm in the UK except for index trackers; yet even some of those have the audacity to charge initial fees – avoid them if they do.

It's common to accept blindly that initial fees are an inevitable sunk cost, but that attitude will cost you dear. If you pay an upfront fee of 6 per cent on a £10,000 investment, over thirty years this would be equivalent to almost £3,000 of your future purchasing power given up. General advice is to avoid paying initial fees wherever possible. The only exception is a dilution levy that covers the cost of you entering the fund. This is only fair. Once you are in the fund you will not suffer the cost of entry or exit of others.

Cost 4: Total expense ratio (TER)

The fund manager will be paid an annual management fee calculated as a percentage of your assets; but that's only the start of the annual cost story. Several additional costs are charged annually to the fund, reducing the overall performance of your investments. In aggregate, these annual costs are known as a fund's *total expense ratio* (TER). Fortunately, Fitzrovia provides excellent industry-wide coverage of fund TERs and these can be accessed on websites described later. Fitzrovia's TER calculation is defined as:

*'The annual percentage reduction in investor returns that would result from largely fixed operating costs if markets were to remain flat and the fund's portfolio were to be held **and not traded** during a period.'*

We will come to the issue of costs associated with trading a portfolio in a moment. First, take a look at Table 14.1, which illustrates the TER of a specific fund using data from Fitzrovia. You can see that the total costs are far more than just the management fees. In this case, annual management fees are 1.3 per cent a year, yet the TER of the fund is actually 2.27 per cent, a whole 1 per cent higher.

Furthermore, as you can see from Figure 14.1, average TER levels are high –
too high for the rational investor. Index tracker funds have the lowest
average TER, which is still far higher than in the USA, where the best are
around 10 basis points, or 0.1 per cent. Put simply, the UK investor deserves
better. Careful screening for funds, in particular index funds, that control
costs and thus have low TERs, will pay rich dividends for you.

Table 14.1 Annual management fees are just the start

Fee category	Annual cost	As %
Management fees	**£316,000**	**1.30%**
Registrar's fees	£30,000	
Marketing fees	£41,000	
Secretarial fees	£58,000	
Custodian's fees	£28,000	
Audit fees	£7,000	
Professional fees	£15,000	
Directors' fees	£31,000	
Other expenses	£27,000	
Total expense ratio	**£553,000**	**2.27%**

Average net assets over 365 days £24,336,692.
Source: Lipper Fitzrovia.

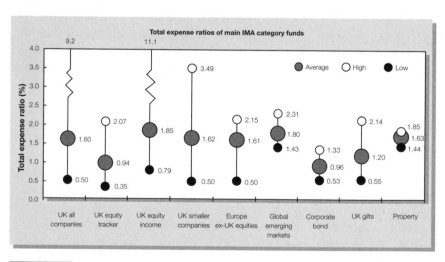

Figure 14.1 TERs are surprisingly high in the UK

Source: Lipper Fitzrovia data from Investment Management Association website, December 2002.

Cost 5: Portfolio turnover

As you can see from the definition above, the TER is based on a scenario where 'the fund's portfolio were to be held and not traded during a period'. Yet this is not realistic, because an active fund manager will be making decisions all the time to try to beat the market, buying and selling investments regularly. This activity is known as *turnover* on the portfolio, which is usually measured as a percentage of the value of the total portfolio that is sold and bought each year.

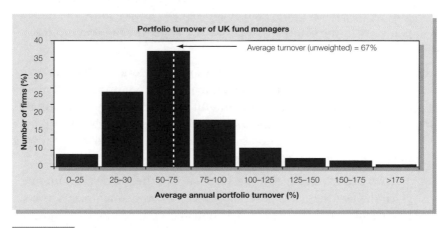

Figure 14.2 **Investment managers are busy people**

Source: Lipper Fitzrovia, December 2002.

Levels of turnover have risen significantly over the past couple of decades with portfolios in some cases looking more like speculative short-term trading strategies rather than longer-term investments. In the USA, around forty years ago, turnover was about 15 per cent, meaning that a portfolio's holdings turned over once every six years or so. Today, with turnover of 100 per cent on average, portfolios are changed completely every year.

It appears that today's managers believe that they can spot undervalued securities, which then achieve a price that reflects their value in under a year. Wow, they must be good! Turnover costs. A study in the UK, again by Fitzrovia, looked at portfolio turnover for UK fund managers. On average, it is pretty high, as you can see in Figure 14.2, at around 67 per cent of the portfolio every year.

There are several components to the cost of turnover:

■ **Broker's commission**: Fund managers sell and buy shares through brokers who get paid a commission for each trade they make. Ideally these arrangements should ensure best execution, i.e. the best price, for the client. Unfortunately an issue called 'soft dollars' has, in the past, meant that trades have been directed towards certain brokers and in return managers have received things such as research and software systems, at the cost of best execution. This costs you money.

■ **Bid/offer spread**: This is the difference between the cost of buying and selling a share. A broker will buy shares at below the mid-point price of the shares in the market and sell you shares above the mid-point. So, in the course of trade you will suffer the bid (buy) /offer (sell) spread.

■ **Price effects**: This is a cost that arises if large blocks of shares are either being bought or sold. Market makers, who set prices, will move the price during the trade. Demand for shares, i.e. a buy, will push the price of shares up before the completed purchase is made. Big fund management group insist on secrecy when they trade to avoid moving the price against themselves too far.

■ **The taxman**: Of course, he gets his hand in the pie. This is amazing given the fact that large portions of money invested represents assets that people are trying hard to accumulate to provide for themselves in their retirement, an activity so encouraged by the government. Stamp duty is paid on the purchase of shares.

Table 14.2 Turnover is costly

Cost of a round-trip trade (selling and buying)

Commission	30 basis points
Bid/offer spread	75 basis points
Price impact	25 basis points
Stamp Duty	50 basis points
Total	**180 basis points = 1.8%**

Source: James (2000).

So what does turnover cost? The answer is that it probably costs somewhere in the region of 1.5 per cent to 1.8 per cent for a round-trip in the UK market, i.e. selling a share and replacing it with another as you can see from Table 14.2. You can therefore calculate the cost that a fund manager incurs by multiplying 1.8 per cent by the level of turnover activity they create on the fund. In some cases the costs may be higher, in others lower, depending on the firm's relationship with its brokers, the shares being traded and the size of trade. This figure is good enough for our purposes. With turnover of 67 per cent for the average fund, the cost associated with it is 1.2 per cent a year. The hurdle for the active manager grows.

Cost 6: Taxes

In the UK, unit trusts and OEICs do not incur capital gains tax on sales of securities held within them, although they may pay income tax on some forms of income. If you own such a fund, as far as you are concerned, you will pay capital gains tax between the cost of buying a fund, indexed up according to the chancellor's latest rules, and the value you sold it for. So, turnover has no effect from a tax perspective within the fund. Other structures such as pension plans, PEPs and ISAs are tax-free for most income and all capital gains. Check with your tax adviser if you want details.

If your assets fall outside tax-efficient structures you will incur capital gains tax once you have used up your annual allowance, paying cash to the chancellor that could otherwise have been compounding in your portfolio. Some estimates put this tax cost at somewhere between 1 per cent and 2 per cent a year with turnover of 50 per cent. It is evident that for a taxable investor, portfolios with low turnover are better than portfolios with high turnover. By and large, well-managed index funds have a turnover below 5 per cent for broad market exposure.

Assessing the effect of your 'all-in' costs

All-in, you have upfront fees, everything that goes into TERs, turnover costs and possible tax consequences to suffer. Controlling costs is important. The best way of demonstrating just how much of your return pie the industry will take is to consider two hypothetical funds: High Cost Fund and Low Cost Fund.

Let's assume that these are both managers who can produce an annualised return of 10 per cent before factoring in any costs. With inflation at, say, 3 per cent, the annualised increase in the purchasing power of your money, or in other words your real return, is 7 per cent. High Cost Fund has an investment process that turns over the portfolio 100 per cent every year. Low Cost Fund turns over 10 per cent of the value of the portfolio. Not only are their investment styles different but also their marketing departments have created different fee structures (Table 14.3).

As you can see there is almost a 3 per cent difference between the two managers. High Cost Fund's manager has to be considerably better at beating the market to beat Low Cost Fund's manager, simply because of its turnover strategy and pricing policies. Taking an initial investment of £10,000 we can work out just what a difference these two different approaches make to your long-term wealth accumulation. With High Cost Fund you head to Bognor and with Low Cost Fund the Bahamas beckons. Over thirty years you give up well over 50 per cent of your future purchasing power (Table 14.4). The choice is yours.

Low Cost Fund is essentially a well run index fund; you can see why an index fund is such a compelling proposition; the hurdle that high cost funds set themselves is very high, requiring significant market-beating decisions, simply to catch up.

Table 14.3 The effect of costs and fee structures

Cost	Low Cost Fund	High Cost Fund
Initial charge	**0%**	**5%**
Initial amount invested (£10,000)	£10,000	£9,500
Annual management fee	0.10%	1.50%
Other expenses	0.20%	0.30%
Total expense ratio (TER)	**0.30%**	**1.80%**
Turnover	5%	100%
Turnover costs*	0.08%	1.50%
Total annual costs	**0.38%**	**3.30%**
Nominal return	10.00%	10.00%
Real return before costs	7.00%	7.00%
Real return after costs	**6.63%**	**3.70%**

*Estimated conservatively at 1.5%.

Table 14.4 Costs matter, as John Bogle would say

Fund	Amount invested after initial fee	10 years	20 years	30 years
Low Cost Fund	£10,000	£18,993	£36,073	£68,513
High Cost Fund	£9,500	£13,662	£19,647	£28,254
Difference	**£500**	**£5,331**	**£16,426**	**£40,259**

14.3 Summary: costs – what a drag

■ You need to get a handle on costs because they really will make a significant difference to your investment programme.

■ In the UK, costs remain ludicrously high for most products.

■ Avoid paying initial fees; they add nothing to your investment programme. Never pay an initial fee for an index fund.

■ Costs are far more than just annual management fees. Always look at total expense ratios. Avoid paying over 0.5 per cent TER for developed market equities and defensive assets – aim for lower.

■ All in all, know who is dipping their hands in your pocket, give them a sharp slap on the wrist by avoiding their products, and avoid dealing with them in future. Keep as much in your pocket as you can. After all, it is your money, you are taking the risks with it and it is your future that is being affected.

References

Autif (1998) as quoted in FSA (2001) *Comparative tables: Bulletin No.1*. London: FSA, Annex A, p. 5. Available from: http://www.fsa.gov.uk.

James, K. R. (2000) *The price of retail investing in the UK*, London: FSA, FSA Occasional Paper.

15

Standing firm on index funds

In an industry dominated by managers trying to beat the markets for a living and advisers who rely on the fees and commissions that active investment products provide, you should not be too surprised if you come across resistance to accepting the validity of the index fund and its rightful place as the default vehicle at the core of a portfolio. A number of arguments are used to dissuade investors from using index funds. Have the confidence to know that you are right and stand your ground.

15.1 Common put-downs

The common arguments that you will face are easy to refute. Remember that just because they may be able to find isolated cases to support their arguments, you are playing a game of probabilities, which always lie in favour of using index funds unless an active manager can really demonstrate their superior and sustainable skills.

Argument 1: You don't want all that rubbish

Telling you that you shouldn't be forced to hold rubbish in your portfolios simply because it is in the index is a common put-down. The argument suggests that active managers can avoid this rubbish and choose to own only 'good' stocks.

At one level you may find yourself agreeing with this – after all, why would you want to hold the stock of a company that has a poor outlook? Remember, though, that markets appear to be quite efficient and the price of each company's shares should reflect all available public information about it. There is a big difference between a good company and a good investment, as many astute investors have pointed out. Perhaps the rubbish is priced appropriately; owning rubbish is therefore not a problem if the price reflects its outlook. Remember, a higher cost of capital delivers a higher expected return.

The empirical evidence tells us that the majority of active managers are beaten by index funds in the long run, suggesting that it is hard to pick the good investments from the supposed rubbish to a degree that covers their all-in costs.

Argument 2: Active managers can hold cash in falling markets

Active managers have an advantage over index funds because they can move into cash when markets are overvalued, and then shift back into equities once markets are set to rise; or that at least is how the argument goes.

If active managers can pick these market turning points before they happen, you would expect to see cash levels in funds to be at their highest at market peaks, in anticipation of market falls and at their lowest at the bottom of the markets. This seems like a reasonable case, but the evidence again suggests otherwise.

In 1973 cash held in US equity funds was around 4 per cent at the height of the market and 10 per cent at its lows in 1974 (Malkiel, 1999). Before markets began to fall in 2000 cash was 4 per cent of US equity funds but increased to 6 per cent a year later after equities had fallen substantially. In fact this is borne out in almost every market fall – 1987, 1990, 1998. Simon Keane, professor of finance at Glasgow University, comes to the following conclusion (Keane, 2000):

'There is no way of anticipating the phases of a bear market except by luck or with the advantage of hindsight. The notion that active fund managers can systematically anticipate the start or duration of a bear market with sufficient accuracy to give them an advantage over index funds is insupportable.

'Even if it could be shown that all active managers outperformed all index funds during a bear market, it would still not follow that investors would be better off in an active fund. It would only be valid if investors were better off in an active fund under normal growth conditions – but the evidence is clear that this is not so. Holding a bank deposit is the ultimate defensive strategy but overall it is a relatively poor investment.'

Table 15.1 The market tends to beat active managers

Equity fund category	Comparison index	2008	3 years	5 years
All US domestic funds	S&P SuperComposite 1500	64%	70%	66%
All US large cap funds	S&P 500	54%	65%	72%
All US mid cap funds	S&P Mid Cap 400	75%	71%	79%
All US small cap funds	S&P Small Cap 600	84%	78%	85%
International funds	S&P 700	64%	77%	84%
Emerging markets funds	S&P/IFCI Composite	65%	84%	90%

Bond fund category	Comparison index	2008	3 years	5 years
US Government Int.	Barclays Int. Govt	91%	91%	94%
Global income funds	Barclays Global Aggregate	78%	86%	79%

Source: Standard & Poor's Indices Versus Active Funds Scorecard, Year End 2008.

Keane's research demonstrated that in 1998, when equity markets around the world fell, US active managers underperformed the market by 2.5 per cent on the downturn and by 5 per cent on the upturn. He postulates that the accumulated evidence indicates clearly that bear markets are by and large unpredictable and that investors are better rewarded by adopting a buy-and-hold-policy than trying to establish defensive positions.

The period under review spans the period to the end of 2008 covering both rising and falling markets. The myth that active managers will outperform in bear markets has been well and truly shattered. The evidence seems convincing to me. Could you truly have picked in advance those that beat the index? If you could, you have a great future as an investment consultant. In 2008 active managers again failed to live up to their claims based on the UK All Companies Manager Universe compared to the broad UK market.

Argument 3: Indexing creates inefficiencies

As more people index, and research into the true or intrinsic value of companies by both buy and sell side analysts declines, then inefficiencies will appear, which the astute active manager can exploit to beat the market. Again, at first glance, this argument seems reasonable, but if we look a little deeper, it appears to be a little shallow. First, indexing represents only around 20 per cent of all institutional equity assets and 10 per cent of retail equity assets in the UK. Very few index bond funds exist in the UK. As such, we are a very long way from the stage of such inefficiencies being pronounced.

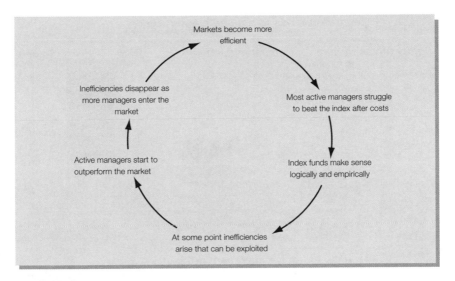

Markets become more
efficient

Inefficiencies disappear as
more managers enter the
market

Most active managers struggle
to beat the index after costs

Active managers start to
outperform the market

Index funds make sense
logically and empirically

At some point inefficiencies
arise that can be exploited

Figure 15.1 **The cycle of efficiency**   *Source: WM Company.*

Remember, too, that active managers, analysts and market makers play an important role in setting the fair price of stocks and providing liquidity. I have no idea at what level between indexed assets and actively managed assets that these inefficiencies begin to creep in, but I am pretty certain that the markets in the UK and USA are today scoured pretty thoroughly for inefficiencies. If inefficiencies increase then active managers will exploit them and outperform. More money and resources will flow into active funds and the inefficiencies will disappear, again favouring index investing. And so the cycle continues, as Figure 15.1 illustrates.

Argument 4: Active managers win in inefficient markets

When markets are inefficient, or to put it another way, when information is unevenly available to investors, possibly due to a lack or reduced level of market coverage by analysts, those investors who seek out and use information wisely may be able to outperform the market. This argument suggests that active managers are a better option in less efficient markets such as smaller company stocks, international and emerging markets.

You might think this reasonable too, but recall the logic we used earlier. All investors are the market and the average investor will be the market before costs. After costs, which tend to be significantly higher in these markets, the average manager will by definition underperform the index by these

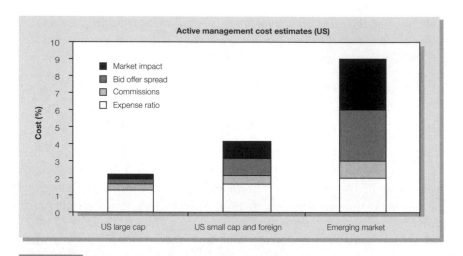

Figure 15.2 **Hurdles for active managers are high**

Source: Bernstein, W.J., The Intelligent Asset Allocator © 2001, McGraw-Hill, reproduced with permission of the
McGraw-Hill Companies.

costs. As index funds have lower costs, they will beat the majority of active funds. Maybe a few managers, with their insight, will end up with skill-based performance that persists.

It seems that the significantly higher costs of playing in these markets mops up most of the skill-based gains that may be achieved by smart professional managers. In inefficient markets transaction costs are often far higher due to wider bid-offer spreads (the difference between the price you can buy a share at versus the price you can sell it at) and other brokerage costs. This is true for small-cap stocks, some international stocks and emerging market stocks. In addition, management fees are usually higher. Less liquid stocks, more common is smaller, less heavily traded, markets, may also incur a higher price effect cost. Figure 15.2 outlines the increased cost hurdles faced by active managers between efficient large-cap markets and other suppos-edly inefficient markets. In the UK, expense ratios are generally a little higher.

A closer look at small-cap funds

Research by Garrett Quigley and Rex Sinquefield (2000) looked at UK unit trusts between 1987 and 1998, and reached the following conclusion:

'Contrary to the notion that small-company shares offer abundant "beat the market" opportunities, we find that small company unit trusts are the worst performers. In fact their performance failure is persistent and reliable.

'Overall, this study, like all mutual fund studies, does not enlighten us about what kinds of market failures [inefficiencies] occur. It does say that if there are any, UK equity managers do not exploit them.'

You saw in Table 15.1 that the market beat the majority of managers.

Argument 5: Index funds success is self-fulfilling

During the bull market of the late 1990s, some commentators claimed that the flow of funds appeared to push the prices of a handful of large companies up just because they were included in the index. However, this would seem to suggest that somehow passive index funds are dictating prices to the market, which seems a little absurd. The vast majority of funds are still managed in an active way and active managers must dictate prices of stocks. The buying of large company stocks by index funds probably represents less than 5 per cent of trading volumes. Surely this passive voice, that does not attempt to price the stock, merely to buy it, can't be dictating to the 95 per cent of active money trading the stock. In addition, if this were the case, then wouldn't all stocks in the index have risen by the same amount during this period? They evidently did not. Any effect would be likely to be short lived.

Argument 6: Why accept certain failure?

Finally, an argument that plays on your emotions is often used: the suggestion is made that either you miserably accept that you are guaranteed to underperform the market, by costs, if you invest in an index fund or you can have the hope and chance of beating the market. No one likes to be a loser and the manager will play on your emotions by showing you a fund with a few years of good returns, and hoping that you will forget about performance persistence, luck, efficient markets, manager costs and reversion to the mean.

Don't be a loser and play the loser's game. Stand up to this emotional pressure, confident in your understanding of where the chances of success really lie long term.

15.2 Bond investing: active or index?

In the great active versus index debate, the arguments and research largely revolve around equity investment. However, you should not overlook the efficacy of index investing for bonds, which up to now has been whispered rather than shouted from the rooftops. The evidence is compelling and comes down firmly in favour of investing in index funds, and exchange-traded funds.

According to Morningstar, over the ten-year period 1988–1998, US bond index funds returned 8.9 per cent a year against 8.2 per cent for actively managed bond funds. Because bond returns are more closely grouped than equities, this translated into index funds beating 85 per cent of all active funds. This differential is largely due to fees.

To date, bond index funds only represent around 3 per cent of all US mutual fund assets and much of this is institutional money. Outside the USA, bond index investing is either non-existent or at a very rudimentary stage, and this applies in the UK.

15.3 Summary: favour index strategies

■ Over longer periods of time index investments have generally beaten a majority of actively managed funds. The logic that the average index funds will outperform the majority of actively managed funds due to differences in cost is borne out by a mounting pile of empirical evidence.

■ Index funds are likely to float towards the top and many of today's winning managers will sink back as their performance fails to persist. Some will beat index funds in the long run – picking them today is the challenge.

■ This result is largely expected and widely known for more efficient markets where it is harder for active managers to find value-adding opportunities such as UK large cap stocks.

■ Surprisingly, though, index fund vehicles tend to outperform a majority of actively managed funds in less-efficient markets including small-cap stocks, and emerging markets. This is generally a consequence of the higher fees charged and the significantly higher transaction costs associated with these markets, negating the potentially larger gains from exploiting inefficiencies.

■ The claim that active managers will outperform index funds in bear markets has been shown to be lacking in supporting evidence. What research there is points to the fact that active managers have a poor record, as a group, in anticipating downturns and subsequent upswings in markets. A buy-and-hold strategy is in all likelihood a better option.

■ Much of the empirical data does not take into account the problem of survivorship bias or the effect of the high turnover, and thus tax costs, for taxable investors, which would significantly improve the efficacy of index investment vehicles over active vehicles.

■ While index funds have outperformed a majority of active funds, some active funds do and will outperform them over different periods. The evidence would seem to suggest that short-term outperformance is rarely sustained. The very small number of active funds that outperform over longer periods could in many cases be attributed to luck. However, it is possible that it may in some cases be down to exceptional manager skill.

■ Any material evidence of performance persistence usually relates to persistent underperformance caused by high fees, rather than any persistence in outperformance. Any persistence is generally too limited actually to act on.

■ There is no useful methodology for selecting them in advance. Past performance is no guarantee or predictor of future returns.

■ Statistically, even the best active managers need to provide fifteen to twenty years of data for you to know whether they have outperformed by luck or judgement.

■ Many managers move around so frequently that it is hard to know whose performance you are actually looking at.

As we have seen earlier, good investing is about maximising the probability of reaching your goals and index funds are the best practical way for most investors to attain performance that captures the bulk of the characteristics that you want from each of your building blocks.

References

Keane, S. (2000) *Index funds in a bear market*. A monograph published by Glasgow University in association with Virgin Direct: as quoted by Anon (2003) *Active fund managers add to market misery*. Virgin Direct, March. Available from: http://www.virginmoney.com.

Malkiel, B. G. (1999) *A random walk down Wall Street*, New York: W. W. Norton, 188–189.

Quigley, G. and Sinquefield, R. (2000) 'Performance of UK equity unit trusts', *Journal of Asset Management*, 1(1), 72–92.

Standard & Poors (2007) SPIVA Report.

Conclusion

This book has, I hope, been useful to you both in getting you into a smarter investing mindset and in allowing you to decide what type of portfolio makes sense and how you can put this into practice. If you take anything away from this book, then let it be these six points:

1 Getting the mix of investment building blocks right is the most critical factor. Remember that diversification makes good sense and is the only free lunch that investing provides you. Spread your portfolio into a number of building blocks to create a portfolio that will help you through the seasons.

2 Remember that risk and return go hand in hand with few, if any, exceptions. If it looks too good to be true, it probably is.

3 Make a pact with yourself only to make investment choices that increase your chances of being successful. Remember that you are always aiming to lose the fewest points relative to the market, which means controlling all costs at every point of the process.

4 Stick with your chosen mix at all times, but rebalance your portfolio if the proportions move significantly out of line using cash flows from the portfolio or additional contributions wherever possible.

5 Implement the portfolio using low-cost index funds (or exchange-traded funds) as the default vehicle to give yourself the greatest chance of capturing the bulk of the market returns that each of your portfolio building blocks delivers. Use active managers if index funds or equivalent are not available or where they can truly convince you, on terms that you set, that they have the people, process and commitment to deliver market-beating returns for you in the future. If you're not sure, don't risk it.

6 Try your hardest to control your emotions: avoid feeling covetous of building blocks doing better than your own; don't be tempted by greed or paralysed by fear. If you have been diligent in establishing your investment portfolio (1–4 above) then, when times get tough, as they will, choose to do nothing as your default strategy!

Finally, be confident that you are now a *smarter investor* than most and enjoy your investing and the wealth it brings you, with any luck!

Bibliography

The following resources are well worth taking a look at. They have been a considerable source of information, wisdom and thought-provoking debate for me in writing this book.

Websites

These websites are in addition to the sites already referenced in Chapter 12.

www.vanguard.com is excellent if you want basic education on investing. While the site is US-orientated, its basic ideas and principles still apply. Especially read the speeches given by John C. Bogle, which can be found via the link to the 'Bogle Financial Markets Research Center'.

www.indexinvestor.com where you can find excellent articles and analysis on the efficacy of index investing. Much of this is free and an annual subscription to the rest is good value at $25 a year.

www.dfaus.com is the public website of a leading index firm which has Eugene Fama and Kenneth French as directors, both leading investment academics. There is a link to a library that has an assortment of articles, research and video clips.

www.myrisktolerance.com is where you can undertake the FinaMetrica Risk Profile questionnaire online to find out more about your attitude to financial risk.

Insightful books

The books below have influenced my thinking over the years and I thank the authors for putting their knowledge and ideas on to paper for all of us to share. It is worth noting that these are all US-focused books, a point not lost on me and my decision to write a book for UK investors. The concepts and ideas apply across borders, but the evidence tends to come from US data.

***Winning the Loser's Game*, Charles D. Ellis, McGraw-Hill** (ISBN 0–07–138767–6).

This is an excellent book that I read in 1994, and wished I had done sooner. It is Charles Ellis' insight into the *'losing-the-fewest points'* strategy that underpins the philosophy that we developed. An easy and entertaining read.

***Common Sense on Mutual Funds*, John C. Bogle, John Wiley & Sons, Inc.** (ISBN 0–471–29543–4). An insightful and valuable book from one of the true visionaries of the industry, a frequent thorn in the side of the active investment management industry, and a true champion of investors. I owe a considerable amount to his insight, wisdom and integrity.

***Pioneering Portfolio Management*, David F. Swensen, The Free Press** (ISBN 0–684–86443–6). David Swensen is the Chief Investment Officer at Yale University in the USA and is responsible for the management of the University's endowment fund. He is one of the most progressive thinkers in the business, with a clear philosophy of where his team can and cannot add value. Yale has been at the forefront in the move into alternative investment products such as private equity and absolute return strategies (hedge funds). An excellent read for those of you who want to see what a leading investment team are doing.

***The Index Fund Solution*, Richard E. Evans and Burton G. Malkiel**. (ISBN 0–684–85250–0). This book establishes sound arguments for why most investors should invest in index funds. It also provides some straight-talking guidelines for establishing an investment plan for you. US orientated.

***Fooled by Randomness*, Nassim Nicholas Taleb, TEXERE Thompson** (ISBN 1–59799–184–5). This is a wonderfully written book, the focus of which is best described in its full title: *Fooled by Randomness: The Hidden Role of Chance in Life and in the Markets*. A stimulating read.

Data-oriented books

***Stocks, Bonds, Bills and Inflation (SBBI) – Yearbook*, Ibbotson Associates** (ISBN 1–882864–012–3). This book provides the definitive data that is used widely throughout the US investment management world. It goes back to 1926, and is the cleanest data available. The book also contains some interesting commentary and observations on the long-term data series. It is an annual publication.

***Triumph of the Optimists*, E. Dimson, P. Marsh and M. Staunton, Princeton University Press** (ISBN 0–691–09194–3). This book provides the best UK data available for equities, bonds and cash, and data on 15 other countries. However, unlike the SBBI, above, it does not provide you with the underlying data, which can only be purchased via Ibbotson. It is a useful book though. The analysis in my book is derived from the underlying data, which I purchased. I thank them for what must have been an unenviable task.

Asset allocation software

Portfolio Pathfinder: One of the very few packages that focuses on the real risk that investors face, which is that of not being able to meet their purchasing power obligations, needs and goals during their lifetimes. It uses mean-variance optimisation to find efficient portfolios and helps you, via a series of educational and decision-making graphs, to decide which portfolio structure is likely to meet your purchasing power goals most effectively. It uses Monte Carlo simulations to do so. It is a reasonably straightforward piece of software that most advisers and reasonably interested investors can use. At the moment it is a US-oriented model that needs a bit of fiddling around to use for other investors. Well worth a look at the website and a call to Dick Purcell, the driving force behind it: *www.planscan.net*.

MC Retire: This software is from Efficient Solutions and can be found at *www.effisols.com*. It uses a Monte Carlo simulation to help you evaluate the chances of success of different investment and withdrawal strategies. At less than $30 it is worth a look. Playing with it provides you with an insight into the issues that you face in the distribution phase of your investing. You can also buy a simple optimiser programme relatively cheaply if you want to play around with one.

Additional sources

Bernstein, W. (2001) *The four pillars of investing*. New York: McGraw-Hill.

Bogle, J. C. (1994) *Bogle on mutual funds: New perspectives for the intelligent investor*. New York: Dell.

Brennan, J. (2002) *Straight talk on investing: What you need to know*. New York: Wiley.

Isaacman, M. (2000) *How to be an index investor*. New York: McGraw-Hill.

Markovitz, H. (1952) 'Portfolio selection', *Journal of Finance*, vol. VII, no.1.

Nofsinger, J. R. (2001) *Investment madness: How psychology affects your investing ... and what to do about it*. Upper Saddle River, NJ: Financial Times Prentice Hall.

Shiller, R. J. (2001) *Irrational exuberance*. Woodstock, UK: Princeton University Press.

Appendix 1

Data used in Smarter Portfolios simulation

Note: All data are in GBP and represent total returns (i.e. income reinvested)

FTSE All-Share Index	FTSE data published with the permission of FTSE.
Dimensional UK Small Cap Index	Courtesy of Dimensional Fund Advisors: not available for direct investment. Performance does not reflect the expenses associated with the management of an actual portfolio. January 1994 – present: simulated by Dimensional from Bloomberg securities data. Returns computed from the average of four staggered, market cap-weighted annually rebalanced portfolios of small company securities. Small companies defined as the bottom 10% of the market ranked by market cap. REITs are excluded. Maximum index weight of any one company is capped at 10%. July 1981 – December 1993: simulated by Dimensional from StyleResearch securities data. Includes securities in the bottom 10% of market capitalization, excluding the bottom 1%. Rebalanced semiannually. January 1970 – June 1981: Elroy Dimson and Paul Marsh, *Hoare Govett Smaller Companies Index 2009*, ABN-AMRO / Royal Bank of Scotland, January 2009.
MSCI UK Value Index (gross div.)	Data copyright MSCI 2009, all rights reserved.
MSCI World ex UK Index (gross div.)	Data copyright MSCI 2009, all rights reserved.
MSCI World ex UK Value Index (gross div.)	Data copyright MSCI 2009, all rights reserved.
Dimensional US Small Cap Index	Courtesy of Dimensional Fund Advisors. June 1927 – present: Dimensional US Small Cap IndexComposition. Market-capitalization-weighted index of securities of the smallest US companies whose market capitalization falls in the lowest 8% of the total market capitalization of the Eligible Market. The Eligible Market is composed of securities of US companies traded on the NYSE, AMEX, and Nasdaq Global Market. Exclusions: Non-US companies, REITs, UITs, and Investment Companies Source: CRSP and CompustatCurrency: GBPDimensional Index data compiled by Dimensional (refer to Acknowledgements).
MSCI Emerging Markets Index (gross div.)	Data copyright MSCI 2009, all rights reserved.
S&P Global REIT Index (gross div.)	The S&P data are provided by courstey of Standard & Poor's.
RJ CRB Commodity Index	CRB Index from January 1990 to December 1994, RJ CRB Index thereafter. Source: www.crbtrader.com.
One month UK T-Bills	HM Treasury.

Other data series used in the book

Dimensional UK Value Index	Courtesy of Dimensional Fund Advisors: not available for direct investment. Performance does not reflect the expenses associated with the management of an actual portfolio. January 1994 – present: simulated by Dimensional from Bloomberg securities data. Returns computed from the average of four staggered, market cap-weighted annually rebalanced portfolios of value company securities. Value breaks are formed by country on the top 30% of large companies ranked on book-to-market capitalization. Utilities and REITs are excluded. Maximum index weight of any one company is capped at 10%. 1955 – December 1993: UK Large Value Index. Source: Elroy Dimson, Stefan Nagel and Garrett Quigley (2003) 'Capturing the value premium in the UK', *Financial Analysts Journal*, vol. 59, no. 6, 35–45. Simulated Returns, converted from GBP to USD using the WM/Reuters at 4 p.m. EST (closing spot), from PFPC exchange rate.
Dimensional International ex UK Value Index	Courtesy of Dimensional Fund Advisors: not available for direct investment. Performance does not reflect the expenses associated with the management of an actual portfolio. January 1994 – present: simulated by Dimensional from Bloomberg securities data. Returns computed from the average of four staggered, market cap-weighted annually rebalanced portfolios of large value company securities. Value breaks are formed by country on the top 30% of large companies ranked on book-to-market capitalization. Large companies are defined by country. Utilities and REITs are excluded. Maximum index weight of any one company is capped at 5%.Countries included are Australia, Austria, Belgium, Canada, Denmark, Finland, France, Germany, Greece, Hong Kong, Ireland, Italy, Japan, Netherlands, New Zealand, Norway, Portugal, Singapore, Spain, Switzerland, Sweden, United States. January 1975-December 1993: Fama/French International Value Country Indices (ex UK) and Fama/French US Large Value Research Index combined using Market Cap Weights. Currency: GBP. Dimensional Index data compiled by Dimensional.
Dimensional International ex UK Small Index	Courtesy of Dimensional Fund Advisors: not available for direct investment. Performance does not reflect the expenses associated with the management of an actual portfolio. January 1994 – present: simulated by Dimensional from Bloomberg securities data. Returns computed from the average of four staggered, annually rebalanced portfolios of small company securities (REITs are included). Maximum index weight of any one company is capped at 5%. Countries included are Australia, Austria, Belgium, Canada, Denmark, Finland, France, Germany, Greece, Hong Kong, Ireland, Italy, Japan, Netherlands, New Zealand, Norway, Portugal, Singapore, Spain, Switzerland, Sweden, United States. July 1981-December 1993: Dimensional US Small Cap Index plus Dimensional International Small Cap Index less Dimensional UK Small Cap Index combined using StyleResearch Small Portfolio Weights. January 1970-June 1981: 67% Dimensional US Small Cap Index, 33% Dimensional Japan Small Cap Index. Currency: GBP. Dimensional Index data compiled by Dimensional.
Fama/French Emerging Markets Value Index	Courtesy of Fama and French: total returns in USD. January 1989-present: Fama/French Emerging Markets Value Simulated Index. Courtesy of Fama/French from IFC securities data. Simulated strategy of IFC investable universe countries in the upper 30% book-to-market range; companies weighted by float-adjusted market cap; countries weighted by country float-adjusted market cap; rebalanced monthly. Source: 'Value versus Growth: The International Evidence', *Journal of Finance* 53 (1998), 1975–99. Currency: GBP. Fama/French and multifactor data provided by Fama/French.

Index

accumulation phase 33–5, 37, 124
  length of 133
AC Milan 114
action-orientation 97
active funds 263–6
  vs index funds 64
active investors 55, 70
active management/managers 15–18, 53,
    56, 79–80, 145, 168, 247, 276–8
  appeal of 54
  beating market after costs 57–66, 63
  evaluating and testing 70–1, 152
  hurdles faced by 61, 280
  and inefficient markets 279–80
  long-term performance 56–7, 63–6
  market-beating confidence 90–1
  opportunities for 57–9
actual returns 34
advice 44, 87
advisers 14, 44
  checklist for finding 234–5
  conflicts of interest 231–3
  fee-based 44, 231–2
  hiring 229–31
  key attributes 231–4
  management insight and robust
    solutions 232–3
  remuneration structure 231–2
affordability 161
AIM stock markets 249
alpha/excess return 69
amateurism 113
annual fees 15, 18
annualised (compound) return 199

anomalously-priced securities 62
asset allocation:
  market diversifiers 171
  models 156
  and time-series variation 66
asset classes/building blocks 23, 27, 51,
    106, 250–2
  assumptions made 223
  benchmarking 250–2
  choosing 155, 161–3
  combining for growth and return
    156–9
  contributions to portfolio 163–4
  correlation 169–71
    matrix 170
  currency as 168
  defensive 175–80
  diversification 247
  excluded from mix 222–3
  functional attributes 160–1
  key 193–219
  moving between 52
  rate of return of UK 147
  selecting 159–64
  for smoothing returns 157
  types 159–60
asset mix 20, 35–7, 39, 51, 79
  choosing 39, 66
  equity/bond 42
  growth/return 158, 159
  life-cycle investing 41
  maintaining 42
average investors 2, 70, 279
  performance 2–4, 84

average managers: underperformance
279–80
AVIVA 257

backwardation 218
Barber, Brad 101
Barclays iShares 258
Barclays Stockbrokers 236
basic concepts 21–38
basic financial survival 128–38
  case study 138–9
  contributions to pool 135
  goals 128–38
  investment plan 138
basic survival 121
beating the market 14–18, 40
bed-and-breakfasting 245
behavioural finance 87–88, 101–2, 281
behavioural rules 102–3
benchmarking 249–52
Berkshire Hathaway 71, 198
Bernstein, William 155, 185
Big Mac Index 168
Bogle, John 61, 64, 71, 83–4, 154, 196,
  210, 212, 274
Bolton, Anthony 4, 70, 72–4
bonds: 148, 156
  active and index funds 40, 281–2
bottom-up approach 53
BRIC economies (Brazil, Russia, India,
  China) 207
brokerage charges 15, 32, 40, 59, 237,
  252
brokers 15
  remuneration 15
Buffet, Warren 4, 71–2, 87, 198, 248
building blocks/asset classes 23, 27, 51,
  250–2
  asset mix 24–5
  benchmarking 250–2
  choosing 155, 161–3
  combining for growth and return
  156–9
  contributions to portfolio 163–4

correlation 169–71
correlation matrix 170
currency as 168
functional attributes 160–1
moving between 52
selecting 159–64
for smoothing returns 157
types 159–60
bull markets 21, 100, 169
burgernomics 168
buy high, sell low 85–7
buy low, sell high 85
buy-to-let 214

cantango 218
Cap funds 145
capital, cost of 146–7
Capital Asset Pricing Model 148–9
Carhart, Mark 68
cash 219
Chartered Financial Planners 44
chasing returns 42, 216
Cheung Kong Holidays 165
China 216
commercial property 214–15
commissions 15
commodities 238
commodity futures 216–19
  correlation with traditional financial
  assets 216, 219
  rebalancing basket 218
  returns 217, 218
  strategy premium 218
company ownership: risks 144
company pensions 138
compounding and time 30–2, 37–8, 132,
  198–9
concentration risk 146
confidence 90–1, 100
confusion and noise
  ignoring 42–3
  simplifying 18–19, 20
  sources 53
contributions: drip feeding 132

corporate bond funds 145
corporate bond index 145
corporate bonds 40
costs 2–3, 15–16, 18, 32, 44, 55, 59, 101,
    256, 268–71
  impact on wealth 267–8, 273, 274
  minimising 27, 40
counterparty risk 145
Credit Crunch 154, 173
credit risk 149–50
currency:
  as a diversifier 167
  risk 145, 167–8
    hedging 168
  as a separate asset 168

debt instruments 177
decisions 45, 59–60
  abrogating to professionals 91
  challenges to 87–98
  evidence-based 24–5
  investment 86
  rational 83
  regretting consequences 93–4
default risk 149–50
defensive asset classes 162–3, 168, 185,
    219–21, 238
  mix 175–80, 180
  role 179
defined contribution pension plans 4
deflation 154
derivatives 256
Dimensional Fund Advisers 257–8
dilution level 252–3
Dimensional Fund Advisors 209
distribution phase 35–6, 37, 124 *see also*
    income
  interim 132
diversification 25–6, 40, 172–3, 252–3
  growth oriented equities 169
  mathematical description 157–8
DIY investing
  administration of 239–40
  asset mix 242–4

diversification 238
  getting started 237
  harvesting and offsetting losses 245–6
  inflation index 242
  lump-sums 238–40
  pension savings 244–6
  plans 234–46
  points to bear in mind 240
  portfolio maintenance 241, 242
  portfolio purchasing power 242
  and tax efficiency 244–6
dot.com bubble 154
downside insight 183
due diligence 234

earnings per share 197
Easy ETF 258
efficient frontier 157
Efficient Market Hypothesis (EMH) 62–3,
    66
Einstein, Albert 31
Ellis, Charles 50, 79, 101–2
emerging economies 152
  equities 169
  risks 207
emerging markets
  investment benefits 206–7
  return enhancing equities 206–7
  volatility 207
emotional demons 89–98
emotional perception: and stock price
    195–6
emotional risk tolerance 105, 155, 183–4
emotions 27, 42, 45, 281
  managing 28–9, 83–103
Equitable Life 14
equities 148, 156
  allocations to 171
  capitalisation of earnings 196
  diversifiers 171
  diversifying risk 214–15
  dividends 196
  emerging economies 169
  exposure 168

equities (*continued*)
   future performance 205–6
   growth oriented 169
   investment performance 101
   long-term returns 199–200
   market risk premium 151–2
   performance 194
     long-term 199–200, 205
   risk premium 204–5
   risks and returns 151–2, 153, 178
   selection 52–3
   size premium 151–2
   smaller companies for return
     enhancement 210–12
   summary of asset classes 213
   thrills and spills 193–4
   value premium 151–2
equity/bond mixture 39, 42, 179
equity funds 40 *see also* unit trusts
   UK 2–3, 61
   US 2–3
equity managers 145
equity markets 63
   crashes 154
   emerging economies 173–4
   falling 86
   returns 198–200, 204–6
   volatility 202–4
equity market trauma 178
estimation error maximisation 157
eurobond managers 145
evidence-based decisions 24–5, 233–4
excess return/alpha 69
excess risk/residual risk 69
Exchange Rate Mechanism (ERM) 63
Exchange Traded Funds (ETF) 193,
   247–8, 254, 258
   ring-fencing 253
extra income bonds 40
eye-openers about investing 1–4

Fama, Eugene 149, 151, 209–10, 212
fear and greed 91
Fidelity Investments 64, 70, 257

financial goals:
   basic survival 128–38
   defining 121–8, 126–8
   determining 140
   roadmap to 129
financial risk profile 109–11
   exploring 112–16
   psychometric 113–14
Fitzrovia: total expense ratio calculator
   269
fixed income markets 63
fluctuating returns 34
focus points 24–37
Ford Foundation 169
forecasting 59, 61
France 201
French, Kenneth 149, 151
FT Funds 262
FTSE 100 87, 90, 113, 165
FTSE All-Share index 40, 65, 148, 242, 249
FTSE Indices 258
fund managers 14, 17
   choosing 263–4
   market-beating 14
   prima donnas 56
   remuneration 15–16
   turnover 69
funds 40
   choosing 264–5
   information on 259–62
funds of hedge funds 222
futures contracts 216–17

gambling 21–2, 94–5, 196
Germany 201
gilts/government bonds 40, 149, 177–8,
   178
   longer-dated 221
global bond exposure 168
global diversification 171–2
global equity funds 165
   tracker 2
global equity markets 166
   real returns 201

global pension fund assets 248
global style tilts portfolio 174–5
global value premium 208–9
goals 105–6, 116
    defining 121–8
    emotional 112
    importance 118–20
    for individuals 120–1
good investing 23
Graham, Benjamin 83, 195, 196, 201
growth oriented portfolios 164–72

hedge funds 17, 146, 203, 222
higher-level 126–7
higher-level financial goals 126–7
higher returns, risk of 25
high income bonds 40
high-quality domestic bonds 40
high-risk loans 149–50
high yield bonds 40
hindsight expertise 92–3, 98–9
history and research
    and investor performance 63–6
    wise use of 26–7, 36–7
History of Interest Rates, A (Sidney
    Homer) 31
home market bias 165–6, 171–2, 205,
    247
horizons, investment 122–3, 125–6, 134,
    141
    long-term 123–4
housing market 154
HSBC 165, 257

Icesave 143, 144
illusions and biases 88
implementation products 172
income *see also* distribution phase
    from portfolios 41–2
income preservation 35
incremental risk premia 151–3
independent advice *see* advisers
index funds 16, 40, 250–2
    benefits 248–9, 282–3

common put-downs 276–81
default investment vehicle 276
long-term performance 64–5
selection criteria 254–5
trading volume 281
underperformance due to costs 65
index funds *vs* active funds 278
index-linked gilts 40, 168, 178, 220
    short-dated 185, 193
index-linked securities 177–8
index/passive investing and investors 54,
    57, 61
    endorsed by active managers 71–4
    favoured by balance of probabilities
    74
index-replicating products 74
index tracker funds 65, 193
India 216
indices 250
indices: information on 258–9
inflation 40, 150, 154, 163, 176–8, 186,
    268–9
    effect over time 22–3, 28, 29
    planning for 28–9, 37
    protection from 2, 185, 198–9, 207,
    219–21
    returns above 201–2
inflation-linked investments 2
Institute of Financial Planning 234
insurance-wrapped products 40, 94–5
interest rate risk 151
intrinsic value 196
investing 22
    basic facts about 1–4
    interest in 89
    points to ponder 284–5
    rational 98–9
Investment Analysts of Chicago 83–4
investment behaviour *see* behavioural
    finance
investment calculators 36–7
investment decisions 88–98
    gender effect 101–2
investment grade bonds 40

investment horizons 122–4, 125–6, 134, 141
Investment Management Association 257, 259
investment managers/professionals 2–3
  market-beating skills 69
  outperformers over time 66–70
    validating 74
  selecting 80
  star 60–1
  truly talented 69–74
  validating outperformance 74
investment period 39
investment phases 32–6
investment philosophy 45–50
  author's 76–9
  case study 47–9
  foundations 50–6
  rules 79–80
investment plan 97
  building 139–41
  calculations for 141–2
  choosing a platform 236–7
  getting started 129–30
  needs 119
    and administration choices 236
  processes and goals 128
  rate of return 141
  summary of goals 142
investment policy/strategic asset
    allocation 51, 65–6
  maintaining 80
  and time-series variation 66
investment returns: link with market
    returns 198
investment risks 144–6
investments:
  rational and irrational 98–101
  total returns 65–6
investment strategy/market
    timing/tactical asset allocation 37–8,
    52, 58, 209
  importance 66
  maintaining 84

investment tracking software 95
investment trusts 253–4
investors:
  competition for 17–18
  loss of confidence 14
  paradox of 87
irrational investing 83, 87–88, 100–1
irrational preferences 94–5
ISAs 41

Japan 201
  market crash 16, 93, 166
junk bonds 40

Keane, Simon 277–8
Keynes, John Maynard 218
knowledge 88–90

Lee, MI 243–4
Legal & General 257
Lehman Brothers 17, 143–6
lending: risks and returns 144–5, 149
less-than-zero-sum game 54, 55
life-cycle investing 41
lifestyle options 121, 126
lifetime cashflow modelling 233
liquidity 161
  risk 145
Lloyds Bank 148
long-shots 94–5
long term buy-and-hold strategy: beating 53
Long Term Capital Management 64, 203
long-term data 27
long-term investments
  equities 204–5
  inflation risk 176–7
long-term investors
  asset allocation of less cautious 178–80
  cautious 176–7
long-term loans 150–1
long-term optimism 165
long-term policy *vs* short-term active
    management 65–6

long-term success 56–7, 71–4
lose-the-fewest-points strategy 70, 79,
    248
lot sizes 256
luck 60–1, 68, 90
lump-sum investing 137, 238–40
Lynch, Peter 72
Lyxor Asset Management 258

Macquarie Bank 165
Madoff, Bernard 17, 146
Malkiel, Burton 62–3
management fees 16, 32, 40, 268
manager investment risk 145–6
managers:
  experience 256–7
  fraud 146
  market-beating 14, 53
    confidence 90–1
  skill (alpha) 4, 222
market-based returns (beta) 222
market corrections 100
market crises 14, 202–4
  responses to 27
market efficiency 62–3
market exposure 249–50
market indices:
  1990–2008 185
  choosing 249–52
market returns: link with investment
    returns 198
market risk 148–9, 151–2
markets see also confusion and
    noise
  beating 40
  efficiency of 66
  long-term 196–8
  overvalues 200
  relationship to real life 195
  replicating 17, 61, 255
  return to mean 210
  reversion toward the mean 200–1,
    210
  short-term 195–6

UK 66
  worst-case 186
market-timers 52, 63–4
market timing/tactical asset
    allocation/investment strategy 52,
    58, 61, 66, 95, 209
  importance 66
  short-term 165
market-timing tools 247
market trauma 178
  global 207
  tolerance for short-term 94
Markowitz, Harry 157, 174
Maslow's hierarchy of needs 119
maturity risk 151
means-variance software 157
Megellan Mutual Fund (Fidelity
    Investments) 64
Meriwether, John 64
Modern Portfolio Theory 157–8
money illusion 29–30
Monte Carlo simulation 133, 185, 186,
    213
Morningstar 262
Motley Fool 236
M&S 165
Multi-factor Model 149
Munger, Charlie 71
mutual funds 15 see also equity funds;
    unit trusts
MVOPlus software 185
Myers-Briggs test 114
Myners Report 19–20

National Savings Certificates 154, 168,
    177–8, 185, 193, 220–21
nest eggs 121, 126, 139
net asset value (NAV) 253–4
Niederhoffer, Victor 64
noise and confusion 14
  ignoring 42–3
  sources 53
non-UK assets 166–7
  risks 145

Northern Rock 143, 144

occupational pension plans 4
Odean, Terrence 101
oil crises 154
online broking accounts 21, 95, 236–7
opaque products 40
open-ended investment companies
 (OEIC) 86, 252–3
opportunity costs 150
optimisation, unconstrained 157
optimism 92
outcomes:
 and expectations 27, 94
 visions of 122
outperformance 200, 209–10
overconfidence 91, 92
 and wealth destruction 101–2

pain-to-gain 94
paradox of investors 87
passive/index funds 281
passive/index investing and investors 54,
 57, 248–9, 253, 257–8
 endorsed by active managers 71–4
 favoured by balance of probabilities
 74
passive product providers 257–62
past performance:
 as proxy for future returns 2–4, 27,
 67–9, 70
pension plans 4, 19–20
pensions 126, 129–30, 145
 contributions 41
 savings 244–6
perception of risk 185
performance:
 persistence 66–8
 short-term 18
personal investment philosophy of
 author 76–79
perspective, big picture 95
philanthropic works 121, 126
philosophies *see* investment philosophy

philosophy-free investing: case study
 47–9
pitfalls, avoiding 4–5
points-winning strategy 71
Ponzi scheme 17, 146
poor outcomes 90
portfolio building 19–20, 106, 154–82
 see also asset classes/building blocks
 aggressive 123–4
 allocations of money 122
 choice 106, 183–92
 importance 111, 112
 consequences of failure 125–6
 construction approach 156–60
 contributions 134–7
 diversification 154–5
 effectiveness 173–5
 estimation error maximisation 157
 excessive conservatism 123
 global market participation 172
 growth engine 198
 growth oriented 171–5
 identifying structure 157
 monitoring 138
 process 116–17, 155
 risk and return comparisons 174
 simulations 133
 smarter 187–92
portfolio matrix:
 comparison of portfolios 184
 understanding and using 183–6
portfolio strategy 116–17
 growth oriented 164–71
 practical implementation 161
portfolio structures: and the risk
 spectrum 180–2
portfolio turnover: costs 271–3
practical investing 40–1
price-earnings ratio 205, 238
price indices 250
principal-protected products 40
private banks 233
private client portfolio managers 17
private equity 223

probabilities 53–5
product engineering 16–17
products
  buyer beware 262–3
product searches 260–1
product selection 247
product structures 252–4
property 141, 169, 238
  commercial 214–15
  correlation to equities 215
psychometric risk profiling 113–16,
  183–4
purchasing power 28, 199, 213
  maintaining 198
  regaining after crash 203
purchasing-power parity 168

Quigley, Garrett 280–1

Random Walk Down Wall Street, A
  (Burton Malkiel) 62–3
'rate tarts' 144
real estate investment returns (REIT)
  214–15
real returns 28–9, 130, 132, 140, 199,
  213
rebalancing bonus 218
research and history:
  and investor performance 63–6
  wise use of 26–7, 36–7
residual risk/excess risk 69
Retail Price Index (RPI) 177
retirement 4, 33, 35–6, 41, 51, 120–1,
  124–5, 129–30, 133, 138–9, 140, 186
returns 213 *see also* variation (returns
  over time)
  actual 34
  beating 51–6
  chasing 42, 80
  estimates of future 39, 133–4, 137–8,
  147
  fluctuating 34
  future 39
  on global equities 201–2

historical context 27, 160
market-based 160, 197
nominal 28
property, unleveraged 214
real 28–9, 130, 132, 142, 199, 213
role of asset allocation 65–6
sensitivity to changes in yields 150–1
smoothing 157, 169, 199
standard deviation 181
straight-line 34
total market 196–7
zero per cent 186
return tilts 247
risk 14, 17, 65
  inflationary 176–7
  perception of 185
  premiums 204
  spreading 40
  tolerance 106, 109–11, 155
risk and return
  comparison between UK assets and
    global assets 174
  interpreting the numbers 181–2
risk-free assets 185
risk number: definition 181
risk/return relationship 134, 144, 146–7,
  150, 157
  trade offs 157
risk spectrum 157
  position on 180–2
risk taking 143–53
risky asset classes/building blocks 161–2,
  163
RJ CRB Commodities Index 217
Robertson, Julian 64

sampling/partial replication 255
saving 22
scepticism 97–9
school/university fees 36, 121, 124, 125,
  126
Schwab, Charles 72
security selection 52–3, 62–3
  winning points through 62–3

Separation Theorem 158
Sharpe, William 148
Shiller, Robert 93, 238–9
short-term active management *vs* long-term policy 65–6
short-term changes 196
short-term data 27
short-termism 95–6
short-term performance 18, 66, 68, 165
  as proxy for long-term performance
  54–5
short-term random sequences
  seeing as patterns 92
Siegel, Lawrence 169
Singer & Friedlander 144
Sinquefield, Rex 209, 280–1
size risk 151–2
  premia 169
small cap funds 280–1
small cap premium 210–12
smoothing returns 157, 199
Soros, George 63–4
Special Situations fund (Fidelity
  Investments) 70
specific risk 148
speculation 22, 198
S&P500 Index 84
star investment managers 60–1
stock-pickers 52–3
stoicism 91
straight-line returns 34
strategic asset allocation/investment
  policy 51, 65–6
  maintaining 80
  and time-series variation 66
structured notes 17
sub-investment grade bonds 40
survivable outcomes 25
Swenson, David 70, 178, 215, 243

tactical asset allocation/investment
  strategy/market timing 52, 58, 209
  importance 66
Tanous, Peter 212

target pool 130–1, 132
  size 135–6
taxes 15, 32, 59, 273
  capital gains 41
  minimising 41
taxpayers: risks 147
T-bills *see* treasuries
TD Waterhouse 236
Tech Wreck 173
temptation, avoiding 87–88
terrorism 154
Tiger Funds 64
time, power of 30, 37, 198
timing 61
Tobin James 158, 175
top-down approach 52
total expense ratio (TER) 40, 269–70
total market 40
total market returns 196–7
tracker funds *see* index funds
tracking errors 254–7
transaction fees 15, 32, 40, 59, 237, 252
treasuries 40, 185
Trustnet 259
turnover 256

UCITS-II 253
UK banks: nationalisation 146–7
UK equities 165
  funds 2–3, 17
    beaten by market 65–6
  risks 199
UK equity market 186, 202
  returns 1900–2008 185
UK market; winners and losers 58
UK plc 148
unit trusts 40, 86, 252–3
unrealistic expectations 94
upfront fees 18, 32, 40, 44, 269
upside opportunity 183
US equity funds 2–3

value (less healthy) companies 174,
  208–10

premia 169, 208–9
   risks 151–2
Vanguard (US) 257
variation (returns over time) 66
Vinik, Jeff 64
Viyella 144
voting machine: short-term 195–6

war 154
Waring, MB and Siegel, LB 70
Waterford 143
wealth:
   accumulation 34, 35
      preserving 193–4
   destruction 80, 85–7, 101–2, 113
      by markets 203
   management companies 233
   management process 232
   preservation 23
wealth outcomes 88
Wedgwood 143, 144

weighing machine 201
   long-term 196–8
Where are the Customers' Yachts? (Fred
   Schwed, 1995) 3
whip-sawing 85
whisky and water approach 158, 159,
   161–2, 171, 175, 193
Wilshire 5000 40
winning points 60, 62–3
Winning the Losers Game (Charles D.
   Ellis) 50, 101–2
with-profits endowments 40
WM Company 65, 66
Woolworths 143, 144

Yale University Endowment 70
yields 150–1
   price sensitivity to changes 178

zero per cent return 186
zero-sum game 55–6, 216